The Archaeology of Ancient
Judea and Palestine

The Archaeology of Ancient
Judea and Palestine

Ariel Lewin

Photographs
Dinu, Sandu, and Radu Mendrea

The J. Paul Getty Museum, Los Angeles

I dedicate this book to my family. To Valentina, David Carlo, Benedetto Aron, my mother, Bassevina (Betty), and my father-in-law, Giovanni Ferrara. And to the ever-alive presence of my father, Jona.

—Ariel Lewin

Italian edition © 2005 Arsenale-EBS

English translation © 2005 J. Paul Getty Trust

First published in the United States of America in 2005 by Getty Publications
1200 Getty Center Drive, Suite 500
Los Angeles, California 90049-1682
www.getty.edu

Christopher Hudson, *Publisher*
Mark Greenberg, *Editor in Chief*

Ann Lucke, *Managing Editor*
Robin H. Ray, *Copy Editor*
Brian D. Phillips, *Translator*

Library of Congress Cataloging-in-Publication Data
Lewin, Ariel.
  [Giudea e Palestina. English]
  The archaeology of ancient Judea and Palestine/
Ariel Lewin; [Brian D. Phillips, translator].
     p. cm.
  "The ancient cities, by Ariel Lewin in collaboration with Leah
     Di Segni."
  Includes bibliographical references and index.
  ISBN-13: 978-0-89236-800-6 (hardcover)
  ISBN-10: 0-89236-800-4 (hardcover)
  1. Palestine—Antiquities. 2. Excavations (Archaeology)—Palestine.
  3. Cities and towns, Ancient—Palestine. I. Di Segni, L. (Leah)
  II. Title.
  DS111.L4913 2004
  933—dc22
                             2004017938
Printed by EBS Editoriale Bortolazzi-Stei, Verona, Italy

Photograph Credits
Archives of the Studium Biblicum Franciscanum Jerusalem; Photos Custody of the Holy Land and Garo Nalbandian: pp. 47, 53, 58, 68, 72, 73 (above), 106, 108, 109, 120, 126, 142–44, 148, 179, 184–85

Building plan drawings on pages 48, 63, 119, 122, 140, 147, and 150 by permission of Oxford University Press.

Contents

Preface

This book is intended not for the specialist scholar but for cultivated people who wish to find in a single volume both an account of the history of Judea/Palestine and an introduction to the most important archaeological sites in the area. Readers who wish to delve deeper into the subject can make use of the appended bibliography.

I must clarify my reasons for choosing a very specific geographical area: I have examined in detail only the archaeological sites situated within the state of Israel and the emerging state of Palestine. I have thus not considered sites beyond the Jordan, which were ruled over by the Herodian kings of Judea for a certain period, nor those towns in present-day southern Jordan that the Romans incorporated into the province of Palaestina III in late antiquity. Editorial considerations of space necessitated a painful process of selection, which in the end meant neglecting important sites even within the chosen area. I therefore decided not to deal with places beyond the Jordan, which were only briefly within the political and administrative sphere of Judea/Palestine. It may well be asked why I have included Negev towns among the sites examined even though they only became part of Palaestina III in late antiquity, but in this case—a debatable one, I admit—I decided to include archaeological sites that are situated within the modern national boundaries of my country. It also occurs to me that I have used the technical terms "late antiquity" and "Byzantine period" without differentiating between them, so I must emphasize that the latter refers, strictly speaking, to a period beginning with the age of Constantine, not that of Diocletian.

Quite apart from these considerations, concentrating attention on a region that is still without peace may serve to encourage the hope that in the not-too-distant future Israeli and Palestinian states may live side by side in times of mutual political, religious, and cultural respect!

I wish to thank Billy Propp and Leah Di Segni for their collaboration in realizing this volume and my colleague Carlo Maria Simonetti of the University of Basilicata for his help in revising this work.

Ariel Lewin

Introduction to Historical Events

Jewish Origins

William H. C. Propp

During the Iron Age, from the thirteenth and twelfth century B.C. onward, a new people settled on the hills of Palestine (ancient Canaan, that is to say, which covered not only the modern state of Israel but also the occupied territories and Lebanon), which formerly had been heavily wooded. The small villages that grew up survived on a mixed agricultural and pastoral economy, and there is little evidence that their internal organization involved economic stratification or social differences. Due to the lack of documentary evidence, we do not even know the name of this people. Nor do we know where they came from: whether they were foreigners settling in a new region—maybe nomadic shepherds anxious to cultivate the land—or an indigenous people who had been living in the plain and now sought a new frontier and better security, as their pottery suggests. There is also doubt as to whether these hill dwellers were related to the various nomadic peoples mentioned in Late Bronze Age texts (ca. 1550–1200 B.C.). Although it is difficult to establish ethnicity at such an early period, especially where there is a paucity of documentary evidence, the fact that this people refrained from eating pork and avoided representing male figures in their statues would seem to be significant. Since their villages were situated in the midst of

what was, according to the Bible, an Israelite settlement, most scholars think the inhabitants were Israelites. In that same century, the thirteenth, the pharaoh Merneptah claimed that he had encountered a group called "Israel" and had eradicated it: "Israel is destroyed, but not its seed!"

It may perhaps seem odd to begin Jewish history with archaeology and Egyptian texts, for after all the Bible seems to state with confidence who the Israelites were, where they came from, and when they arrived in the land where they settled. But archaeology has not confirmed the biblical narrative. Researchers have concluded that there could not have been a mass exodus from Egypt followed by a dramatic conquest of Canaan in the fifteenth and fourteenth centuries B.C., as the Bible would have us believe. Since the nineteenth century, furthermore, scholars have shown that the Bible was composed at different times, and that although the Torah is attributed to Moses, it was not in fact composed by a single person. The stories in the Bible were written centuries or even millennia after the events they narrate, and therefore archaeology offers a more solid basis for a historical reconstruction. As one might imagine, biblical sources can be considered better informed only for the later periods.

Both biblical and Mesopotamian sources assert that from the ninth century B.C. onward, two kingdoms ruled the land: the kingdom of

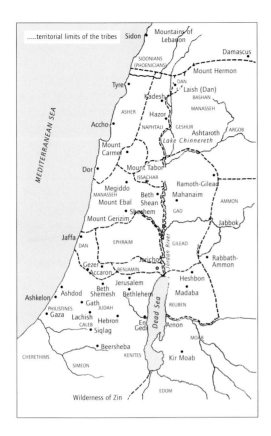

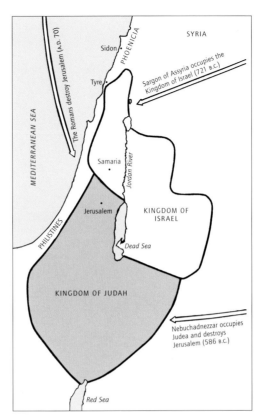

Opposite: Figure of the god Bes, from the Megiddo Ivories (Jerusalem, Rockefeller Museum). Megiddo is a very ancient site at a strategic point in the most important pass in the Mount Carmel chain. The name first appears in an inscription in the temple at Karnak in Upper Egypt, containing an account of the city's conquest by Pharaoh Thutmose III in 1468 B.C. Megiddo plays an important part in the Book of Revelation (16:16), where we are told that the final battle between the forces of God and evil will take place at Armageddon (Har Megedon: the "mountain of Megiddo").

Left: The Twelve Tribes in the Palestine of the Judges

Right: The kingdoms of Judah and Israel

Israel to the north, and that of Judah to the south. Israel stretched north from Bethel to Dan, near Mount Hermon, while Judah stretched south from Jerusalem to the Negev. The Bible says that they were two branches of the same people, the "children of Israel"; and material remains do indeed suggest that, in spite of regional differences, their culture, language, and religion were the same. According to the Bible, these kingdoms were the remains of a united tenth-century monarchy: a small empire that had held sway over Canaan and Transjordan. The capital of this political unit was Jerusalem, with its royal palace and a splendid temple dedicated to the national god. Archaeologists, however, have come to believe that no imperial Israel ever existed; and there is still debate as to the historical reality of Saul, David, and Solomon, those early kings who are supposed to have reigned approximately from 1020 to 922 B.C. There is an Aramaic stele attesting that in the

ninth century B.C. the kingdom of Judah was known in Syria as "the house of David." But no one has ever discovered a document pertaining to these early kings.

The Bible tells of an age before the kings when there had been a loose tribal federation led by charismatic "judges" who were really more military commanders than jurists. This period may be the time of the first Iron Age settlements in the thirteenth and twelfth centuries B.C. Before that—so the Bible tells us—the Israelites had dwelt in the land for centuries but had then moved to Egypt to escape a famine. In Egypt they had been enslaved but were finally freed in a miraculous manner. Archaeology has little or nothing to say about the stories of Abraham, Isaac, Jacob, Joseph, and Moses, although there are certain isolated aspects of the tradition, such as a pastoral way of life, tribalism, and the pre-eminence of Asians in Egypt, that have parallels in known historical events and circumstances.

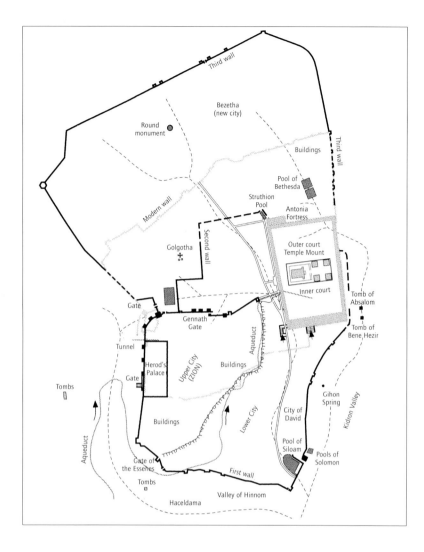

According to the authors of the Bible, the religious ideal was monotheistic. While both the Bible and archaeology confirm that polytheistic tendencies also existed, scholars have pointed out that almost all Hebrew divine names refer to the single god *YHWH*, who appears quite frequently in Hebrew inscriptions as well as occasionally in foreign texts referring to the Israelites. Ancient Hebrew writing did not indicate vowels, but scholars have given this divine name the pronunciation "Yahweh," which is apparently a form of the verb "to be." This concentration on a single male god is part of a regional tendency in the first millennium B.C., and it coincides with the rise of centralized states. While most civilizations recognized a multitude of gods, only one was raised to the status of representing the state and the sovereign.

One special metaphor governed Israel's conception of its relationship with Yahweh. Adopting the terminology of contemporary vassal treaties in the Middle East, the people as a whole defined themselves as the servants of Yahweh, obeying the terms of a covenant that placed the entire group under an obligation for a favor received in the past. The people were consequently forbidden to serve any other gods and were obliged to recite the content of their covenant with God in public. This privileged relationship brought them great blessings and terrible punishments, depending on the extent of their faithfulness to God. The many laws in the Torah are the terms of the covenant.

Although prophecy was a widespread phenomenon in the Near East, it seems to have been an Israelite specialty: They had schools of prophets who conveyed messages from Yahweh, either by pronouncing them while in a state of trance or setting them out in poems of great artistic merit. It is not surprising to learn that since the prophets were in competition, their prophecies often contradicted one another. Historical experience, however, acted as a filter, and inaccurate predictions were thus brushed aside and forgotten. What remains in the Bible is an extremely coherent corpus of prophecies, which threaten Israel with terrible consequences for its recurrent lack of faithfulness to God.

The Israelite kingdoms and the neighboring civilizations of Philistia, Phoenicia, Aram, Moab, Ammon, and Edom rose and flourished at a time in the first millennium B.C. when both Egypt and Mesopotamia were in decline. However, Egyptian and Assyrian power increased again in the ninth century, and in the end the small nations of Syria and Palestine became subservient to the policies of the great powers. They took part in conspiracies in favor of one or other of the great powers in the region and periodically rose up in rebellion, with the inevitable result that all the kingdoms in the region were subjugated. First Israel (722/721 B.C.) and then Judah (587/586 B.C.) had to suffer the fate reserved for rebels who succumbed to the might of Assyria and Babylon: They were scattered and deported to other lands. However, it is still not clear whether this deportation affected the whole population or just certain elites. The ancient northern kingdom disappeared into the mists of legend as the "ten lost tribes," though the Samaritans still claim to be their descendants.

The fate of the southern kingdom of Judah was different, largely because the new empire of Babylon was short-lived (626–539 B.C.). At this time of decline in the kingdom of Judah, the prophet Jeremiah had predicted not only a hard fate but also a revival. In 539 B.C., Cyrus the Persian conquered Babylon and immediately afterward sent the Jews back to their ancient land. There they were subject to the Persian satrap but tried to revive their ancient way of life, rebuilding the temple on a smaller scale and restoring the rite of sacrifice. Zerubbabel, a descendant of the royal line, gained temporary preeminence as governor under Darius I (522–485 B.C.), but the Davidic monarchy was never restored, and prophecy languished. The old propaganda about the eternal rule of David was converted into hope for an eschatological messiah or a consecrated king.

The Persian province of Judah has left us scarcely any written texts. It seems likely that its religion retained most of its pre-exile aspects, with priestly sacrifices in the temple at Jerusalem. Scholars also maintain that this was the period when almost the whole of the Old Testament or Tanach was written (with the sole exception of the Book of Daniel), and that it was completed in the fourth century. Most of the raw material of the Old Testament—its historical sources from Genesis to the Second Book of Kings, the books of the prophets (Isaiah through Malachi), and the Psalms—must already have existed in some form before the exile. The Jews seem to have been part of an international movement that tended to express national sentiment in terms of the study and compilation of its history and laws. In this period, under the influence of Zoroastrianism, Judaism developed strong dualistic tendencies, seeing the cosmos as a field of battle between the forces of good and evil.

With a series of resounding victories in the years 334–326 B.C., Alexander III of Macedonia (Alexander the Great) destroyed Persian power in Egypt, Syria, and Palestine. Judah was incorporated into the province of Coele-Syria with Samaria as its capital and became known as Judea. When Alexander died in Babylon, his generals divided up the empire, and Judea became an object of contention between Ptolemy I, king of Egypt, and Seleucus I, king of Syria. From 301 to 198 B.C., Judea was under the control of Egypt. The Jews in Egypt now had a flourishing culture, especially at Alexandria, where the Bible was translated into Greek (the Septuagint). However, in 198 B.C., the Seleucid king Antiochus III the Great annexed Palestine to his Asian empire. In Hellenistic times, Judaism was in permanent contact with Greek culture, and Greek language and Greek thought began to influence Hebrew and Judaism. To some extent the hellenization of the Jews was a natural and peaceful process, but internal disagreements soon emerged and erupted into violence, as for instance when Antiochus IV Epiphanes (175–164 B.C.) tried to hellenize Judea by force.

Roman Judea and Palestine
Ariel Lewin

Hellenization encountered resistance in the world of Judea, a small region with its center at Jerusalem; but while part of the populace and the ruling classes were opposed to any kind of contact with things Greek, there were some exponents of Hebrew society who looked upon the values of Hellenistic culture with interest.

The highest religious position among the Jews at that time was that of high priest of the Temple of Jerusalem. This temple, in which animals were daily sacrificed to God, was of fundamental importance to the Jewish people. The key factor in their religious sentiment and morality was a strict observance of the books of the Bible (the Torah), whose authority was beyond all question. The life of the people was also regulated by detailed rules of ritual purity. The name of God could never be spoken, and the representation of human or animal figures was forbidden. This last prohibition derived from a strict interpretation of the second commandment: "You shall not make for yourself a graven image, or any likeness of anything that is in heaven above, or that is in the earth beneath, or that is in the water under the earth; you shall not bow down to them or serve them."

A moment of crisis in the Jews' relationship with their Seleucid overlords came when King Antiochus IV Epiphanes not only deposed the high priest of the Temple but insisted on imposing his own candidate for the position; later, in 167 B.C., he went so far as to ban temple worship altogether. A rebellion against this draconian provision was led by members of the Maccabees, who rallied a peasant army imbued with a spirit of nationalistic determination. After various wars, which did not always turn out in their favor, the Jews managed to achieve political independence in 129 B.C. The Maccabees then founded the Hasmonean dynasty. One of the descendants of the Maccabees who had rebelled against Antiochus took the title of king. This was either Aristobulus (104–103 B.C.) or, more probably, Alexander Jannaeus (103–76 B.C.). The Maccabees also insisted on monopolizing for themselves and their relatives the position of high priest of the Temple, which continued to be the highest religious position among the Jews.

The little Hebrew kingdom was based geographically on Judea, with Jerusalem at its center. Under the command of several warlike kings, especially Alexander Jannaeus, it took advantage of the dramatic weakening of the Hellenistic kingdoms to increase its size considerably. In this way it took control of Galilee, certain territories beyond the Jordan, Idumea, and part of the coastal region. The Hasmonean kings looked favorably on Hellenistic culture, and Aristobulus went so far as to call himself "philhellenic." These new attitudes often aroused unrest among the population.

In 66 B.C., when the Roman general Pompey was returning from a series of conquests in the East, he used the quarrels that had arisen in Judea after the death of the Hasmonean ruler Alexandra in 67 B.C. as an excuse to intervene there. Alexandra's sons, Aristobulus and Hyrcanus, quarreled over both the kingly title and the posi-

tion of high priest, and although Hyrcanus was the elder brother and therefore the legitimate heir, he was pushed aside by Aristobulus. Pompey skillfully entered the quarrel and restored Hyrcanus to power. His victorious military campaign concluded at Jerusalem in 63 B.C., but while there he committed an act that the Jews thought sacrilegious: He not only entered that part of the Temple reserved for the Jews alone but dared to make his way into the Holy of Holies, which was forbidden to all but the high priest. The ill feeling aroused by this odious act did not die down with the passage of time, and in the second century A.D., during a Jewish revolt at Alexandria, Pompey's tomb there was destroyed.

Roman intervention in Judea put Hyrcanus back in power, but only as high priest. The title of king was abolished, and, being a somewhat weak character, Hyrcanus made no attempt to get it back. Judea, like the other lands that had belonged to the Hasmoneans, had fallen once more into the hands of a foreign power that demanded tribute from it. In 57 B.C., the Roman general Gabinius decreed that Jewish territory be divided into five districts administered by leading local citizens. In some ways this was a further loss of power and prestige for Hyrcanus, who was under the influence of Antipater, the powerful governor of Idumea. The latter was an expert military commander and totally loyal to the Romans.

When Antipater died in 43 B.C., his son Herod inherited his position as strongman of the regime and ally of Rome. As the years went by, Mark Antony and Cassius, the murderer of Julius Caesar, rewarded him with various responsible tasks, and he went on to form a close friendship with Augustus. His extraordinarily cold and calculating nature is revealed by his ability not merely to survive unscathed during the various changes at the head of the Roman world but even progressively to increase his own power.

In 40 B.C., the Persians invaded Judea, took Hyrcanus prisoner, and put Antigonus, son of Aristobulus, on the throne, appointing him high priest as well. Antigonus had Hyrcanus's ears cut off, a mutilation that, under Jewish law, made

him ineligible for the position of high priest. The Romans entrusted the reconquest of Judea to their faithful ally Herod, who was given the title king of Judea. Military operations against the Persians came to an end in 37 B.C., their success being largely due to the intervention of Roman legions. Antigonus was beheaded, and his death brought Hasmonean domination to an end forever.

The reign of Herod

Herod had thus become a king and ally of the Romans, a *rex socius et amicus populi romani*. However, it is important to note the limits that Roman power placed on these so-called client kings. They were, in fact, chosen or deposed at the whim of the Romans, who in practice consid-

ered such client kingdoms to be as much part of the Roman Empire as its provinces.

Herod remained in power until his death in 4 B.C., and thanks to Roman support he managed to add new territories to his kingdom, such as Trachonitis, Gaulanitis, Batanaea, Perea, and Banyas (Paneas). But his regime was viewed with hostility by a large part of the Jewish population. For various reasons, the Hasmoneans had often had to face the hostility of their subjects, who saw them as tyrants. But Herod's position was different: Not only did he exert his power with cruelty, using an army of mercenaries, but he was also disliked because he was considered only half Jewish. His father was in fact an Idumean (the Idumeans had in any case been converted to Judaism for decades) and his mother, Cypros,

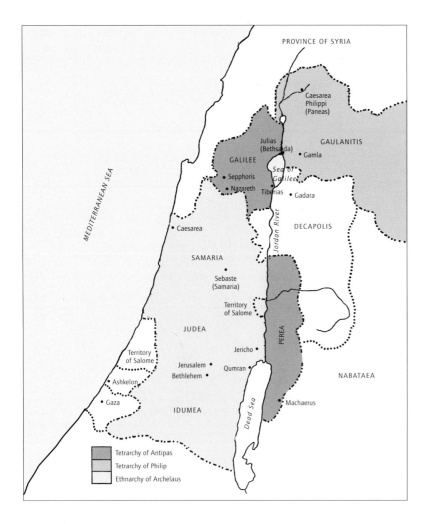

Tetrarchy of Antipas
Tetrarchy of Philip
Ethnarchy of Archelaus

was a Nabataean. By marrying Mariamme, a niece of Hyrcanus, he tried to give himself dynastic legitimacy, but this step does not seem to have gained him popular sympathy.

Since his condition precluded him from becoming high priest of the Temple, he appointed to the post people who were beholden to him, rather than members of the old aristocracy. Also under Herod, the high priest ceased to be appointed for life, serving instead at the pleasure of whoever held the reins of political power. In thirty-three years, Herod chose a total of seven different high priests.

Among the more brutal deeds of Herod's reign were the execution of forty-five members of

the Jewish aristocracy and the confiscation of their property; the execution of his brother-in-law Aristobulus, a seventeen-year-old who had risen to the rank of high priest, but whose popularity turned him into an object of suspicion; and the elimination of Hyrcanus immediately after Octavian's victory at Actium. As a loyal ally of Antony, Herod was now fearful for his future, and he thought it wise to get rid of a possible rival for the throne.

Not long afterward, in 29 B.C., he also eliminated his wife Mariamme. This crime was committed within an atmosphere of intrigue in a palace dominated by his mother-in-law Alexandra on the one hand, and by his mother, Cypros, and sister Salome on the other. Herod's extraordinary jealousy fed on false rumors of Mariamme's infidelity until he finally accepted them as true.

The years from 25 to 13 B.C. were on the whole the calmest of Herod's reign, and he devoted his energies to constructing monumental public buildings in various cities. Theaters and hippodromes sprang up and a whole series of public events was instituted. A new city, called Caesarea, was founded, and the ancient city of Samaria was rebuilt and renamed Sebaste. As an ally of the Romans, Herod was thus organizing his kingdom in such a way as to situate it firmly within the cultural climate of the Graeco-Roman world, at the same time stressing his total loyalty to imperial Rome. He built a royal palace at Jerusalem as well as luxurious leisure complexes at Masada, Jericho, and Herodion. He renovated an ancient fortress at Jerusalem, calling it Antonia, and built a series of outlying fortresses whose purpose was not to defend against outside attack but to imprison political opponents. His most ambitious project, the rebuilding of the Temple in Jerusalem, was started in 20 or 19 B.C. and completed in 12 B.C. A huge workforce was involved, and the operation certainly acted as a safety valve under conditions of social unrest and high unemployment.

In the closing years of his reign, Herod had to face a new drama, and once again its origins lay in family intrigue. In 7 B.C., Herod had his two sons by Mariamme, Alexander and

Aristobulus, put to death at the instigation of Antipater, a son by his first wife, Doris. However, Herod soon learned of a plot organized by Antipater, and when the latter failed to produce any evidence in his own defense, the king had him imprisoned. But everyone knew that Herod was now very ill and his fate sealed. Two influential rabbis therefore incited the people to get rid of the blasphemous eagle, symbol of Roman power, which the king had installed at the entrance to the Temple. When Herod heard about this, he ordered that the instigators of the deed be burned alive. A few days before his own death, he also gave orders that the death sentence on Antipater be carried out. And finally, knowing that the Jews would rejoice at his demise, he arranged for prominent inhabitants of the villages of Judea to be held in the Jericho hippodrome, ready to be slaughtered on the day of their sovereign's death. Fortunately, this deathbed wish was ignored and the intended victims were released. Herod's life thus came to an end in an atmosphere of extreme violence, which very much reflected the character of his whole reign. In order to preserve his own power he had not hesitated to commit any crime. His chief occupation had been to preserve his close friendship with those in power in Rome, and to that end he relied on the loyalty of his armed forces. This pleasure-loving king had ten wives and many children, but he died unmourned by his family and hated by the whole nation.

The sons of Herod

In his last will, Herod had chosen Archelaus as his successor. This decision inevitably caused resentment in Antipas, a son by his Samaritan wife Malthace, who had been preferred in his first will.

In this atmosphere of tension and uncertainty, the members of Herod's family appeared before Augustus in Rome to present their rival claims. As we have seen, the client kingdoms were really an integral part of Roman dominions, and consequently Rome reserved the right to choose sovereigns and establish the borders of these kingdoms. Since power in Rome lay in the hands of Augustus, it was he who made all the deci-

sions; hence it was at his court that Archelaus and Antipas presented their dispute. At a later stage, a delegation from the people of Judea also came to Augustus, to request that neither of the two claimants be appointed and that the Jews of Judea be allowed to govern themselves in accordance with their own laws, though under Roman sovereignty. With fresh memories of Herod's tyrannical regime, the Jews greeted with dismay the prospect of seeing one of his descendants on the throne.

In the meantime, however, there had been uprisings in Jerusalem, Galilee, and other parts of Herod's kingdom against the representatives of Roman power who had provisionally taken over the reins of government until Augustus reached a decision. The insurrection was put down by Varus, the Roman legate in Syria, who brought in his army and destroyed the city of Sepphoris, sold its inhabitants into slavery, and crucified two thousand rebels.

In the end, Augustus partly confirmed the decisions made by Herod: Archelaus obtained Judea, Samaria, and Idumea. But he lost control of some cities that were formerly part of the kingdom, including the important commercial center of Gaza, which now became part of the province of Syria. In addition, he did not receive the title of king but had to make do with that of ethnarch. Antipas was given Galilee and Perea (two non-contiguous areas) and the title of tetrarch, while Philip, another son of Herod and half-brother of Archelaus and Antipas, received Batanaea, Auranitis, Trachonitis, and Banyas (areas with a mixed Jewish and Syrian population, but with an overall preponderance of the latter), and he too was given the title of tetrarch.

The rule of Archelaus was such a failure that in A.D. 6 a delegation of Jews and Samaritans arrived in Rome to complain to Augustus. The complaints must have been reasonably well founded, for Augustus decided to relieve Archelaus of his position and exile him to Gaul. The Romans thereafter decided to install their own administration in the land of Judea, headed by an official of equestrian rank, but Philip and Herod Antipas continued to rule as tetrarchs.

Philip ruled until his death in A.D. 33/34, and he is recorded in sources as a just and peace-loving ruler. His claim to fame lay in having rebuilt and embellished the city of Banyas at the source of the Jordan, calling it Caesarea in honor of the emperor. It subsequently came to be known as Caesarea Philippi in order to distinguish it from the other Caesarea, founded by Herod on the Mediterranean. He also rebuilt Bethsaida on the north shore of the Sea of Galilee, naming it Julias in honor of Augustus's daughter.

The rule of Antipas was quite different. It was noteworthy for the rebuilding of Sepphoris and the founding of the new city of Tiberias, which became the capital of his tetrarchy. Though he was a cunning and cruel man, Antipas scrupulously carried out his duties as a Jew in relation to the Temple in Jerusalem, which he visited for religious festivities and defended against the outrages of the Roman administrators in Judea. In accordance with the practice of "political" marriages among eastern dynasties, he married the daughter of the Nabataean king, but while on a journey to Rome he fell in love with Herodias, the wife of his half-brother. Being an ambitious woman, she agreed to marry Antipas; the latter's wife fled when she heard what had happened, taking refuge with her father. The result was great tension between Antipas and the king of the Nabataeans. It was at this time that the preaching of John the Baptist became famous in Judea and within the tetrarchy of Antipas. John's outright condemnation of Antipas's marriage to Herodias increased the tetrarch's irritation, perhaps decisively: He had John imprisoned and then beheaded at the fortress-prison of Machaerus in Perea (almost certainly in A.D. 35). The special part played in this episode by Salome, the young daughter of Herodias, is well known. Having performed a sensual dance before Antipas, she succeeded, at the behest of her mother, in persuading him to give her John's head.

Source of the Jordan River with the famous temple of Pan at the ancient city of Banyas (Paneas), renamed Caesarea Philippi when Philip, son of Herod the Great, rebuilt it

Judea becomes a Roman province

The first Roman administrator in Judea was a man named Coponius. The Roman presence there was apparently rather light, since only auxiliary forces were retained to keep order. The power of the Roman military machine lay in the legions, but none were sent to Judea. For the Romans, Judea was a sort of appendix to the great province of Syria, where there was indeed an imposing military presence. Since the governor of Judea was of equestrian rank, he was in practice a subordinate of the powerful legate of Syria, who was a senatorial governor of consular rank.

Greek sources describe the equestrian official in charge of the Judean government as an *epitropos*, and scholars used to think that he was a procurator. But the discovery of the famous Pontius Pilate inscription at Caesarea in 1961 by Italian scholars (it records that Pilate was responsible for an important building, perhaps a temple in honor of Tiberius) reopened the whole question by providing new and unexpected information, for in the inscription Pilate is described as a prefect. It seems clear, therefore, that the early prefects were only replaced by procurators at the time of the emperor Claudius (A.D. 41–54), and that this change in the rank of the official in charge of administration was a result of the increasing preeminence of the emperors in relation to the senate. The title of prefect, although it originally specifically described an administrator of imperial property, emphasized the military nature of the post, whereas that of procurator was related to property administration.

The headquarters of the Roman prefect was a palace in Caesarea, but he also used Herod's former palace in Jerusalem as a *praetorium*.

The presence of a prefect also had a striking consequence for the religious life of the Jews, for now that there was no king to exercise authority over the nation, the right to appoint the high priest of the Temple was given by the Roman emperor to his local representative. And Herod's practice of appointing the high priest for an indefinite term rather than for life was continued.

Governing Judea was not an easy task for the prefects. Converting it into a province meant car-

rying out a census in order to organize tax collection, and putting this procedure into effect aroused such general discontent that there was some danger of it leading to a full-fledged rebellion. Some quite substantial uprisings took place, in fact, thanks to the activities of Judas the Galilean, who was a vigorous opponent of Roman government. He and a Pharisee called Saddok are remembered as the founders of a "philosophy" that proposed the rejection of any kind of government—by the Jewish kings as well as the Romans—and submission to the will of God. Judas and his followers also attacked the property ownership of the rich pro-Roman Jews. In the end he was killed and his followers scattered, but hostility toward the Romans and collaborationist Jews nevertheless continued to thrive among various sectors of the population, where a strong nationalist feeling was permeated with an extraordinary kind of religious inspiration. And we also have to remember that social discontent created a latent tension that could sometimes explode into acts of banditry.

The A.D. 6 census was ordered by Quirinus, the Roman legate in Syria. The Gospel of Luke tells us that it was this procedure that obliged Joseph to go with his wife from Nazareth in Galilee to Bethlehem in order to register, since that was his home town. As is well known, this seems to run counter to the whole rest of the story in the Gospels, according to which Jesus was born during the reign of Herod.

This was a time when the quarrels between Jews and Samaritans grew fiercer, and it was only the firm action of the prefect Coponius that prevented an outbreak of violence. The Samaritans hated the Jews because they held them responsible for the fact that their temple on Mount Gerizim in Samaria had been destroyed by the Hasmonean king Hyrcanus I and had never been rebuilt.

As we have mentioned, it was in A.D. 6 that the Roman authorities began the practice of themselves appointing the high priest. Quirinus was responsible for deposing Joazar, who had encountered popular hostility, and appointing Ananus, whose family succeeded in nearly monopolizing the post for the next sixty years, until the outbreak of the Great Revolt. All five sons of Ananus became high priest in turn, and it seems that Caiaphas, who succeeded Ananus after he had been high priest for about ten years, was his son-in-law. The high priest came to be the head of the Jewish nation under Roman rule; in addition to his position as religious leader, he was also head of the Sanhedrin, the nation's supreme council.

It is important to note that in general the prefect tried not to interfere too heavy-handedly in the life of Judea, except in cases of serious public disorder and the collection of direct taxes. Indirect taxes were farmed out, but as a result of a reform instituted by Augustus, the grasping Roman tax collectors were forbidden to operate in the provinces. The tax collectors who operated in Judea were therefore Jews who had bought concessions. For their part, the high priest and the Sanhedrin had plenty of scope for exercising power over the people, and it also appears that the Sanhedrin enjoyed the right to issue and carry out sentences of death, though perhaps only when so authorized by the Roman authorities.

That Pontius Pilate remained prefect of Judea for many years (A.D. 26–36/37) was in accordance with the normal policy of the emperor Tiberius, who liked to keep provincial administrators in office for lengthy periods. During Pilate's rule, there was a good deal of tension and friction between him and the Jews. Philo of Alexandria describes Pilate as cruel, inflexible, corrupt, and violent. Shortly after his arrival in Judea, he ordered the transfer of a new military unit to Jerusalem. These units had portraits of the emperor among their insignia, while Jewish law prohibited the representation of human or animal figures. The operation was obviously carried out with some discretion: The new garrison arrived by night and their banners were kept covered. But as soon as Pilate's action became known, the Jews' anger quickly erupted, as they could not tolerate the presence of these images near the Temple. Pilate returned to Caesarea but was followed by a crowd of Jews who demonstrated at his palace, demanding that the military unit be removed

from Jerusalem. Pilate refused and followed his refusal with threats, but the Jews would not give up. Five days later he summoned them to an audience in the stadium. This was simply an attempt to terrorize them: He had them surrounded by soldiers, implying that they would be massacred if they did not leave and abandon their claims. To Pilate's amazement, they all offered their necks to the sword, proclaiming that they preferred to die rather than contravene the Law; Pilate was forced to give in. The guilty military unit was removed from Jerusalem.

Some time later, another of Pilate's acts caused ill feeling and unrest. In order to improve the water supply to Jerusalem, he had had an aqueduct built. This in itself was certainly a worthy undertaking, but the work was financed by appropriating money from the Temple treasury. Tensions rose, Pilate called in the army, and many demonstrators were killed.

Later on, probably toward the end of his period in office, Pilate arranged to have some inscribed gilded shields hung in his palace in Jerusalem. They did not bear any human or animal images, but for some reason they upset the Jews. Protests were therefore lodged, and a letter was even sent to Tiberius, who reprimanded his official and ordered him to transfer the shields to the temple of imperial worship at Caesarea. The scholar Luisa Prandi has made an interesting reconstruction of an incomplete inscription suggesting that Pilate's intention was to place the shields in the temple and thus to celebrate its embellishment in honor of Tiberius.

The name of Pilate is indissolubly linked to the Passion of Christ. Various theories have been put forward as to the part played by Pilate in the events leading to the Crucifixion. Over the centuries, the Jews have been branded and persecuted as deicides because they condemned Jesus to death. This attitude has now fortunately been abandoned for the most part, but it has to be pointed out that, if accepted, it has certain juridical implications, for it suggests that though operating within a Roman province, the Sanhedrin still had powers of criminal jurisdiction and also the right to issue sentences of death. This view

Opposite, above: Coin minted by Pontius Pilate, the Roman procurator of Judea. The crooked staff is a sign of the Roman augur, the priest who foretold the future.

Opposite, below: Bronze coin celebrating the Roman conquest of Judea, represented as a defeated woman

has caused scholars much perplexity, for they believe that the Sanhedrin had no such powers, and that only the prefect was vested with that authority. In more recent years, a new and thoroughly rigorous study has clarified the terms of the problem and provided a fresh interpretation of the events leading to the Crucifixion. In this context, the prominent historian Fergus Millar has pointed out that, in the first place, the Gospel of John shows a better understanding of Jewish society before the destruction of the Temple than the synoptic Gospels (Matthew, Mark, and Luke). John provides an excellent description of the nature of Jewish life, built as it was around the Temple, with a regular pattern of pilgrimages to Jerusalem from the countryside and other towns on the occasion of traditional religious festivities. It is in the Gospel of John that the events leading to the arrest, interrogation, and crucifixion of Jesus are presented with considerable consistency, and in a way that can reveal the exact nature of the problem of the so-called trial of Jesus from a strictly formal point of view. Jesus was taken before Pilate by some Jewish notables led by the high priest Caiaphas on the eve of the Jewish Passover, and when the Jews asked the Roman prefect to condemn him, Pilate told them to take him and judge him (but he did not say *execute* him). However, the Jews pointed out that they were not allowed to condemn anyone to death. At first sight this statement seems very odd, because it is surely impossible to suppose that Pilate was unaware of the limits on the juridical authority of the Jewish notables. The point made by the Jews has a certain logic, however, if we keep in mind that the Jews were trying to remind Pilate of the particular significance of the moment. For this was the eve of the Passover, a day of preparation for the feast, and on that and the following days they were not allowed to hold trials involving a possible death sentence. It was not Roman law that placed a limit on their authority to act, but their own religion. Furthermore, as Millar has shown, we have to remember that it was then normally the case that trials involving a possible death sentence were the responsibility of the high priest and not the Sanhedrin. In such cases, in

fact, the high priest would select a group of citizens to assist him by acting as a jury. As we have seen, the high priest was chosen by the Romans and was therefore a kind of "collaborator" at the heart of society, whose attitude to the ruling power was quite different from most. The decision to have Jesus executed was thus a concession granted by Pilate and dictated by political considerations, as a result of pressure brought to bear by the high priest and a crowd of his supporters. And finally, let us point out that a study by Nikos Kokkinos has established convincingly that the Crucifixion took place in A.D. 36.

In order to understand the nature of the Jewish religion at the time of Jesus, it must above all be remembered that it still centered on strict observance of the written Law (the Torah), temple worship, the celebration of religious feasts, and the observance of prescribed ritual purity. The written Law contained basic advice about almost every aspect of daily life: agriculture, dress, festivities, and offerings for priests and Levites. Saturday was the day of rest and prayer to the Lord; the most important feasts were Passover, which commemorated the flight from Egypt and the crossing of the Red Sea; Pentecost, so called because it fell fifty days after Passover and celebrated the offering of first fruits in the Temple; New Year's Day; the Day of Atonement; and the Feast of Tabernacles of Sukkoth, during which four types of plant were taken in procession to Jerusalem, and tents were raised to commemorate the wanderings in the desert. Alongside the written tradition, there was also a parallel oral tradition, in which consideration was given to matters treated in only a vague and general way in the former.

The works of Josephus, a first-century historian, point out the important role played in Jewish national life by three schools of thought: the Pharisees, the Sadducees, and the Essenes. Each had its own particular characteristics. There is clear evidence for the existence of these sects at the beginning of the first century B.C. The priestly aristocracy gravitated to the Sadducee group, and judging by Josephus's description, they were not pleasant people to know. They were proud and quarrelsome and considered themselves to be guardians of the strictest cultural tradition; but they were also rationalists who did not believe in the immortality of the soul. The sect of the Pharisees, however, did believe in it, and for them, personal relationships were chiefly about establishing mutual understanding and assistance. The Pharisees were scholars devoted to the interpretation of the written Law and the formulation of oral law. The sect of the Essenes has aroused a great deal of interest over the years, because of its asceticism and because its adherents enjoyed a particular reputation for sanctity among their contemporaries. The discovery of the Dead Sea Scrolls at Qumran has stimulated great debate as to the nature of the Essenes. We will devote further attention to evidence concerning the Essenes in the section given over to the Qumran site.

Friction between the Jews and the Roman authorities continued in the years that followed. In A.D. 40 it was learned that the emperor Caligula, in an act of megalomania, had ordered that a statue of himself be placed inside the Temple in Jerusalem. Rebellion seemed inevitable, but Caligula's death and the subsequent abandonment of the project restored tranquility to Judea, at least temporarily.

Agrippa I

It was in these years that Agrippa (son of the Aristobulus put to death by Herod in 7 B.C. and hence the latter's grandson) began his ascent to power. Sources portray him as something of an adventurer: He spent his youth in Rome, where he became friendly with Drusus, son of Tiberius, but squandered all his wealth in luxuries and banquets. When Drusus died in A.D. 23, Agrippa lost his chief ally. Pursued by his creditors, he fled back to his native country, taking refuge in a fortress in Idumea, the land of his forefathers. He contemplated suicide but subsequently gained the support of his sister Herodias, who sought help from her husband, the tetrarch Antipas. Agrippa was thus welcomed by his brother-in-law and succeeded in restoring his finances. He was also

The famous inscription in honor of the emperor Tiberius containing the name of Pontius Pilate, prefect of Judea from A.D. 26 to 36/37

given the important post of supervisor of markets at Tiberias, the capital of Antipas's tetrarchy. A quarrel with his brother-in-law and various other escapades precipitated Agrippa's return to Rome in A.D. 36, this time with sufficient funds to pay off his old creditors. But it was not long before he resumed a dissolute life and struck up a friendship with Caligula. At a banquet one day, he made the mistake of expressing the hope that his friend would soon be emperor, causing Tiberius to throw him in prison. Agrippa suffered six months of harsh imprisonment, from which he was finally freed when Tiberius died and Caligula ascended to the throne (A.D. 37). The latter immediately rewarded his friend by giving him the former possessions of the tetrarch Philip, together with a small piece of land on Anti-Lebanon; he even gave him the title of king. Agrippa's return to the East to take possession of his kingdom was a flamboyant affair: On his way through Egypt he aroused the jealousy of the local prefect because his guards wore gold and silver armor. But within a few months, Agrippa was back in Rome, where he plotted against Antipas, who was finally deposed and exiled by Caligula (A.D. 39). In this way, the tetrarchy of Antipas was added to Agrippa's dominions.

When Caligula died (A.D. 41), Agrippa was once again in Rome and was able to play an important part in the negotiations between the senate and the army that led to the ascent of Claudius. Out of gratitude, Claudius ordered that Judea and Samaria be added to Agrippa's realm. It is important to note, however, that Claudius awarded the territory of Chalcis, in Lebanon, to a brother of Agrippa called Herod, who was also given the title of king.

Agrippa had thus gradually and rather unexpectedly become king of all the lands that had belonged to Herod the Great. Expectations as to the nature of the new regime were by no means optimistic, but Agrippa suddenly revealed another side to his character. When he reached Jerusalem, his first act was to hang inside the Temple the gold chain that Caligula had given him as a memento of his imprisonment. He declared that this chain bore witness to his past misadventures and the change in his destiny and showed that while the greatest men can suffer a fall, God can raise up the fallen.

Agrippa was a pious king who observed Jewish Law and often resided at Jerusalem, where he took part in religious festivities. He was liked by both the people and the Pharisees.

Beyond the borders of his own kingdom, however, he showed support for Greek culture, like his grandfather Herod, and gave theaters, amphitheaters, and baths to the towns. The amphitheater at Berytus was inaugurated with impressive gladiatorial games, at which fourteen hundred criminals were forced to fight one another to the death. And acts of cruelty were carried out even within Agrippa's own kingdom, such as the imprisonment of his former friend Silas.

To some extent Agrippa invigorated the national spirit. He began work on the construction of new northern walls at Jerusalem and offered himself as a leading figure in Near Eastern politics by gathering together some of the kings who were allies of Rome for a conference at Tiberias. But these arrangements did not please the Roman authorities, and the Syrian legate ordered him to suspend work and close the conference. Agrippa's death was as dramatic as his life: He appeared in the theater at Caesarea to public acclamation, dressed in sparkling silver raiment, but was suddenly gripped by agonizing pain. He was taken to his palace and died five days later, in A.D. 44.

The reintroduction of provinces and the reign of Agrippa II

Although the excesses of Agrippa I made him an object of some suspicion to the Romans, his death nonetheless deprived Judea of a king who appeared capable of ruling evenhandedly over a difficult land, where social, national, and religious aspirations effectively hindered the reintroduction of provinces. The natural heir to the kingdom seemed to be Agrippa's only son, also called Agrippa, but Claudius's advisers urged caution on the grounds that he was only seventeen. The entire realm consequently passed into the hands of Roman procurators, and thus for the first time the Roman province also included areas that had been part of the realms of Philip and Antipas. Herod of Chalcis was given supervisory powers over the Jerusalem Temple and its treasures, as well as the right to appoint the high priest.

Although the first two procurators are given credit by sources for managing to maintain peace in the land, they had to deal with tense situations and episodes of open hostility. It is interesting to note that the second procurator, Tiberius Julius Alexander, a Jew from Alexandria, was a nephew of the philosopher Philo and hence a member of one of the most illustrious families in the city. But he had abandoned the religion of his ancestors, preferring to embark on a career in the imperial administration.

When Alexander's successor, Cumanus, was procurator, clashes repeatedly broke out between the Jewish population and his soldiers, and in one case he ordered reprisals that caused the deaths of twenty thousand people. In this same period, Samaritans slaughtered a group of Jewish pilgrims as they passed through Samaria on their way from Galilee to Jerusalem. Cumanus, having taken bribes from the Samaritans, refused to take any action against those responsible; a band of Jews therefore took matters into their own hands, making their way into Samaria and slaughtering women, children, and the elderly. Only at this stage did Cumanus and his soldiers intervene, killing or capturing many of the Jews who had attacked the Samaritans. Subsequently, two embassies, one Jewish and the other Samaritan, came seeking justice from Ummidius Quadratus, the Roman legate in Syria. After carrying out a personal investigation in Samaria, Quadratus ordered that the captured Jews be executed, and he sent the leaders of the two peoples to Rome, to justify the conduct of their fellow countrymen before the emperor. Young Agrippa had in the meantime managed to gain control of the possessions of the late Herod of Chalcis, as well as the right to appoint the high priest. Thanks to his intervention, the Jews succeeded in having the leaders of the Samaritans condemned to death and Cumanus removed from office and exiled (A.D. 52).

The high priest Jonathan was keen to persuade Claudius to appoint Felix, a powerful imperial freedman, to the post of procurator of Judea, but this appointment had disastrous consequences. During the years of his governorship (A.D. 52–60), Felix behaved in an utterly tyrannical manner, and his misdeeds led to a series of rebellions against Roman rule. Arrests and crucifixions were inevitably followed by more anti-Roman unrest, and there was also a dramatic increase in the activities of the *sicarii*, whose name derived from the dagger (*sica*) that they customarily used to strike surreptitiously against collaborators or political opponents in the crowded streets of Jerusalem. Making use of nationalist and religious propaganda, the *sicarii* succeeded in arousing a good portion of the population, and the country soon became prey to repeated acts of rebellion.

Fearing the hostility of his fellow Judeans for having supported the appointment of Felix, Jonathan tried to reestablish his credibility by openly urging Felix to conduct a more equitable administration. But this behavior simply caused Felix to hire bandits to kill Jonathan. At about this time the Jews tried to have Paul of Damascus

condemned to death when he was brought to Caesarea to be judged by Felix. Taking advantage of the fact that he was a Roman citizen, however, Paul sought and obtained permission to be judged by the emperor himself.

The unrest in Judea did not die down when Porcius Festus succeeded Felix as procurator, but the former did manage to arrest many of the rebels, and some death penalties were imposed. He died while still in office, and it was in the period between procurators that the high priest, Ananus the Younger, summoned a meeting of the Sanhedrin to condemn James, brother of Jesus, to death by stoning. But the new procurator,

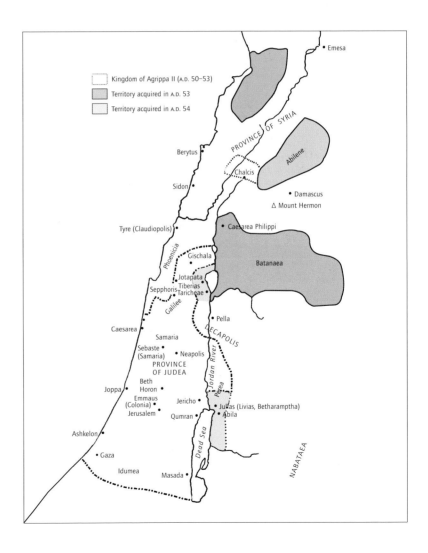

Albinus, criticized the Sanhedrin for failing to observe the correct procedure: Apparently the approval of the Roman authorities was needed before the Sanhedrin could be summoned to meet. King Agrippa therefore had Ananus removed from his post.

Tension continued to mount during the governorship of Albinus (A.D. 62–64). He was a corrupt man, ready to take bribes not only from Ananias, a former high priest who was still very influential, but also from the *sicarii*. The situation finally came to a head during the governorship of Gessius Florus (A.D. 64–66), "compared with whom even Albinus seemed a paragon of virtue," according to Josephus (*Jewish War* 2b.14.2). Sources emphasize that he carried out his misdeeds quite ostentatiously, sacking whole cities.

The Great Revolt

According to Josephus, Gessius Florus was afraid of being brought before the emperor to answer for his misdeeds, and so he decided to provoke the Jews into rebellion. He reckoned that his misdemeanors would be forgotten if events were sufficiently momentous.

In the spring of A.D. 66, the preconditions for a revolt were certainly in place: Various revolutionary groups drew on their common messianism and apocalypticism to prophesy the advent of a new world, the political struggle had reached a peak of extreme violence, and social unrest was widespread. In this context even the more moderate elements were swept up in the general climate of opposition to imperial rule.

Nor was King Agrippa II capable of playing a pacifying role, for he was openly pro-Roman. He had ruled over the so-called kingdom of Chalcis, a small realm in Lebanon, since A.D. 50 and had acquired the right to nominate the high priest. Then, in A.D. 53, he was given Batanaea, Trachonitis, Gaulanitis, and some other small districts in Lebanon. He was also granted some territories in Galilee and Perea, including the important cities of Tiberias and Taricheae, but the kingdom of Chalcis was taken away from him. As far as one can judge from the evidence,

Agrippa completely lacked charisma, and what is more, he was strongly suspected of having an incestuous relationship with his sister Berenice. On the positive side, he displayed some level of concern for Jewish religious life; he also ordered that new white paving stones be laid in Jerusalem, in order to provide work for those left unemployed after the completion of work on the Temple. Nevertheless the Jewish population continued to hold him in low esteem.

Two serious events sparked off the revolt: a bloody clash between Graeco-Syrians and Jews at Caesarea led to the unjustified arrest of some Jewish notables by Florus; and at Jerusalem, the procurator appropriated seventeen talents kept in the Temple treasury, provoking popular indignation. In order to ridicule the perpetrator, the Jews armed themselves with baskets and pretended to take up a collection for "poor" Florus. This in turn aroused Florus's resentment; he brought his troops from Caesarea, sacked Jerusalem, and killed a great many people, including some of elevated birth.

Hatred of the Romans then became uncontrollable. Agrippa made a fruitless attempt to pacify the Jerusalem Jews, but he was forced to flee the city pursued by a stone-throwing mob. In the wake of his departure, young Eleazar, son of the high priest Ananias, persuaded the Temple worshippers to abolish sacrifices on behalf of the emperor and the Romans. This was an unequivocal sign of rebellion, and some leading citizens and high priests tried to protect themselves by asking Agrippa and Florus to intervene with their troops. However, the presence of these soldiers in Jerusalem proved insufficient to deal with a situation that was now completely out of control. The troops were annihilated, Agrippa's palace was set on fire, and various pro-Roman Jewish notables were put to the sword. In this situation, the *sicarii* faction, commanded by Menahem the Galilean, tried to seize control, but Menahem was eliminated by another group of angry revolutionaries: the Zealots, commanded by Eleazar ben Simon. The surviving *sicarii* abandoned the city and took refuge in the fortress of Masada, which some of them had already occupied.

The conflict soon spread. Throughout the procurator's territory and beyond, vendettas broke out between Jews and Syrians, resulting in thousands of deaths. In Caesarea, the Jews got the worst of it, with ten thousand of them losing their lives.

Meanwhile, the Roman legate in Syria, Cestius Gallus, made his way to Jerusalem to put down the revolt, accompanied by many more soldiers than Florus had had at his disposal. In fact, Cestius Gallus arrived with a whole legion, as well as some legionary detachments and auxiliary and royal forces. Nonetheless, not only did he fail to take the city, but as he was withdrawing, in A.D. 66, he suffered a major defeat in the defiles of Beth Horon, with the loss of almost six thousand men.

In order to solidify resistance against the inevitable Roman reaction, the rebels organized themselves under the leadership of Ananus the Sadducee (the high priest who had had Jesus' brother James put to death) and Joseph, son of Gorion. Military chiefs were appointed for each region, and Josephus, the future historian of the revolt and a noble descendant of the Hasmoneans on his mother's side, was put in charge of Galilee. His job was to organize the defense of Galilee and, more generally, to keep the region tightly under his control, but this was made extremely difficult by the machinations of a certain John, son of Levi, who controlled the city of Gischala. These fierce internal struggles were only a pale anticipation, however, of what was to happen the following year, when the skilled Roman commander Vespasian, to whom Nero entrusted the crushing of the revolt, arrived in Galilee with a powerful army of about sixty thousand men. The principal episode of the campaign was the capture of Jotapata, a city whose defense was commanded by Josephus himself. The city fell after a month and a half of heroic resistance. Josephus took refuge in a cave but was finally captured by the Romans; they spared his life, however, and took him away as a prisoner. His rival John abandoned his native town of Gischala, which was therefore easily taken by the Romans, and he retreated with a faithful band of followers to Jerusalem. This Great Jewish Revolt was to some extent supported for a brief period by an uprising of Samaritans. Thousands of them gathered on their sacred mountain, Mount Gerizim, and proclaimed their independence. But this uprising was rapidly crushed by Vespasian's army.

Meanwhile, at Jerusalem, irreparable divisions appeared in the rebel camp. The Zealots, who were opposed to the traditional power group headed by Ananus, insisted that the high priest be chosen by lot from a list of ordinary people. This move permanently damaged the prestige of Ananus and the notables; they in turn tried to rouse the populace against the Zealots, who in the meantime had been joined by John the Levite and his armed band. This outbreak of civil war was finally resolved by the arrival in Jerusalem of a powerful group of Idumeans, whose intervention had been sought by the Zealots. They made their way into the city, massacred Ananus and the most important members of his faction, and also fell upon the populace, slaughtering eighty-five hundred of their number. But in the end, the regime of terror imposed by the Zealots disgusted even the Idumeans, who left the city.

Vespasian realized that the civil war raging in Jerusalem would in the end exhaust the Jews. In A.D. 68 he decided to attack the city, but in the meantime a few months had sufficed for him to take control of Perea, Samaria, the coastal region, and Jericho. Then, at the beginning of the following summer, even the districts nearest to Jerusalem fell to the imperial authority. In this way the center of the revolt was isolated, and only the fortresses of Masada, Herodion, and Machaerus were still in the hands of the rebels.

Meanwhile, a new figure had carved himself a portion of power in Jerusalem. This was Simon bar Giora, a native of Gerasa (modern Jarash). He had already distinguished himself militarily at the time of Cestius Gallus's arrival, when he assembled a band of armed men and terrorized the countryside in Judea and Idumea. Within a few months, news of these enterprises motivated the people of Jerusalem and the Idumean group—tired as they were the tyrannical regime of the Zealots, now headed by John, son of Levi—to ask for Simon's assistance. As Josephus tells us:

"Haughtily consenting to be their master, he entered as one who was to rid the city of the Zealots, acclaimed by the people as their savior and protector; but, once admitted with his forces, his sole concern was to secure his own authority, and he regarded the men who had invited him as no less his enemies than those he had been invited to oppose" (*Jewish War* 4.9.11).

By now it was the spring of A.D. 69, and the civil war had reached its culmination. John's men occupied the Temple area and managed to hold up Simon's advance by virtue of their higher position. Soon, however, a split appeared within the Zealot camp, caused by the irritation of Eleazar, son of Simon, at the preeminent position of John. Eleazar and his men occupied the inner part of the Temple, with the result that John was now obliged to deal with attacks on two fronts. Here is Josephus's famous description of the dreadful events that followed:

> Old men and women in their helplessness prayed for the coming of the Romans. . . . Loyal citizens, for their part, were in dire despondency and alarm, having no opportunity for planning any change of policy, no hope of coming to terms or of flight, if they had the will; for watch was kept everywhere, and the brigand chiefs, divided on all else, put to death as their common enemies any in favor of peace with the Romans or suspected of an intention to desert, and were unanimous only in slaughtering those deserving of deliverance. The shouts of the combatants rang incessantly by day and night, but yet more harrowing were the mourners' terrified lamentations. . . . No regard for the living was any longer paid by their relations, no thought was taken for the burial of the dead—negligences both due to personal despair; for those who took no part in sedition lost interest in everything, momentarily expecting certain destruction. The rival parties, meanwhile, were at grips, trampling over the dead bodies that were piled upon each other, the frenzy inhaled from the corpses at their feet increasing their savagery.
> (*Jewish War* 5.1.5)

During the conflict, Simon and John even set fire to the stores of grain and other foodstuffs, thereby laying the foundation for the tragic situation that soon developed when the Romans laid siege to the city.

A few days before Passover in the year 70, Titus, who had been given command of operations by his father Vespasian, appeared before the walls of Jerusalem. Three legions, namely the XV Apollinaris, the XII Fulminata, and the V Macedonica, together with many auxiliary units and troops supplied by Agrippa II, camped on Mount Scopus, while the X Fretensis took up a position on the Mount of Olives. In all, Titus must have had at his disposal about 60,000 men, whereas, from what Josephus tells us, the Jewish factions had a total of 23,400 armed men. (Simon had 10,000 followers and 5,000 Idumeans as well; John had 6,000 men; and Eleazar was at the head of 2,400 Zealots.)

Some semblance of an agreement between the rebel factions seemed to be emerging. But then John, son of Levi, took advantage of the fact that Eleazar and his men had allowed access to the Temple for the Passover celebrations and sent some of his men into the sanctuary. There they drew their weapons and fell upon their enemies. Eleazar and his men managed to flee, however, and took refuge in underground passages, while John's men slaughtered those who had crowded into the Temple for the celebrations.

Titus, meanwhile, surrounded the city with his legions. He decided to attack a section of the city walls on the northwest side, where Jerusalem's complex defensive system, based on a triple ring of walls, seemed less impregnable. Only when the Roman battering ram seemed about to collapse a section of the wall did John and Simon realize that they needed to concentrate their energies on the enemy without. A Jewish sortie succeeded in setting fire to many of the siege engines, but the bravery of some Roman soldiers and the courageous intervention of Titus himself prevented the destruction of the wooden towers and the structures erected to support the earthworks. It was not long before the outer wall was breached by Titus's troops, and nine days

later, having dealt with the second wall, they took possession of the district of Jerusalem called Bezetha, which means "new city." The Jews mounted a vigorous defense, taking advantage of their elevated position to strike at the Romans with artillery: John was defending the city from the Antonia Fortress and the northern portico of the Temple, while Simon occupied the sector near Herod's palace in the Upper City. Still, it seemed that the innermost wall must soon be breached and the revolt therefore defeated. Titus made an unsuccessful attempt to arrange a peaceful surrender, for which Josephus, now a Roman captive but once a person of note in Jerusalem, vainly offered himself as an intermediary.

While the people were in the grip of hunger and their desperate situation was exacerbated by the violence meted out by the various armed factions, the fighting between Titus's army and the rebels continued with renewed vigor. The besieged forces successfully wrecked some earthworks that the Romans tried to build for their siege engines, so Titus decided to build a wall around the city in order to impose a complete blockade. In addition, he soon began to build new earthworks in front of the northwest part of the Temple. Finding it impossible to knock down the very substantial stonework of the outer Temple wall, however, he gave orders to set fire to the gate. Once this was destroyed, a Roman soldier got into the courtyard and, contravening a decision that Titus had made hours earlier at a council of war, threw a torch into a room of the Temple. In the general confusion that followed, other soldiers set fire to the whole of the inner sanctuary. The Romans slaughtered everyone they encountered, including women and children, while the Zealots took refuge in the upper part of the city. That is how the Temple, symbol of the Jewish nation, was destroyed on an August day in the year 70. The date given by Josephus corresponds to the fateful 10 Ab in the Jewish calendar, the very day on which the first Temple had been destroyed by Nebuchadnezzar in 587 B.C. In a later age, however, the date for both tragedies was accepted as 9 Ab.

The southeastern wall of Masada by the Dead Sea

The rebel chiefs refused to surrender and they shut themselves up in the so-called Upper City, where the palace of the Hasmoneans, subsequently rebuilt by Herod, still stood. After setting fire to a large part of the city, the Romans spent a little over two weeks building new earthworks. As soon as these were complete, the Romans managed to breach the last defenses, and the rebels sought safety in underground passages. So the Jewish War came to an end, with the whole of Jerusalem falling into Roman hands after a five-month siege. John subsequently emerged from his hiding place, ravaged by hunger. He asked to be spared and was imprisoned for life. Simon also eventually emerged from the underground passages and was taken prisoner.

According to Josephus's estimates, the war caused the death of 1,100,000 Jews, and a further 97,000 were taken prisoner, many of whom met their deaths at gladiatorial games or were torn to pieces by wild animals in the amphitheaters of Rome or other imperial cities. Others were used as slave labor in the mines of Egypt.

The victorious army seized enormous riches, and some of the most sacred objects from the Temple, together with seven thousand selected prisoners, were paraded through the streets of Rome during the triumph of Vespasian and his sons Titus and Domitian. The climax of the triumph was the ritual execution of Simon, the rebel leader. Two monuments to the victory over the Jews can still be seen in Rome: the Arch of Titus and the Flavian Amphitheater, or Coliseum. The reliefs on the Arch of Titus, which was erected only after Titus's death, show the triumphal procession and the seizure of the precious objects sacred to the Jews, which had been kept in the Temple. Another arch was erected for Titus in the Circus Maximus, but it has not survived. Regarding the Coliseum, it is worth noting that only a few years ago, the prominent scholar Geza Alföldy studied the position of the holes that held the letters, now lost, of the monumental inscription recording the completion of work on the building. He was able to prove that the text explained how booty from the Jewish War had been used to finance its construction. A series of

coins was also struck, on which the motto *Iudaea capta* emphatically stressed the successful outcome of the military campaign.

The rebellion effectively ended with the elimination of the last pockets of resistance at the fortresses of Herodion, Machaerus, and Masada. The first of these was taken without much difficulty. The second, however, put up a certain amount of resistance, until the besieged men saw that one of their number had been captured and was about to be crucified by the Roman governor, Lucilius Bassus. They decided to surrender in return for their companion's life. The taking of Masada was a much more difficult matter. It fell in the spring of 73 or 74 after the implacable siege imposed by the governor Flavius Silva. The military operations and the collective suicide of the rebels, who belonged to the sect of *sicarii* led by Eleazar ben Jair, are narrated in a famous passage by Josephus. The historian acknowledges the heroism of these fighters but considers their gesture to be a tragic consequence of the futility of rebelling against the Romans.

As for Josephus, he became a friend of Vespasian and Titus and after moving to Rome composed a vast fresco of Jewish affairs, concentrating particularly on the Great Revolt and the years leading up to it. In this work, titled *The Jewish War*, he tried both to console the Jews who had had to endure the Roman victory and to dissuade them and other peoples from rebelling against the imperial power. He tried in his book to emphasize that the Jews and the Romans were two great peoples. The war between them had not been inevitable, and peaceful coexistence had been a real possibility, but such a positive relationship had been thwarted by corrupt and violent procurators on the one hand and fanatical extremists on the other. By means of his friendship with Roman emperors, his residence in the capital, and the composition of his passionate literary work, Josephus wanted to present himself as an outstanding intellectual and political figure, dedicated to encouraging the Jewish people after the tragic outcome of the war. In the years that followed he wrote more books, including *Jewish Antiquities*, *Against Apion*, and *Life*. This noble

Jewish survivor became famous in Rome. He was awarded the imperial family name, libraries stocked his works, and his statue was erected in the capital. But he was also subjected to bitter attacks: In a book that has not come down to us, one of his political enemies, Justus of Tiberias, tried to discredit him.

From the First to the Second Jewish War

The disastrous outcome of the Great Revolt brought dreadful turbulence to life in the Jewish world. The glorious Temple, which had been a symbol of the nation and the heart of its religious life, lay in ruins. The practice of sacrifice in the Temple lapsed, as did that of regular pilgrimages to Jerusalem on festive occasions. The Jews had previously earmarked a certain tax for temple worship; the Roman authorities now ordered that it be diverted to the imperial coffers and administered by a special department called *fiscus iudaicus*. It should be noted, however, that while the temple tax had been paid only by freedmen and by freemen aged between twenty and fifty, the new tax applied to both sexes and all ages, though women over sixty may have been exempted. On the other hand, slave owners had to pay for their slaves. And the Sanhedrin, the organization that had governed the Jews in their own land, was not revived.

Caesarea was reorganized as a colony called Flavia Augusta Caesariensis, and two population centers—Joppa (modern Jaffa, on the coast) and Neapolis (in Samaria)—that had previously only had the status of villages were raised to the rank of city. It is difficult to be certain whether these new institutional arrangements also involved colonization from outside; as far as we know, the Jewish community at Joppa and the Samaritans at Neapolis, who were the nucleus of the population, continued to enjoy their rights. Only in the case of Emmaus are we explicitly informed that eight hundred Roman army veterans settled there.

We also have to take note of another significant change within the sphere of Jewish religious history: From the period following the end of the revolt onward, we no longer find any mention of the three Jewish sects. This does not represent a clear break with the past, however, because a number of important rabbis fled from Jerusalem to the city of Jabneh (Jamnia) and with Vespasian's permission founded an important center for teaching the Torah and oral Law, thereby reestablishing a connection with the tradition of priestly and Pharisaic teachings. As far as we know, however, the characteristic qualities of Essene thought disappeared. The elimination of sectarianism led to a substantial spirit of unity, and it is therefore interesting to note that the people accepted as binding the interpretations of law and cultural prescriptions issued by the sages of Jabneh. The head of the school, or rabbinate, could enjoy the title of *nasi*, which means "president" or "prince," and it is likely that appointment to the position was recognized by the Roman authorities.

While the last embers of the revolt were still dying, the Roman authorities also decided to alter the administrative and military status of Judea. It was considered appropriate that a legion be there permanently, and so the X Fretensis was quartered in Jerusalem; and in accordance with normal practice, the province was ruled by a senatorial governor: a *legatus Augusti propraetore* of praetorian rank. It was, in fact, normal for a province with a single resident legion to be governed by a *legatus* of praetorian rank, whereas those with more than one legion were placed under a *legatus* of consular rank.

The only faint hope for those with notions of Jewish independence was to be found in the faded figure of King Agrippa II, whom the Flavian emperors left to rule in the territories granted to him by Claudius and Nero. Agrippa II died around 93, or perhaps as late as 100, and no successor was appointed. He was the last of the Jewish kings.

As early as about 117, the Romans stationed a second legion, the II Traiana, at Caparcotna in Lower Galilee, between the Jezreel Valley and Mount Carmel. From that time onward, the governor of the province was therefore a *legatus* of consular rank, and we are bound to deduce from this reinforcement of the military presence that fires of unrest were still smoldering beneath the surface. Judea was not in fact a frontier province requiring defense against potential enemies from outside, or from which it was likely that attacks on enemy territory would be launched. But the 116 and 117 revolt of the Jews in Cyrenaica, Egypt, and Mesopotamia, which the Romans briefly occupied in the years of Trajan's Persian campaign, was likely to have had repercussions in Judea.

It was only in 132, however, that a genuine rebellion broke out. Its origin seemed to be closely connected to orders issued by the emperor Hadrian that the Jews considered to be a real provocation. Hadrian had in fact ordered the prohibition of circumcision, despite the fact that it was a fundamental part of Jewish religious practice; he also gave orders that a colony to be called Aelia Capitolina (Aelius was the emperor's family name) be founded on the soil of Jerusalem. A grand temple to Zeus was to be built on the ruins of the Jewish Temple. Through these measures, Hadrian intended to nurture Hellenistic culture and religion, but it was at the expense of a religion that was, after all, still recognized and permitted under Roman law. In 130 he had visited Judea during a journey through the whole of the Roman East, and his plan to refound Jerusalem as a colony was in all probability launched on that occasion. The bloody revolts of 116 and 117 had certainly intensified anti-Jewish sentiment in his mind.

Unlike with the first revolt, the rebel command in this case was entrusted entirely to one man, Simon bar Kosiba. Because of a sort of assonance between his patronymic Kosiba and Kokhba, he also acquired the name Kokhba, which means "son of the star." This name echoed messianic expectations, and indeed he did proclaim himself the Messiah. He was recognized as such by distinguished rabbis, including the authoritative Akiba. On the coins minted by Bar Kokhba for the rebels, on the other hand, he described himself as "prince of Israel."

The lucky discovery of a series of letters written by Bar Kokhba, along with other documents about the revolt, has thrown light on the character of this Jewish leader. He was meticulous in organizing his army and severe in maintaining

discipline, ordering harsh punishment for his own men when necessary.

In all probability the revolt began in the spring of 132 and lasted until early 136. The armed conflict played out in a rather peculiar manner. As far as we know, the rebels wisely avoided attacking the enemy in the open, concentrating instead on guerrilla tactics: hiding in natural hollows in the land and in a series of interconnecting underground passages of their own construction. These underground systems not only served as refuges and places to store arms but also provided bases from which to launch attacks. The governor of Judea, Tineius Rufus, may initially have been caught unaware by the revolt and its methods, and he asked that reinforcements be added to the two legions and auxiliary units (of which there must have been between twelve and sixteen) that were already stationed in the province under his command. The coins minted by the rebels clearly show the aims and ideals being pursued: They were inscribed in ancient Hebrew—the language of worship—a fact that testifies to the combined religious and nationalist nature of the uprising. Images of the Temple figured largely in their iconography, as did the Ark of the Covenant and other characteristic symbols of Jewish ritual. The aspirations of the rebels thus lay in rebuilding the Temple and reviving an independent Jewish state.

We do not have a detailed source like Josephus for the Second Revolt. Hence we know only the broad outlines of events, and many questions remain unanswered. We do not even know whether the rebels succeeded in taking Jerusalem.

In the early years of the war, Tineius Rufus managed to inflict enormous losses on the rebels, but he evidently did not succeed in crushing his enemy. In 134, the post of *legatus* was given to Sextus Julius Severus, a military commander of great experience, who was then governing distant Britannia. Various pieces of evidence lead us to believe that the choice of Severus was dictated by very serious, indeed quite exceptional, motives: The Roman army was having great difficulty in dealing with the Jewish revolt and had suffered terrible losses. It was therefore necessary to send the best general in the empire to Judea. Severus finally managed to crush the rebels thanks to a strategy of doggedly isolating individual enemy groups, depriving them of supplies, and then exterminating them. The decisive operation was the capture of Bethther, a fortress situated ten kilometers southwest of Jerusalem, where Bar Kokhba himself had retreated with his followers. The siege went on for some time, until hunger and thirst forced the defenders to surrender. Other pockets of resistance were eliminated in the months that followed. We know that during those years, some of the most authoritative exponents of the Jewish religious world, including Rabbi Akiba himself, were tortured and killed.

So ended a war that had proved extraordinarily difficult for the Romans, who lost thousands of men and probably had to suffer the annihilation of a legion as well. The Jewish revolt must have extended to neighboring provinces where thousands of Jews lived, and it is significant that at the end of the war extraordinary triumphal honors were granted not only to Severus but also to Publicius Marcellus, the governor of Syria, and T. Haterius Nepos, governor of Arabia.

For the Jewish world, the outcome of this war was even more disastrous than that of the First Revolt. The historian Dio Cassius records that 580,000 Jews perished in battle, and there were countless victims of starvation, disease, and fire. Thousands of villages were destroyed. The land of Judea around Jerusalem became depopulated and the Jews became a minority in the south of the country and along the coast. Close-knit communities remained in a few places, such as Jericho, Hebron, Lydda (modern Lod), and other areas of Perea and the Plain of Sharon, but the center of gravity of Jewish life soon moved decisively toward the fertile and well-populated region of Galilee.

There is no proof that the Samaritans rebelled against the Romans as well, but Neapolis coins from the years following the revolt show a temple of Zeus on Mount Gerizim. Hadrian likely thought that the Samaritan religion was a variant of Judaism and therefore ordered that it, too, be eradicated. On the other hand, recent studies have suggested that the temple of Zeus, shown on the

coins as having a large flight of steps, was not built on the site of a Samaritan temple but on another peak of the same mountain.

The Roman authorities issued a special order changing the name of the province, and so from the years immediately following the war onward it was no longer called Judea but Syria Palaestina. It seems clear that by choosing an apparently neutral name—one juxtaposing that of a neighboring province with the revived name of an ancient geographical entity (Palestine), already known from the writings of Herodotus—Hadrian was intending to suppress any connection between the Jewish people and that land.

From the Second Revolt to late antiquity

The death of Hadrian in 138 removed a bitter enemy of the Jewish religion. According to rabbinical tradition, Hadrian not only refounded Jerusalem as Aelia Capitolina and prohibited circumcision but at the end of the war forbade the observance of the Sabbath, the ordination of rabbis, and the study of the Law. He even prohibited the Jews from setting foot in Jerusalem,

on pain of death. Where the Temple had once stood there now rose a temple of Jupiter Capitolinus.

When a new emperor, Antoninus Pius, ascended the throne, he made significant improvements in relations between the Roman authorities and the Jewish world: The prohibition against circumcision was lifted, or rather an exception was made for the Jews so that an ancient practice fundamental to their religion became legal again.

The chief surviving rabbis gathered in the little town of Usha, between Sepphoris and the coast, in order to reestablish a study center that could hope to act as a linchpin for Jewish religious authority. Contrary to what many scholars have supposed, however, this assembly of sages was not a national institution representing the whole Jewish community. Similarly, the rabbinical academies that flourished later on were quite different from the Sanhedrin of the period preceding the destruction of the Temple.

A significant step had been taken, however, in transferring the main religious schools into the populous and prosperous world of Galilee. An important new stage in the development of Jewish cultural and religious life was reached when an influential rabbi called Judah ha Nasi (Judah the Prince, ca. 140–225) came upon the scene. He obtained the position of patriarch and enjoyed friendly relations with the Roman authorities, to the extent that he is recorded in rabbinical sources as a personal friend of an emperor, possibly Caracalla.

Judah had previously lived and taught at the little town of Beth Shearim, but he spent the last seventeen years of his life at Sepphoris, where he oversaw the preparation of a work of extraordinary import: the Mishnah. This text, arranged by subject, preserved the interpretations of the Law made by important religious authorities from the years preceding the destruction of the Temple to the early third century. It is important to note that over time the sages had continued to offer interpretations of various aspects of sacrifice, temple furnishings, and the organization of the feasts that were celebrated at Jerusalem. Everything seemed to continue as though the Temple and its rituals still existed, and this fed the hope that the center of Jewish religious life might be rebuilt.

It is believed that from the time of Rabbi Judah on, the patriarchs had obtained substantial powers from the Roman authorities in the areas of tax collecting, trial procedures, and the supervision of education and the Jewish religion.

From the third century on we find the first specific evidence of rabbinical academies in the cities of Tiberias, Sepphoris, Caesarea, and Lydda (Lod). In addition, there were minor schools in other towns and even in villages, especially in Galilee and Golan. In order to maintain institutional continuity, the post of school leader was filled immediately upon the death of the incumbent.

Although the members of the rabbinical academies defined themselves as a separate group, superior to the Jewish society of the time, they were fully integrated into communal life and did not shrink from enjoying positive relations with various classes of people. Furthermore, the relationship with Hellenistic culture became more open, and the prohibition against the representation of human and animal figures was abandoned. Clear evidence of this change is found in the reliefs and mosaics representing mythological scenes and animal figures that have been found in synagogues and private houses, attributable to the third century or later.

The destruction, poverty, and depopulation caused by the Second Revolt must have dissipated by the time of Judah ha Nasi, for the sources describe him as a wealthy man and a substantial landowner. At the time of the emperor Septimius Severus, two villages were raised to the rank of city under the names Eleutheropolis and Diospolis (Lydda). And it was also at this period that the prohibition against Jews visiting Jerusalem except on 9 Ab was withdrawn, and it is actually possible that a small Jewish community once again settled in the colony there.

Although the third century was a time of economic crisis for a large part of the Roman Empire, it must have been a period of comparative prosperity for Palestine, since no particularly serious events occurred there. In fact, rabbinical sources and archaeology seem to suggest that the whole area enjoyed a certain level of economic prosperity.

In the last decade of the third century, as part of a series of administrative reforms that Diocletian carried out throughout the empire, the frontiers of the Syria Palaestina province were substantially altered: The whole of the Negev and part of Transjordan, which had previously been in the province of Arabia, were now incorporated into Syria Palaestina. It was probably about this time that the two legions stationed in Palestine left their bases: The X Fretensis was transferred to Aelana (Aqaba) on the Red Sea, while the VI Ferrata, it seems, acquired a new base at Udruh in Transjordan. It was also at this time, or shortly afterward, that the imperial authority ordered that civil and military powers be separated, as was happening in other provinces. Palestine consequently had a governor responsible for civil administration, and a military commander for the whole province: the *dux Palaestinae*.

When Constantine defeated Licinius in 324, becoming sole emperor and taking over the Eastern Empire, Palaestina seemed to be a peaceful province in which the Jewish population showed deference to the authority of the patriarch, who in turn saw his rights respected by the imperial power. The patriarch received taxes from Jews residing outside Eretz Israel, sending his own

Opposite: Catacombs at Beth Shearim

representatives into the lands concerned. But the profanation of Jerusalem continued to be a subject of mourning: The temple of Zeus and the statues of Hadrian and Antoninus Pius rose up where the Jewish Temple had previously stood. A Christian pilgrim who visited the Holy Land in 333 records how the Jews who were allowed to visit Jerusalem on the anniversary of the destruction of the Temple rent their clothes and pierced the air with their lamentations.

When the first Christian emperor came to the throne, the world of Palestine received an unexpected shock: Having previously been a marginal province as far as imperial events were concerned, it now rose to the rank of Holy Land. In Jerusalem, attention shifted to the area of Hadrian's forum, or more precisely to the place where a temple to Venus had been built. The bishop of Jerusalem, Makarios, informed the emperor that according to tradition this was the location of the Holy Sepulcher, and after receiving the necessary permission, he destroyed the pagan temple. The discovery of a tomb cut into the rock was received with great joy, and a colonnaded courtyard was soon built round the Holy Sepulcher. Work on the Church of the Anastasis, which was to enclose the Holy Sepulcher, was probably begun under Constantine but it was only completed at the time of his son, Constantius II. Constantine also took steps to see that a splendid basilica was built on Golgotha and given the name Martyrium, and he also had two churches built: one over the cave on the Mount of Olives where Jesus had preached, and the other over the cave of the Nativity at Bethlehem. The emperor's mother, Helena, went on a pilgrimage to the Holy Land and supervised the building of these two churches, and, according to a tradition (rejected by many scholars), workers found what were thought to be the remains of the Cross of Christ while she was in Jerusalem. More recently, however, it has been suggested that the discovery of these wooden fragments was not a later event subsequently backdated, but something actually attributable to Helena's activities. Be that as it may, there are reports from pilgrims to the Holy Land in the second half of the century showing that at that time the relics of the cross were kept in a gold and silver reliquary in the Church of the Holy Sepulcher.

An outstanding intellectual figure and religious leader in Palestine during the years of Constantine's reign was Eusebius, bishop of Caesarea. He sat at the emperor's right hand during the Council of Nicea (325) and described and praised the emperor's Christian zeal in various works. By writing an ecclesiastical history that served as a model for other writers, he invented a new literary genre: history in which the central subject was the church. Two of his works in particular deal with Palestine: the *Onomasticon*, a sort of geographical dictionary of places in the region with added historical information, and *Martyrs of Palestine*, which is an account of Christian suffering under the tetrarchs.

At the beginning of the fourth century, the ethnic and religious makeup of Palestine was very complex. The Jews were largely concentrated in Galilee and some marginal areas in the Judean hills, while the Samaritans lived in Samaria. Pagans were in the majority in Judea, the coastal plain, and Transjordan and, generally speaking, in all the large towns in the region, with the sole exception of Tiberias, which remained strongly Jewish. However, we must not forget that in many towns, especially on the coast, the population was mixed. According to one rabbinical source, at about the middle of the fourth century the total Samaritan population of Caesarea equaled that of the Jews and pagans together. But these numbers include land under the control of the city, where the Samaritans in particular were numerous. In any case, the provincial governor's staff, now as in previous centuries, had their headquarters at Caesarea, and as far as one can tell, they were preponderantly Samaritan.

In 351, there was a rebellion in Palestine, which scholars generally call "the last Jewish revolt against Rome," although the sources do not elucidate its nature very well. Its epicenter was Sepphoris, but it also affected Diospolis. The rebels succeeded in capturing the weapons of a military unit stationed at Sepphoris and declared a certain Patricius to be their leader.

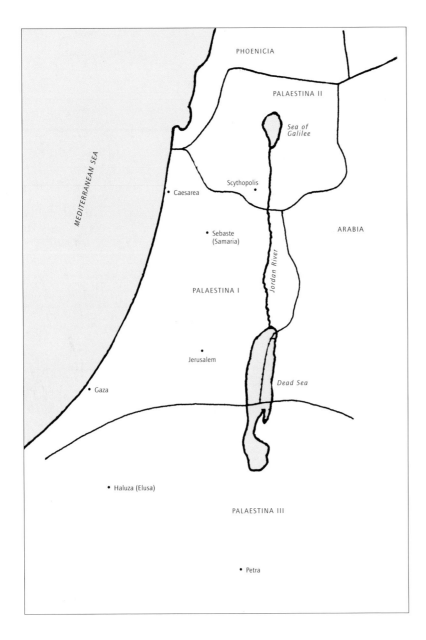

Some passages in the Palestinian Talmud record the existence of a period of emergency at Sepphoris and the presence there of the *magister militum per orientem*, the powerful general Ursicinus, who had contingents of the regional army under his command. He must have put down the revolt without much difficulty. Some ecclesiastical writers of a later period record the event in apocalyptic terms, suggesting that it was responsible for the destruction of whole cities, but there is no reason to suppose that the information they provide is more than polemical exaggeration with the Jews in mind. The revolt was a strictly local event and in all probability was supported by only part of the Jewish population.

Another famous episode involving the Jewish world took place at the time of the emperor Julian (361–363), an intellectual ruler who tried to restore the pagan religion to a dominant position. He ordered the Temple in Jerusalem to be rebuilt, not out of any particular regard for the Jews, but because he wanted to damage the Christians; rebuilding the Temple would have proved that Christ's prophecy of the eternal desolation of the Temple was false. Shortly after work began, Julian met his death during a military campaign in Persia. His successors were Christians, and the project was thus abandoned.

Also in 363, a violent earthquake shook almost the whole of Palestine, causing serious damage to buildings, as archaeological research has clearly shown. But life resumed without any great hesitation. Within a few decades the region began a period of unequaled prosperity, as one can tell from the proliferation of sites in the countryside, the amount of building work undertaken in the towns, and the increasing presence of goods from Palaestina in the cities of the Mediterranean basin.

It should be kept in mind that around 390 the land of Palaestina was divided into three separate provinces: Palaestina I included Judea, Samaria, and the coastal region; Palaestina II covered Galilee and the upper valley of the river Jordan; and Palaestina III, or Palaestina Salutaris, included the Negev and large tracts of land beyond the Jordan. The provincial governors had their headquarters at Caesarea, Scythopolis, and Petra respectively. Military power, on the other hand, remained concentrated in the hands of a single *dux Palaestinae*. The dismemberment of the province, however, should be seen not as a special arrangement resulting from a local emergency, but rather as part of a process of subdividing civil power for administrative purposes that was set in motion throughout much of the empire from the mid-third century onward.

In the course of the fourth century, the Jewish patriarch took up residence at Tiberias and continued to have competence in matters of civil jurisdiction; whoever held the post of patriarch was given the honorary rank of praetorian prefect by the Christian emperors. The intense activity of the sages of Tiberias ultimately produced the so-called Palestinian Talmud, which was drawn up at the end of the fifth century. It consisted of an extremely detailed discussion of the various treatises that made up the Mishnah, including deliberations by the sages and commentary on religious precepts.

Christian sources stress that the Jewish patriarchs were powerful and rich. One particular episode throws light on a situation in which the excessive power of the patriarch was capable of arousing fierce resentment: A governor of Palaestina called Exichius plotted against the patriarch Gamaliel VI in an attempt to find evidence of a (supposed) plot against the Roman authority. He bribed some officials in order to get hold of the patriarch's correspondence, but the protests of the highest authority of the Jews gave the patriarch the upper hand, and Exichius was condemned to death.

However, dissatisfaction at the great power wielded by the patriarch led to an imperial law, issued in 398, by which he was deprived of jurisdiction in civil matters, except when both parties agreed to be judged by the Jewish court. In the following decades, the Christian emperors issued a series of laws that effectively eroded many of the rights that the Jews had acquired. Theodosius II accused Gamaliel VI of building new synagogues, of having Christian slaves circumcised, and of passing judgment in civil cases, and he conse-

quently deprived him of the honorary rank of praetorian prefect. That led Theodosius II to impose a complete ban on the building of new synagogues; those that had recently been built in sparsely inhabited places actually had to be taken down. Despite the fact that the same law confirmed that the Jews could repair their old synagogues and that these buildings were legally protected from hostile acts, the decidedly anti-Jewish tone of the imperial orders is evident. Jewish rights were further limited three years later when the western emperor, Honorius, in conjunction with his eastern colleague, Theodosius II, issued a law denying the Jews access to the most important civilian and military posts. Still to be eliminated was the annoying presence of a supreme Jewish authority endowed with significant prerogatives; in 429, therefore, Emperor Theodosius II took advantage of the death of Gamaliel VI to abolish the position of patriarch, a move clearly intended to humiliate the Jews. The tribute that the Jews had paid to their acknowledged leader now became a tax destined for the imperial coffers.

The Christian religion had in the meantime received a great boost in Palestine thanks to the activities of monks such as Hilarion, whose followers settled as hermits in various parts of the Negev. According to tradition, Hilarion founded the first church in the town of Haluza (Elusa) around 350, during the reign of Constantius II, after converting a large part of the population. In the fourth century it became fashionable for high-society ladies to go on pilgrimages to the Holy Land. However, an aristocratic Roman lady by the name of Melania, not content with a religious trip of the tourist variety, traveled in the company of an intellectual priest named Rufinus. In 374 or 375 she founded a monastery on the Mount of Olives that also functioned as a hostel for pilgrims to Jerusalem from imperial court circles. Melania's activities were continued by her granddaughter Melania the Younger, who came to Jerusalem with her family in 417.

In the 380s, Poemenia, another lady of high rank and possibly a relative of the emperor Theodosius I, financed the construction of a

Opposite: The three divisions of Palestine, about A.D. 390

church on the Mount of Olives, at the place of the Ascension; and at about the same time a noblewoman called Paula, accompanied by Jerome, also arrived in the Holy Land. She founded one monastery for men and another for women at Bethlehem, both of which also provided shelter for pilgrims.

At the beginning of the fourth century, Christians had been no more than a small minority in Palaestina. By the end of the century, however, they were already a majority in the region. A very important influence on this development was the imperial policy of Theodosius I (379–395), which, like that of his successors, aimed to eradicate paganism from the empire. With the support of the bishops and zealous imperial officials, no quarter was given in the fight against pagan temples, which were destroyed. In the fifth century, the activities of the empress Eudocia, wife of Theodosius II, were of particular moment. The life of the emperor and his family in Constantinople was governed by maximum observance of the Christian religion, and on various occasions they sent money to Jerusalem for the needy. The imperial couple also donated a gold cross, which was placed on top of the church on Golgotha. Eudocia herself visited the holy places in 439, taking part in the ceremonies for the inauguration of the sanctuary on Mount Zion, where the relics of Saint Stephen were deposited. Two years later, when court intrigues forced the empress to leave Constantinople, she decided to return to Jerusalem. Although formally deprived of any support from the emperor, Eudocia had very considerable wealth of her own and was hence able to finance various charitable and building activities. Among her projects was the sumptuous rebuilding of the sanctuary of Saint Stephen; it thus became a vast church where the empress herself was buried, at her own request, when she died in 460.

New monastic foundations rose up in the desert on the initiative of various authoritative figures, whether priests or community organizers, such as Euthymius, who arrived in the Holy Land in 405 and died in 473, and Sabbas, who was active there from 457 to 532.

During the course of the fifth century, the Christian world was rent by violent religious controversies: The christological theories put forward by the Nestorians and Monophysites were widely supported, but exponents of orthodoxy used all possible means to counter them. These violent dissensions also troubled Christian Palaestina, where one particular episode demonstrates the intensity of the clashes. After taking part in the Council of Chalcedon (451) at which the Monophysites were condemned, Juvenal, bishop of Jerusalem, rejected their creed in favor of triumphant orthodoxy. As a reward, the imperial authorities elevated the See of Jerusalem to a patriarchate, with primacy over all the churches in Palaestina and Arabia. However, when Juvenal returned to Jerusalem, he was met by hordes of enraged monks and citizens who supported the Monophysites, and they appointed a different priest to the position of bishop. Within twenty months, Juvenal regained his see, but only thanks to the intervention of the army, which restored his authority by slaughtering his opponents.

Palaestina played a very important part in the cultural life of the empire. The so-called School of Gaza, which began to flourish toward the end of the fifth century, enjoyed a great reputation and was active until the time of Justinian. Important intellectuals and rhetoricians, such as Anastasius, Timotheus, John, Procopius, and Choricius added luster to their city by writing rhetorical works and epistles that were based on classical culture inserted into a Christian context. Procopius, the great sixth-century historian from Caesarea, wrote a history of the wars waged by Belisarius on behalf of Justinian in Africa and Italy and against the Persians. In this work, as well as in the *De aedificiis*, in which he described the buildings in the empire for which Justinian was responsible, Procopius exalted the emperor, but later he attacked him as a demoniac despot in the *Anecdota* (secret history).

Palaestina was weakened by a series of conflicts involving the Samaritan community, which was deeply attached to its own religion and traditions. In 484, there was a sharp reaction when the emperor Zeno had a church built to

Maria Theotokos (Mary, Mother of God) on Gerizim, the sacred mountain of the Samaritans. At the same time there were some clashes at Caesarea, caused, according to sources, by the local Samaritans acting under a leader who was subsequently captured and killed. Another important Samaritan uprising took place in 529, when a new charismatic Samaritan leader called Julian gathered together a large body of fighting men in the countryside. Julian and many of his men were massacred by the Roman army, but acts of banditry against the governing powers continued. These acts eventually led to a dramatic explosion of violence in 556, when the very proconsul of the province of Palaestina, Stephen,

was killed by the rebels in the *praetorium* at Caesarea. On this last occasion, the Jews joined the Samaritans, but the army intervened and suppressed the uprising with a heavy hand.

The involvement of Jews in the Samaritan revolt can be interpreted as a reaction against Justinian's laws, which restricted their rights. Justinian in fact completed the work begun by his predecessors, who had issued various laws tending to marginalize the Jews. This imperial policy had taken a radical turn as early as 527 with a law promulgated by Justinus I but in fact ordered by Justinian, who had already taken over the reins of power during the last years of his predecessor. On that occasion, the position of the Jews as well as that of the Samaritans was redefined; the idea that anyone who did not belong to the Orthodox Church was to be considered a heretic now became rigid policy. In this way, the Jews, like the other "heretics," were not only prevented from working in civil administration or the military sphere but also excluded from city senates and from pursuing a career in law. One exception made it possible to work in the lowest ranks of civil administration. Other provisions in later years, such as one that prevented them from acting as witnesses at the trials of Christians, further weakened the Jews' position. As for the Samaritans, they were not even allowed to have synagogues. One thing that is striking about the Justinian legislation, apart from its legal implications, is that it is permeated with a fierce malice toward the Jews and the other minorities. In Novella 45, promulgated in 537, for example, the Jews are described as "abominable."

Palaestina reached a peak of prosperity in the late fifth and early sixth century, at the time of the emperors Anastasius (491–518) and Justinus I (518–527), and in the early part of the reign of Justinian (527–565). One of the most characteristic aspects of urban life at that time was the emergence of commercial and industrial areas within towns. Continuing a trend that was already evident in the fourth century, towns increasingly acquired new civic basilicas and porticoed streets with spaces for shops. The process of christianization in towns—and villages—received a fresh, vigorous boost from the erection of many churches and other religious buildings.

A serious outbreak of plague, which struck a large part of the Roman East in 542, also deeply affected Palaestina, causing a decline or at least stagnation in the provincial economy. To make matters worse, an attack by the Persians, who penetrated into Syria in 614 and even occupied Jerusalem, caused the deaths of tens of thousands of people and forced many others into exile, including Zacharias, the patriarch of the city. The Church of the Holy Sepulcher was destroyed, and the reliquary containing the presumed remains of

the True Cross was removed from the patriarch and ended up in Persia. The taking of Jerusalem caused great consternation in the Christian world, and, rightly or wrongly, it afforded an occasion to accuse the Jews of betrayal and aiding the enemy in the capture of the city. Within a few years, however, the emperor Heraclius succeeded once more in defeating the Persians and recapturing the True Cross, which was returned to Jerusalem in 630. The emperor and his court personally took part in the restitution ceremony: In an atmosphere imbued with great significance, Heraclius entered Jerusalem barefoot and soberly dressed, carrying the cross in his hands. Contemporary sources attest that many witnesses experienced a sense of joy and were confirmed in their belief in the advent of a new age.

Within a few years, however, a new and less expected enemy succeeded in penetrating the Near East: the Arabs. Their first attack came in Transjordan in 629, at a time when Heraclius's army was busy trying to reorganize that territory after the retreat of the Persians. The imperial forces were victorious at Mu'tah, which probably led them to underestimate the threat. Consequently, the Arab tribes succeeded in the next few years in forcing the surrender of Areopolis and Aelana (Aqaba), and then they occupied the Negev as well. In 634, the imperial army was defeated near Gaza, and then again near Eleutheropolis. The Roman army's decisive defeat, however, came at a battle in the defiles of the river Yarmuk in 636. Although they probably had superior numbers, the imperial forces with their Christian-Arab allies were unsuccessful in the opening encounter, and they were ultimately surrounded and massacred. Few managed to escape.

This battle effectively marked the end of Roman domination in the Near East. From then on, the imperial forces no longer had the ability to counter an attack, and all hope of resistance was entrusted to the solidity of city walls. Within a short time all the principal towns in Palaestina fell into Arab hands, and Caesarea was finally taken in 640.

Jerusalem

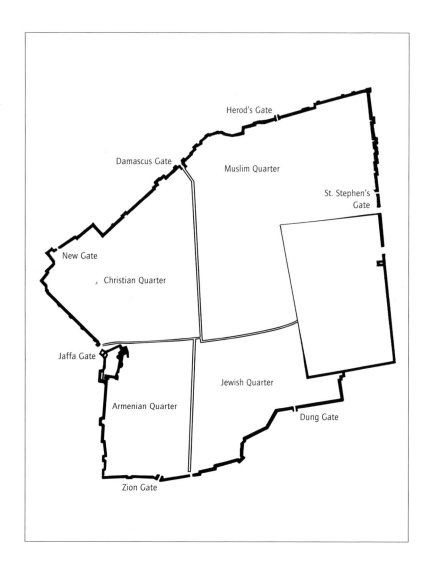

Jerusalem was chosen as the capital of Israel by King David around 1000 B.C. It was destroyed by the Babylonians in 586, rebuilt under the Persians, and conquered by Alexander the Great in 332 B.C., thereafter taking its place in the Hellenistic world. Together with the rest of the region, it was an object of contention between the *diadochoi* (Alexander's successors) until it fell into the hands of the Seleucids at the end of the third century B.C. The Seleucid king Antiochus IV Epiphanes encouraged Jerusalem's transformation into a Hellenistic polis—a change that pleased the city's aristocracy but was opposed by Jewish traditionalists, who objected to the influence of Greek culture. This opposition soon developed into a revolt, led by the brothers Judas and Simeon Maccabeus. In 164, Judas occupied Jerusalem and purified the Temple, and in 141 his brother Simeon succeeded in getting rid of the Seleucid garrison that still occupied the fortress called Acra. That is how Jerusalem became the capital of the Hasmonean dynasty.

A struggle for the succession to the throne between the last two descendants of the royal family, Hyrcanus and Aristobulus, gave Pompey a pretext for occupying Jerusalem in 63 B.C. and making the Hasmonean kingdom a Roman protectorate. Aristobulus was taken to Rome in chains. Hyrcanus was recognized as high priest, but he was not given the title of king and very soon he was effectively deprived of authority by

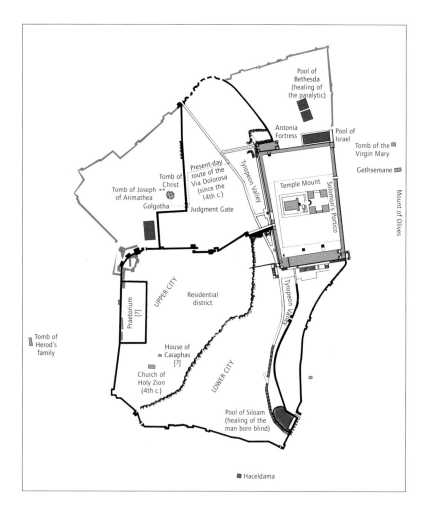

Pool of
Bethesda
(healing of
the paralytic)

Antonia
Fortress

Pool of
Israel

Tomb of the
Virgin Mary

Gethsemane

Tomb of
Christ

Present-day
route of the
Via Dolorosa
(since the
14th c.)

Tomb of Joseph
of Arimathea

Golgotha

Judgment Gate

Tyropeon Valley

Temple Mount

Solomon's Portico

Mount of Olives

Tomb of
Herod's
family

Praetorium
[?]

UPPER CITY

Residential
district

Tyropeon Valley

House of
Caiaphas
[?]

Church of
Holy Zion
(4th c.)

LOWER CITY

Pool of Siloam
(healing of
the man born blind)

Haceldama

his skillful Idumean minister Antipater. Jerusalem and the Temple itself suffered serious damage both during Pompey's siege and in later years, when the sons of Aristobulus tried to regain control of the city. After the battle of Pharsalia (48 B.C.), Antipater, acting in the name of Hyrcanus, supported Caesar and gained his favor. In this way Hyrcanus obtained the hereditary title of ethnarch, and Antipater acquired effective power as procurator of Judea. He was aided in this endeavor by his son Phasael, who was made governor of Jerusalem, and by another son, Herod, who was sent to govern Galilee. In this period Antipater also obtained permission to repair the city walls of Jerusalem.

Caesar was assassinated in 44, and Antipater was poisoned by a rival in 43. During the power struggles that ensued, Herod and Phasael managed to retain power by supporting first Cassius, the murderer of Caesar, and then Mark Antony. Meanwhile, Antigonus, the surviving son of Aristobulus, made a fresh attempt to conquer Judea, with the support of the Parthians. In the year 40, therefore, Jerusalem was taken once more and sacked. Hyrcanus and Phasael were captured and Herod fled to Rome, where, thanks to the support of Mark Antony, he obtained the title of king of Judea, from the senate. After a long war, Herod defeated Antigonus and conquered Jerusalem with the aid of Roman troops (37 B.C.). After the death of Mark Antony, Herod managed to obtain the goodwill of Octavian, in honor of whom he founded Caesarea; but Jerusalem remained the capital of his kingdom, which now included Judea proper, Samaria, Galilee, and Perea, and later on Augustus assigned further territories to him to the north and northeast, lands that today form part of Lebanon and Syria.

During his long reign, Herod rebuilt much of Jerusalem, embellishing it with splendid buildings. When he died in 4 B.C., Jerusalem and Judea passed to his son Archelaus, and the disturbances that this aroused were violently suppressed by the Romans. In A.D. 6, Archelaus was sent into exile and Judea was transformed into a Roman province governed by prefects or procurators. Jerusalem was replaced as capital by Caesarea but continued to grow. At the time of the Great Revolt against the Romans (A.D. 66–70), a new wall had to be built on the north side of the city, to defend the new districts that had grown up outside the old city walls.

The revolt had disastrous effects for Jerusalem. Titus imposed a terrible siege on the city, with the result that it was captured piecemeal and almost totally destroyed. Those inhabitants who survived the hunger, the fighting, and the final conflagration were sold as slaves. Only one part of the city walls on the western side remained standing, together with three towers of Herod's palace; they were to serve as a base for fortifications for the Roman camp that rose among the ruins of the city. Between 70 and 130, when Jerusalem was refounded by Hadrian as Aelia Capitolina, all that stood on the site was the camp of the X Fretensis legion and a wretched civilian settlement whose inhabitants were soldiers' families, the providers of various services (merchants, prostitutes, and so on), and in all probability a few local Jews who had somehow escaped the slaughter. The earliest Christian sources bear witness both to the existence of seven synagogues and a small church on Mount Zion and to the continuity of the episcopal succession at Jerusalem. So some Jews, including christianized Jews, had resettled among the ruins.

Hadrian's decision to rebuild the city as a *colonia civium Romanorum*—as a pagan city, that is, with the usual temples—was one of the causes of the Bar Kokhba revolt (132–135). It seems that the rebels held Jerusalem for a while, but it was not long before the Romans recaptured it. After the suppression of the revolt, the Jews were forbidden to live there, and that prohibition seems to have still been in force in the fourth century when, according to Christian sources, the Jews had to pay to come to Jerusalem in order to mourn the destruction of the Temple on the anniversary date of 9 Ab. Later on, however, the prohibition ceased to be enforced, and the Jews not only began to visit their holy city again during festival pilgrimages but even resumed living there on a permanent basis.

Christian pilgrimages to the holy places had taken place since at least the third century, but when Constantine made Christianity the religion of the empire, they began to increase. The site of Christ's tomb was identified, and Constantine had the large Church of the Anastasis, or Holy Sepulcher, built there. According to tradition, it was Constantine's mother, Helena, who discovered the True Cross while on a pilgrimage to Jerusalem; the holy wood was exhibited in a chapel at the Anastasis church. A number of other churches were built at the holy places during the fourth century, and even more in later centuries, many with adjoining monasteries. In the opening years of the fifth century, however, the city was still partly a scene of desolation, to the extent that plots of land were offered free to anyone who would build on them. Groups of devout Christians who arrived as pilgrims decided to

Below: The western wall, or Wailing Wall, of the Temple Mount. On the left is the Dome of the Rock, also known as the Mosque of Omar.

On p. 44: The Old City quarters as they are today

On p. 45: View of the Old City

On p. 46: Plan of Jerusalem at the time of Jesus

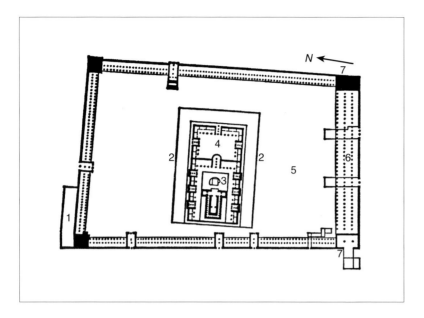

tion pilgrims and residents from Gaul, Spain, Britain, North Africa, Egypt, Ethiopia, Arabia, Syria, Persia, and other countries.

In 438/39, Eudocia, wife of the emperor Theodosius II, arrived in Jerusalem on a pilgrimage, and, some years after she had separated from her husband, she took up permanent residence there, remaining until her death in 460. She was responsible for numerous buildings in the city, not only churches, monasteries, and charitable institutions, but also a new city wall. Soon after the Council of Chalcedon (451), the whole of Palestine was rent by a serious crisis, particularly affecting Jerusalem and the desert to the south and east of the city, where a large number of monks lived. Juvenal, the archbishop of Jerusalem, had accepted the definition of the two natures in one person of Christ, as affirmed by Pope Leo, and had obliged the bishops under him to accept it as well. But the great majority of monks rejected it, forcing the bishops out of their sees and electing others who did not accept the decisions of the Council of Chalcedon. Juvenal himself was ejected and was able to return only in 453, under escort by imperial soldiers. Eudocia sided with the monks and was sufficiently influential to keep the schism alive for years, even after her own death.

In the sixth and seventh centuries too, Jerusalem suffered as a result of internal church strife over doctrinal matters, which often took the form of actual uprisings. However, the city continued to grow and prosper, thanks to the influx of money brought by the pilgrims. It was not until 614 that Jerusalem was struck by a new disaster, when the Persians, in alliance with the Saracens, invaded the region and appeared at the walls of the city. The patriarch Zacharias would have liked to accept the terms of surrender offered to him, but some of the citizens insisted on resistance, with the result that the city was taken by force; many inhabitants were slaughtered, and many churches destroyed. Shortly afterward, however, the Persians withdrew, taking with them the patriarch, numerous prisoners, and the relics of the True Cross. Modestos, who was abbot of the monastery of Saint Theodosius near

settle both in the city itself and on the Mount of Olives, living a monastic life there, or at least spending long periods in prayer at hostels that were sometimes geared toward pilgrims of a particular nationality. The city thus took on an international aspect, which it still retains. From literary sources and inscriptions, we know of the existence of permanent communities of Armenians, Georgians, Cappadocians, Byzantines and other Greeks, Italians and other westerners, not to men-

the city, took over the city's government and rebuilt the churches that had been destroyed. In 630, the emperor Heraclius reconquered Palestine and brought the cross back to Jerusalem, but not many years later the Muslim Arabs attacked the Byzantine Empire and conquered Syria, Palestine, Egypt, and then the whole of North Africa. Jerusalem fell in 638. This time the patriarch, having learned from experience, opened the gates of the city, and its destruction was avoided. At first the Muslims were satisfied with occupying the Temple Mount and building a mosque there; but from that moment on, except for the period of the crusades, Jerusalem ceased to be an essentially Christian city.

Jerusalem in the Herodian period
During the Hasmonean period, the city had already spread west and northwest from the hill of Ophel—the ancient city of David south of the Temple Mount—crossing the Tyropeon Valley (the Lower City) and occupying the western hill (the Upper City). The first city walls enclosed the two hills, and when the inhabited area spread northward toward the end of this period, a second wall was built to enclose that part of the city as well. The line of the wall is not very clear, because the area concerned, lying partly in the Christian Old City and partly in the Arab quarter, is heavily built up and it has been impossible to carry out systematic excavations. It is commonly accepted, however, that the second wall ran to the south and east of the Holy Sepulcher site, which means that Calvary, where the Crucifixion took place, as well as the tomb where the body of Jesus was placed, was outside the second wall at the time of Pontius Pilate (governor of Judea from 26 to 36).

Characteristic of the topography of Jerusalem are the two deep valleys that surround the city on three sides (the Hinnom Valley to the west and south, and the Kidron Valley to the east). This meant that it could expand only in a northerly direction, and indeed that is where the "new city" rose under Herod and his successors. It was protected by a third wall begun by King Agrippa I, Herod's nephew, but only completed at the time of the Great Revolt against the Romans.

Model of Jerusalem in Second Temple times. The Antonia Fortress (Jerusalem, Holyland Hotel)

The Gihon at the foot of Ophel was Jerusalem's only spring, and its water was brought into the city by means of tunnels, the latest of which dates to the time of King Hezekiah, and the earliest to before David's conquest of the city. The Pool of Siloam, at the southeast corner of the walls, was constructed as early as the Hasmonean period, and it was here that water from the Gihon spring was collected. The city had a number of other pools for collecting rainwater; one of the most famous is the Bethesda (also called Probatica or Bethzatha), to the north of the Temple, for it was here that Jesus cured the paralytic (John 5:2–8). The Hasmoneans also built an aqueduct that gathered water from springs to the south of the city and brought it to cisterns in the southern part of the Temple Mount.

Herod built his palace in the Upper City, against the northwest corner of the first Hasmonean wall. The complex stood on an enormous podium, measuring about 330 meters in a north–south direction and 130 meters east–west. Remains of the podium have been found during excavations in the courtyard of the so-called citadel, a barracks in Turkish times and now a police station. On the north side of the palace were three tall towers, which Herod named after people who were particularly dear to him: his

brother Phasael, his friend Hippicus, and the dearest of his wives (he had ten in all), the Hasmonean princess Mariamme, who was put to death in the end by her suspicious and jealous husband. These towers were left standing when Jerusalem was destroyed by Titus, and the base of one of them (probably Hippicus, though some say Phasael) is still visible, incorporated into a later tower, traditionally known as David's Tower, close to the present-day Jaffa Gate on the south side.

The Upper City was Jerusalem's elegant quarter, and it was here that aristocratic families lived, some of them belonging to the priestly class. After the Six Day War, the Jewish quarter in the Old City, which had been abandoned by its Jewish inhabitants in 1948, was found to be completely destroyed. This provided the opportunity—rare in Jerusalem, since it has been densely and continuously populated for more than four thousand years—to carry out archaeological excavations, which brought to light a number of luxury houses dating to Second Temple times. A number of ritual baths have been found in these houses (in some there were one or two, and in one palace, covering 600 sq m, there were six), as well as various bathrooms not intended for ritual use. It seems clear that the families who lived here paid particular attention not only to personal hygiene but also to the purity required of priests who served in the Temple. Some of these dwellings are open to visitors in a vast underground archaeological park, beneath the modern buildings of the Jewish quarter. The houses were all built in the late Hasmonean and Herodian periods and have mosaic floors with geometrical and floral designs and walls frescoed in Pompeian style, but without human or animal figures, as observance of the second commandment required. In the various rooms were found stone tables and vases: local products typical of the Jerusalem area from Herodian times up to A.D. 70.

To the south of Herod's palace, in the area now occupied by the Dormition Abbey, as well as on the slopes of Mount Zion outside the Ottoman walls of the Old City, there are other remains of the same period. Among them is a

The building known as David's Tower, beside the present-day Jaffa Gate. The tower incorporates the base of the Hippicus Tower or, as some think, the Phasael Tower, both of which rose along with the Mariamme Tower on the north side of Herod's palace.

house excavated at the end of the nineteenth century, which Christian tradition holds to be the house of the priest Caiaphas, where Jesus was taken as a prisoner and where he was denied by Peter (Matthew 26:57ff.; Mark 14:53ff.; Luke 22:54ff.; John 18:13ff.; see also below).

The Temple Mount rose opposite the Upper City. The Temple had been rebuilt in the fifth century B.C., but Herod completely reconstructed it, expanding the top of Mount Moriah with the construction of vaults and cyclopean retaining walls supporting an immense esplanade. The temenos, or temple precinct, which now encloses two mosques (el-Aqsa and the so-called Mosque of Omar or Dome of the Rock), is more or less rectangular and measures 485 meters along the west wall and 470 meters along the east wall. It is 315 meters wide along the north side and 280 meters along the south side, where the wall reached a height of 50 to 55 meters from the valley floor. Towers rose at the four corners. The structures within the temenos are known to us only from literary descriptions, the most important of which is in the Middot tractate of the Mishnah. The enormous esplanade was flanked by porticoes supported by columns with gilded capitals. On the south side was the basilica, or royal portico. An enclosure separated the esplanade from the Temple proper, which consisted of the *hekhal*, or Holy of Holies, preceded by a series of courtyards as one moved inward from the esplanade. On the enclosure were displayed inscriptions in various languages, warning strangers not to proceed farther, on pain of death. One complete copy of the text and another fragmentary one, both in Greek, were found in the debris beyond the esplanade. Bronze gates separated the outermost courtyard, called the Women's Court, from an inner courtyard called the Court of the Israelites, where only male Jews were allowed. Beyond was an area reserved for priests, and only the high priest was permitted to enter the Holy of Holies, and then only on Yom Kippur, the Day of Atonement.

The original masonry of the temenos survives to a variety of heights at various points in the walls: more than 40 meters in the northeast cor-

ner, and 20 meters or so in the southern part of the west wall, now known as the Wailing Wall because for centuries Jews have gone there to pray and mourn the destruction of the Temple. The upper part of the walls has not survived; it was replaced by later walls, built of much smaller pieces of stone, hewn in a different way. The Herodian stones are easily recognizable thanks to the characteristic margins of the exposed surface. The walls of the temenos, which had to support the immense weight of the buildings on top of it and the pressure exerted by the fill, are made of enormous stone blocks, particularly at the base. Their height is fairly uniform at 1–1.10 meters but the length varies. Most of them weigh between 2 and 5 metric tons, but many are as much as 10 meters long and weigh 50 tons or more. The whole temenos was surrounded by a girdle of larger stones; this is discernible in the southern part, where a course of stones twice the height of the others can be seen. One of these stones, in the southeast corner, is reckoned to weigh 100 tons. The largest stone in the visible part of the walls is in the northern part of the western wall: it is 13.60 meters long, 3.30 meters high, and 4.60 meters thick and is reckoned to weigh 570 tons.

Two blocked entrances can be seen today in the southern wall. These are the remains of the Huldah Gates described in the Mishnah. There is a double gate toward the west and a triple gate farther east, both providing access to the temenos. The east gate is a later reconstruction, not the original, but the west gate is partly Herodian, although the arch that surmounts it is proto-Islamic. Each of the entrances at the double gate is currently more than 5 meters wide and was originally about 10 meters high. The gates were accessed by a system of monumental steps, and above them were the openings of two tunnels, which ascended toward the Temple esplanade. At the foot of the steps was a square where the remains of public buildings have been found, including ritual baths where pilgrims immersed themselves before entering the Temple.

Toward the south corner of the west wall are the remains of an arch. It is called Robinson's Arch, after the archaeologist who first suggested

that it was the bridge described by Josephus as connecting the Temple and the Upper City. Archaeological research carried out after the Six Day War has shown, however, that Robinson's Arch is not part of a bridge but a single 13-meter arch that spanned the street parallel to the wall at a height of 17 meters. Six vaults, each one lower than the next, began at the west end of the arch and supported a stairway that descended toward the south, forming a right angle with the arch and connecting the street to the royal portico on the south side of the Temple esplanade. This street ran on two levels: The higher level was next to the wall and was supported by vaults, and the vaults opened into the lower level to form shops. This shopping street formed part of the most important arterial road in Herodian Jerusalem: Its solid surface of large stone slabs followed the line of the Tyropeon Valley, down as far as the Pool of Siloam. South of the southwest corner of the Temple the street was as much

as 10 meters wide and crossed two other streets, one of which ascended westward toward the Upper City, while the other followed the south wall of the temenos.

Farther north along the west wall, excavations beside Robinson's Arch have brought to light a public building of considerable dimensions, which may be the city archive mentioned by Josephus. Still farther north along the wall is a blocked gateway known as Barclay's Gate. It was 5.60 meters wide and 10 meters high, with its base at the level of the upper street; traces have been found of a stairway leading down to the lower shopping street. A stepped tunnel led up from this gate to the Temple esplanade. About 100 meters farther north, an arch projects from the west wall: this is known as Wilson's Arch, and modern excavations have shown it to be part of the bridge mentioned by Josephus as linking the Temple and the Upper City. Beside it is a splendid hall dating to Herodian times,

The south wall of the Temple Mount with the triple Huldah Gates

Opposite: The Struthion Pool

The Golden Gate on the east side of the Temple Mount, where, in Jewish tradition, the Messiah will enter

Opposite: The Pool of Siloam, which collected water from the Gihon spring

now covered by a later vault. This may be the Council Building, which according to Josephus stood in this area. Farther north still, the west wall is hidden by later buildings, but after the Six Day War, its base was uncovered by means of a tunnel excavated along the wall to the northwest corner and beyond. About 40 meters north of Wilson's Arch, another gate was identified as long ago as the nineteenth century. It corresponds to Barclay's Gate, and in this case, too, there is a stepped tunnel leading up toward the esplanade. Both tunnel and gate were named after Sir Charles Warren, the archaeologist who discovered them when he was exploring a cistern underneath the modern esplanade. The modern tunnel follows the Herodian street at the foot of the wall as far as the end of the street, just short of the northwest corner of the wall. A water-collection system of Hasmonean construction found here opens onto the Struthion Pool, a Herodian structure whose northern part is now incorporated into the basement of the Sisters of Zion Convent. A small part of the pavement covering it, known as the *lithostrothon*, is inside the adjacent Monastery of the Flagellation. The

modern tunnel comes to an end in the Via Dolorosa, opposite this monastery.

On a spur of rock to the north of the Temple stood the Antonia Fortress, so named by Herod in honor of his patron, Mark Antony. Scarcely any of it has survived, and, thanks again to Josephus's description, we know only that it was a square building adjacent to the temenos, with towers at the four corners. It was once thought to be very extensive and to include the *lithostrothon* and underlying pool, but modern research shows that it was of much more modest dimensions, and that the Struthion Pool was actually outside the Antonia Fortress, on the north side. In Christian tradition, the Antonia Fortress is identified as Pontius Pilate's praetorium, the place where Jesus was scourged and shown to the people. Hence the name Ecce Homo was given to the arch that spans the Via Dolorosa opposite the *lithostrothon*, which, like the *lithostrothon,* is in fact part of the eastern forum of Aelia Capitolina (see below).

Parts of the wall on the east side of the Temple Mount are pre-Herodian. Herod apparently incorporated parts of an earlier wall into his construction: perhaps part of the Seleucid fortress, the

The so-called Tomb of Absalom, which in fact dates to Hellenistic times

Acra, perhaps part of the Persian or Hellenistic wall around the Temple, or perhaps even remains of the wall around the First Temple. At the northeast corner of the wall are remains of the corner tower of the Herodian temenos, and about 200 meters to the south is the so-called Golden Gate, or Gate of Mercy. The structure seen today is later than Second Temple times and has been built over another gate, which is also later; but it seems that this is also where the Herodian gate stood. According to tradition, this is the gate through which the Messiah will enter. Farther south can be seen the remains of another double gate, beneath which are vestiges of an arch similar to Robinson's. Here, too, the arch probably led to an access stairway. This gate may have given access to the underground vaults at the southeast corner of the temenos known as Solomon's Stables.

Other Jerusalem buildings of the Second Temple period are known to us only from the writings of Josephus and other sources (such as the Gospels), and scarcely anything remains to confirm their existence. The city had markets and palaces, towers, pools, a theater and a hippodrome, and monumental tombs such as the famous Tomb of David (which tradition places on Mount Zion, but its whereabouts are in fact unknown). Herod apparently built a second aqueduct, which fell into disuse and was later rebuilt by soldiers stationed at Aelia Capitolina. Deserving particular mention are the cemeteries dating to the Second Temple period, which surround the city on all sides but especially to the east and north. Most of the tombs are hewn out of the rock, with burial niches, or arcosolia, where corpses reposed until only the bones were left. These were then collected and put into ossuaries: small stone boxes, often with a sloping lid, which may be either free of all decoration or richly carved. Some of the tombs are substantial monuments, however, built or hewn out of the rock, with splendidly ornate facades, usually with flower motifs, and sometimes with a colonnaded antechamber. A few, such as the Tomb of Zacharias and the one known as the Tomb of Absalom, are very tall constructions, square in plan and with a pyramidal or conical roof.

Aelia Capitolina

The plan of Aelia Capitolina can be deduced from that of Byzantine Jerusalem as represented in the Madaba map, a mosaic representation of the Holy Land with vignettes showing the various towns and villages. It dates back to the second half of the sixth century and was discovered at the end of the nineteenth century in the Church of the Apostles at Madaba in Jordan. The *cardo* of the city can clearly be seen as a colonnaded street starting at the north gate, the present-day Damascus Gate. The *decumanus* ran along the ancient northern stretch of the first Hasmonean wall. Both streets still exist, and their ancient lines have been confirmed by excavations, though admittedly these have not been systematic: The area is densely built up and it is rarely possible to excavate, and then only on a modest scale.

The north gate was in reality a triple triumphal arch flanked by two towers. It gave on to a semicircular open space, at the center of which stood a column shown on the Madaba map. Even now, the Arab name for the gate is Bab el-'Amud, which means Gate of the Column. The arch and towers have been found underneath the Damascus Gate, but no trace has been discovered of a corresponding city wall, and current opinion is that Aelia Capitolina did not have defensive walls until the late third or early fourth century.

*The Byzantine quarter in the
area to the south of the
Temple Mount*

The Damascus Gate

Opposite: The columns of the Byzantine cardo *in the Jewish quarter*

Various streets led from the square beside the triumphal arch. The chief ones were the *cardo* proper, which ran south and was flanked by columns, some of which have been found incorporated into the walls of the bazaar, and a secondary *cardo,* running southeast along the natural hollow of the valley to the west of Temple Mount. This secondary *cardo* probably crossed the whole city as far as the Pool of Siloam; traces found during excavations show that the street was flanked by a colonnade. As to the route of the principal *cardo*, opinions differ: Because its southern stretch, beyond the point where it crosses the *decumanus*, has revealed only Byzantine remains, most scholars think the Roman *cardo* stopped at the crossroads, its way south being blocked by the Tenth Legion camp. It seems more likely, however, that the *cardo* did continue southward, but that all traces of it disappeared when the Byzantine street was made. For reasons explained below, the Byzantine street was cut into the rock of the southwest hill, at a lower level than the previous *cardo*.

Almost all reconstructions place the X Fretensis (Tenth) Legion camp in the southwest quarter of the city, which corresponds to the Upper City of Herodian times. Josephus, in fact,

tells us that the city walls were not destroyed on that side, since they could be used to fortify the Roman camp. This area has been fairly systematically excavated at various periods, and although a certain number of characteristic tiles bearing the Tenth Legion stamp have turned up, very few remains of buildings of that period have been found, and indeed no trace of fortifications on the south and east sides. This is very puzzling, because it was an absolute rule that Roman camps be surrounded by a defensive wall. Various solutions to this problem have been offered, but none of them is satisfactory. Most recently it has been suggested that the legion was first based provisionally in the area indicated by Josephus and then moved to the Temple Mount, but so far this theory has not been sufficiently confirmed by finds.

To the north of the *decumanus* was the forum, bounded on the north side by a basilica and a temple on a podium, probably dedicated to Venus. According to the earliest Christian historians, in fact, a temple of Venus was built on the site of Calvary. Some scholars, however, prefer to identify the raised temple as that of Jupiter Capitolinus, or rather of the three Capitoline deities who were normally worshipped in Roman colonies, namely, Jupiter, Juno, and Minerva. Substantial remains from this period have been discovered in the area of the Church of the Holy Sepulcher but it is not clear whether they are linked to the basilica or the temple. A second forum, the eastern forum, was situated north of the northwest corner of Temple Mount. Impressive remains of a gate or triple triumphal arch, which constituted the western entrance to the forum, have been found here. Part of the central arch, 5.20 meters wide, is, as mentioned above, now known as the Ecce Homo arch and spans the Via Dolorosa at a height of more than 6 meters. The arch to the north is 2.36 meters wide and 5.20 meters high (like the side arches of the triumphal arch at the Damascus Gate) and is now incorporated into the Convent of the Sisters of Zion. The *lithostrothon*, which is incorporated partly into the convent and partly into the Chapel of the Condemnation inside the Monastery of the Flagellation, was the original forum pavement, part of which rested on vaults covering the Struthion Pool. The pool was still in use and was linked to the forum square by a flight of steps.

East of the forum, along the Via Dolorosa, where the Convent of Saint Anne now stands, more Roman remains have been found: the Bethesda Pool, or Probatica, was still in use in Roman times and it seems that a temple of Asclepius, the god of medicine, also stood there. The Temple esplanade was apparently still in ruins (unless we accept the suggestion that the Tenth Legion camp was here). The temple of Jupiter Capitolinus may have been built here, and a Christian tradition tells of one or more statues of the emperor in this area, but there are no material remains, or even precise information, to confirm this. On the other hand, Roman buildings and a considerable quantity of tiles bearing the Tenth Legion stamp have been brought to light at the southwest corner of the Temple Mount and in the northern part of Ophel, but the rest of the hill—the so-called City of David—remained unoccupied during the Roman period.

A second aqueduct was built by the legionaries at this period, as is indicated by inscriptions on some of the siphons, bearing the names of some of the centuries who had been tasked with building sections of the aqueduct. The aqueduct began at springs south of Bethlehem and traveled at a greater height than the Hasmonean aqueduct, crossing some low-lying land on piers that seem to have been erected first in Herodian times. That would suggest that the work was started by Herod but then abandoned, and that Roman soldiers installed new pipes in order to supply the increasing needs of the new colony. This second aqueduct passed through a tunnel to the west of the city and ended in the Pool of Hezekiah inside the present-day Jaffa Gate.

Christian Jerusalem

Constantine found Jerusalem largely in ruins, though it seems to have been already surrounded by walls—probably built when the Tenth Legion was transferred elsewhere, leaving the city without a garrison. The northern, western, and eastern parts of the walls followed roughly the lines of

the walls that we see today, but the southern part seems to have left Mount Zion and a large part of Ophel outside. It was only in the mid-fifth century, when the city had spread into this area, that Eudocia, wife of Theodosius II, funded the extension of the wall in a southerly direction, along the line of the ancient Hasmonean "first wall." However, not all scholars agree with this reconstruction.

Left: The entrance to the Holy
Sepulcher, with the Stone of
Unction on which Nicodemus
anointed the body of Jesus

Right: The rotunda and
chapel of the Holy Sepulcher

If it is true that after James, brother of Jesus, the succession of Jerusalem bishops was unbroken, there must have been some churches, or at least one church, in the city even before Constantine's building program began. Were they just meeting-houses, or could they have been Judeo-Christian synagogues? We do not know. After the foundation of Aelia Capitolina, however, Jews were no longer allowed to reside there; thereafter the bishops must have been of Gentile origin. It is possible that their see was in the area where the Church of Holy Zion rose in the fourth century.

After the sites of Calvary and Christ's tomb had been identified, Constantine's first concern was to reorganize the area and build a church there. The tomb was a cave cut into the rock, and the first stage was to detach it from the hillside, surround it with a circle of columns, and then build a circular shrine—the Anastasis, or Resurrection—at the top of which was an *oculus*, a circular hole open to the sky. Beside it were a

baptistery and the patriarchate (the bishop's palace), and facing it was a courtyard surrounded by porticoes. Beyond it and to the west was a basilica, the Martyrium, whose west wall abutted the rock identified as Calvary. This complex was inaugurated in 335, but construction was not completed until a few years later. In one of the lower chapels of the present-day church, a graffito has been discovered on a wall built in the time of Constantine. It depicts a boat above the words *Domine ivimus* (Lord, we have come). It is possible that this is the earliest evidence of a pilgrim arriving from the West while the Constantinian church was still being built.

The Church of Holy Zion was built on Mount Zion, probably by Bishop Makarios, in 340. It stood where tradition placed the Last Supper, in the "room upstairs" (Acts 1:12–13), where the apostles gathered after the Passion and where the Last Supper was held. Little remains of this basilica church with four rows of columns, which

stood in the area of the present-day Dormition Abbey. Beside it, in what is known as David's Tomb, Roman remains have been found, probably belonging to a synagogue: This may have been the place chosen by the first Christians for their *ecclesia* (meeting place). Remains of Byzantine mosaics have been found farther to the east, perhaps from a church built where tradition placed the house of Caiaphas. Today an Armenian monastery stands there. On Mount Zion and farther north, in the direction of David's Tower (it had already acquired that name in Byzantine times), there was a concentration of convents, cells of individual monks, and hostels run by monasteries for pilgrims. Remains of religious buildings of the period have been found in various parts of the Armenian quarter. On the eastern slopes of Mount Zion, which were deserted in medieval times and lay outside the Ottoman walls, various public and private Byzantine buildings have been excavated (some

of them lie on top of older buildings dating to Second Temple times). The present-day Church of Saint Peter in Gallicantu stands on the spot where Saint Peter is supposed to have withdrawn to weep after denying that he knew Jesus (Matthew 26:69–75; Mark 14:66–72; Luke 22:56–62; John 18:25–27): A church was built there in Byzantine times. A stepped street has been discovered to the north, rising from the east toward the Church of Holy Zion.

Among the places visited by pilgrims as early as the fourth century was the Pool of Siloam, where a church was built, and the Bethesda Pool, to the east of the eastern forum. Here, too, in the fifth century, a church dedicated to Mary was built, because it was thought that the house of Anne and Joachim, Mary's parents, had stood there. Part of the church was built over the pool and rested on piers standing on the pool floor. The church was rebuilt in crusader times and dedicated to Saint Anne. Excavations carried out

Plan of the Church of the Holy Sepulcher, the fourth-century Constantinian church

1 Atrium

2 Basilica

3 Courtyard

4 Rotunda

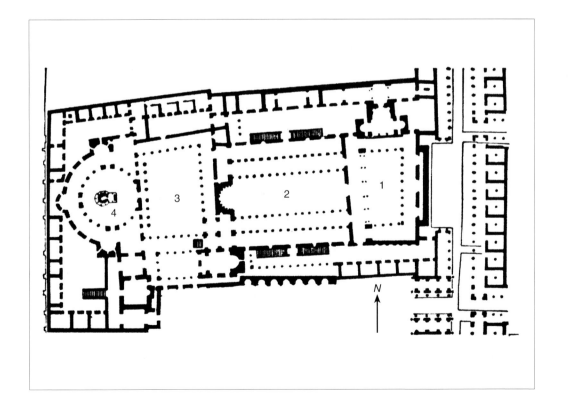

Above: Church of the Dormition on Mount Zion

Below: The Mount of Olives
1 *Chapel of the Ascension*
2 *Church of Pater Noster*
3 *Tomb of the Virgin*
4 *Church of All Nations*
5 *Church of Dominus Flevit*
6 *Tombs of the Prophets*
7 *House of Abraham*
8 *Ancient road*
9 *Ancient road*
10 *Bethphage*
11 *Ancient road*
12 *Bethany in the first century* A.D.
13 *Tomb of Lazarus*

Opposite: Chapel of the Ascension on the Mount of Olives

at the present-day Convent of Saint Anne have brought to light remains from various periods.

A number of churches were founded on the Mount of Olives as early as the fourth century. Even before the time of Constantine, a cave was venerated where Jesus was supposed to have taught his disciples before the Passion.

Constantine had a basilica built there, but scarcely anything of it remains. Beneath its apse there was once a crypt, which may have been an ancient burial cave. A little farther north, on a hillock identified as the place where Christ ascended to heaven (Luke 24:51; Acts 1:9–11), a matron called Poemenia founded a round church in 378: Excavations undertaken by the Franciscans in the 1960s have brought to light the circular base (25 m in diameter) of the Byzantine church, which was rebuilt with an octagonal plan in the crusader period. Another fourth-century church is that of Gethsemane on the Mount of Olives, founded by Theodosius in 385 at the place where Jesus and his disciples spent the night before his arrest. Excavations here have revealed a three-apsed basilica, surrounded by various rooms with mosaic floors. There were also numerous monasteries on the Mount of Olives, the most famous being those of the Latins, as well as various churches built in Byzantine and proto-Islamic times, and funerary chapels from the same period. There was in fact a large cemetery here in late Roman times, and it continued

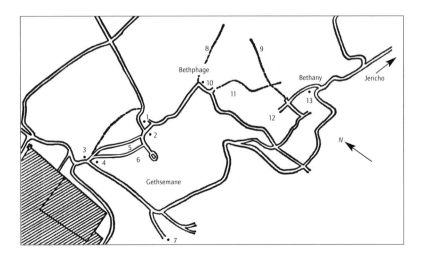

to be used in the Middle Ages, up to the time of the crusades.

A number of funerary chapels with splendid mosaic floors have been discovered in another Byzantine cemetery to the north of the city. In one, the mosaic depicts Orpheus playing the lyre to an audience of wild animals, a satyr, and a centaur. Another has coils of vine tendrils with bunches of grapes hanging from them, and birds of various kinds in medallions. At the edge of this latter mosaic, an inscription in Armenian contains a prayer for the Armenian dead. Not far away, north of the Damascus Gate, another chapel has been excavated. It belonged to a monastery with an attached hospice, and here, too, one of the inscriptions is in Armenian. It was evidently in this area that the community of Armenian residents and visitors was concentrated. In this same area stood the Church of Saint Stephen with an attached monastery, founded by Eudocia and inaugurated in 460. A monk of the time tells us that at the beginning of the sixth century it was the largest in the city, so large in fact that it was able to look after ten thousand monks who were demonstrating against the religious policy of the Monophysite emperor Anastasius. The monastery complex is in the same area as the modern Dominican monastery of Saint Etienne. But the biggest ecclesiastical complex of all was built later on by the emperor Justinian in the form of the church called Nea (New) and dedicated to Mary, Mother of God. It stood at the south end of the southern *cardo*, and its construction is described by a contemporary historian, Procopius of Caesarea. The complex included not only a basilica with a narthex and atrium, but two pilgrim hostels, a hospital, a library, and a monastery. To make room for all these buildings, the top of the hill had to be enlarged by means of vaults. The church columns were massive monoliths cut in a quarry some distance from the city and dragged on rollers to the building site. In order to make their journey possible, openings had to be cut into the rocky terrain so that these enormous loads could be hauled through; it was probably for this reason that the level of the southern

cardo was lowered, eliminating a ridge on the slopes of the southwestern hill and creating a downward slope to the church. This operation removed all traces of the preceding Roman *cardo* in the area. Parts of the Nea Church apses have been uncovered, as well as the colossal vaults on the south side, which were used as a cistern. A dedicatory inscription has also been found there, commemorating the inauguration of the cistern under Justinian.

Capernaum

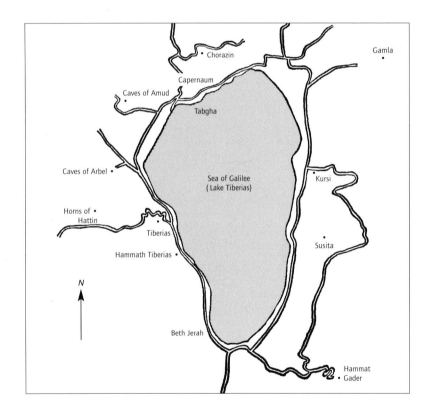

Map showing ancient sites around Lake Tiberias

Opposite: View of Lake Tiberias

Capernaum is a fishing village on the northwest shore of Lake Tiberias. It owes its fame to the fact that Jesus preached and performed miracles here and also chose five of his disciples from among its inhabitants: Matthew and two pairs of brothers, Simon (Peter) and Andrew, and James and John, sons of Zebedee. The Gospels speak of two buildings in the village: the house of Peter and a synagogue built by the Roman centurion whose servant was healed by Jesus (Luke 7:1–10). A medieval text, reporting the evidence of a fourth-century pilgrim, reveals that in about the year 384 Peter's house in Capernaum, now adapted as a church, was shown to visitors; and there was also a synagogue reached by a flight of steps. Excavations have revealed an octagonal church dating to the Hellenistic-Roman period, built on top of a private house. One room in the house was apparently adapted for worship in the first century, and later on, in the fourth century, the house was rebuilt and surrounded by a wall. The house walls were decorated with colored plaster on which graffiti in Greek, Latin, Aramaic, and Syriac, left by Christian pilgrims, have been found. It was in the second half of the fifth century that the octagonal church replaced the previous building.

About 30 meters north of the church is the synagogue, its facade facing south—that is, toward Jerusalem. The building consists of a room with colonnades on three sides and a

Remains of the octagonal church built over the so-called House of Saint Peter

Opposite: Main entrance to the synagogue, dating to the late fourth century A.D.

porticoed courtyard on its east side. A large number of richly sculpted architectural features in white sandstone were revealed during excavation. The synagogue stood on a raised podium and two flights of steps led up to the entrance. According to the Franciscan archaeologists who excavated it, the hall was built in the late fourth century; the courtyard was added later and was not completed until after the mid-fifth century. The remains of ancient dwellings of the Hellenistic-Roman period were found underneath the podium. Under the nave of the synagogue, the archaeologists were able to identify a basalt floor, apparently belonging to the earlier synagogue built by the centurion. Other parts of the village were excavated beyond the church and the synagogue, revealing various private houses and a jetty. In a cemetery to the north of the vil-

lage there is a noteworthy Roman mausoleum with an underground chamber containing a number of sarcophagi.

About 5 kilometers south of Capernaum is the site of Tabgha, ancient Heptapegon (seven springs), where tradition places various episodes from the Gospels: the Sermon on the Mount (Matthew 5–7), the Miracle of the Loaves and Fishes (Matthew 15:32–38), the appearance of Jesus to the apostles after the Resurrection, and Peter given primacy in the church (John 21:1–17). The principal church discovered here is that dedicated to the Multiplication of the Loaves and Fishes: It is a basilica with a nave and two aisles, a transept, a mosaic floor, and an atrium at the front. The mosaic behind the altar shows fish and a basket of bread to commemorate the miracle. There are Nilotic scenes in the transept, with a

Nave of the synagogue

wealth of plants and aquatic birds. The basilica and its mosaics have all been dated to the second half of the fifth century. A more modest church, founded in the fourth century, has been discovered underneath the basilica, and a modern church has been erected over it. Another church, belonging to a monastery, has been found about 300 meters to the north. It is partly built up onto and partly cut out of the rock on the mountain slope and includes a cave where, according to one tradition, Jesus delivered the sermon of the beatitudes, preaching not to a crowd but to his disciples alone. A third church stood on the lakeshore, about 200 meters northeast of the Basilica of the Beatitudes. It is in fact a chapel built in the seventh or eighth century and restored in the Middle Ages, but in its original form it may go back to the fifth or even the fourth century. There is a roughly rectangular rock here known as the Mensa domini (Table of the Lord) where, according to tradition, Jesus prepared food for the apostles after the Resurrection. Another version has it that the Mensa domini is the table on which Jesus

placed the loaves and fish to be distributed to the crowd, and that it corresponds to the large piece of rock under the altar in the Church of the Multiplication, fragments of which pilgrims used to take home as relics.

Opposite: Mosaic floor in the Church of the Multiplication of the Loaves and Fishes

Above: The site of Tabgha, ancient Heptapegon (seven springs), where tradition places several Gospel episodes

Below: Mosaic floor in the Church of the Multiplication of the Loaves and Fishes. This mosaic, behind the altar, shows a basket of bread and two fish, to commemorate the miracle narrated in the Gospels.

Tiberias

Above: Justinian's monastery on Mount Berenice. In the background lies the modern town of Tiberias on the western shore of Lake Tiberias.

Opposite: Remains of the Byzantine church on Mount Berenice

Herod Antipas, son of Herod the Great and heir to part of his kingdom, founded the city of Tiberias around A.D. 20 and made it his capital. The site he chose was on the shore of the Sea of Galilee, later called Lake Tiberias, beside some hot springs near a village called Hammath (hot spring). Because the place had long been used as a cemetery and was therefore unclean in Jewish eyes, Antipas was obliged to populate his city with foreigners, adventurers, and beggars, partly by compulsion and partly by giving them free housing. Legend

has it that in the second century, at a time when the Roman authorities prohibited the teaching of the Law, Rabbi Simeon bar Yohai emerged from a cave where he had taken refuge from persecution, healed his wounds by bathing in the hot springs, and in gratitude purified the city.

The fact that the inhabitants supported the revolt of A.D. 66 against the Romans shows, however, that by that time the majority of the population was Jewish. In 67, the city surrendered to Vespasian, thereby avoiding destruction. On the death of Herod's last heir, Agrippa II, Tiberias was incorporated into the province of Judea. A large temple was built there in honor of Hadrian in the second century, implying that some of the inhabitants must have been pagans. But at the end of that century, once the city had been purified by bar Yohai and so made habitable for practicing Jews, it became the residence not only of the patriarch (who represented the Jewish people before the Roman authorities) but also of students of the Law; an illustrious rabbinical academy here was responsible for drawing up the Palestinian Talmud, also known as the Jerusalem Talmud. Even after the abolition of the patriarchate in 429, the sages of Tiberias retained their positions as spiritual and cultural guides for Jews throughout the world—a role that increased in status at the beginning of the sixth century, when the great sage of the Babylonian diaspora, Mar Zutra, settled at Tiberias and became the head of

Above: The Roman cardo
across the ancient city

*Below: Plan of ancient
Tiberias*
  A Tiberias
  B Hammath Tiberias
  1 Northern synagogue
  2 Water reservoir
  3 Basilica
  4 Marketplace
  5 Baths
  6 Monastery
  7 Cardo
  8 Gate
  9 Synagogue
  10 Baths
  11 Southern synagogue

*Opposite: Remains of the
Roman baths at Hammath
Tiberias*

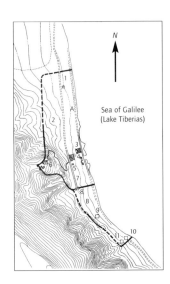

its academy. Here the Jewish calendar was drawn up year by year, and here the definitive text of the Jewish Bible was established.

An attempt to introduce Christianity at Tiberias in the mid-fourth century failed, but in the fifth century the city had a Christian minority and a bishop. The Jews continued to be a majority even after the Arab conquest, when a small number of Muslims settled there and the city was raised to the status of capital of the northern Palestine district. After conquest by the crusaders, it became the capital of the principality of Galilee. The crusaders built a fortress and a church to the north of the old urban area, which had suffered damage in the wars and in disastrous earthquakes, and the remaining inhabitants moved to the new area, which was surrounded by a wall. From the sixteenth century on, the local population became largely Jewish again, and the city remained within the crusader walls until the twentieth century. This meant that the Tiberias of Roman and Byzantine times was unoccupied and therefore available for archaeological exploration.

Tiberias was founded as a Greek polis, with a civic assembly, a council, and magistracies of a Hellenistic type, and it was laid out like a Graeco-Roman city on the strip of flat land between the lake to the east and a mountain to the west. A *cardo* lined with porticoes and shops crossed the city, ending to the south in a square with a monumental gate. Discoveries made along the *cardo* include (starting at the south end): a theater, public baths, and a covered market. A street parallel to the *cardo* followed the lakeshore, where the harbor had a series of jetties and moorings. Excavations along this street have revealed a large semicircular exedra (almost 32 m in diameter) facing the harbor, and a Roman basilica, which became a church in Byzantine times. An aqueduct, which brought water from a spring about 15 kilometers south of Tiberias, ran the length of

Above: Detail of the famous mosaic found in one of the two synagogues at Hammath Tiberias. It represents the pagan sun god, surrounded by the twelve signs of the zodiac.

Below: The Hammath Tiberias mosaic, as reconstructed in a drawing. At the top, flanked by two lighted menorahs and other ritual objects, is the ark of the Torah, in which the scrolls of the Law are kept. In the middle is the sun god surrounded by the twelve signs of the zodiac and the four seasons with their names in Hebrew. At the bottom, flanked by two lions, is an inscription in Greek that names the founders of the synagogue. The symbols of Cancer and Capricorn and the sun god's chariot in the central panel are missing from the original mosaic.

Opposite: Detail of the Hammath Tiberias mosaic showing the ark of the Torah

the city, ending in a large cistern (32 m by 10 m, and about 10 m deep).

According to tradition, there were thirteen synagogues at Tiberias, but only one—at the north end of the Byzantine inhabited area—has been discovered. It may have been built in the sixth century, and it remained in use until the time of the crusades. Another two synagogues, one of which is decorated with splendid mosaics, have been excavated in the area of ancient Hammath, which became part of Tiberias from the fourth century onward.

When the city was founded, it had no surrounding wall, and no defensive wall was built until the time of the Great Revolt. In the sixth century, Justinian built the impressive surrounding wall that can still be seen today. It enclosed not only Tiberias but also Hammath and Mount Berenice, which looms over the city. A church was built at the top of the mountain in Byzantine times, but it was subsequently destroyed and rebuilt in the Arab period, remaining in use until the time of the crusades. Attached to the church was a monastery and perhaps a hostel for pilgrims coming from Nazareth and Mount Tabor, who entered the city by the west gate, just a short distance away.

Sepphoris

Above: Roman-Byzantine-period cistern

Opposite: Remains of the porticoed cardo

The name Sepphoris comes from the Hebrew *Zippori*, a variant of the word *zippor*, meaning "bird." A passage in the Talmud explains that the city was given this name "because it is perched at the top of a mountain, like a bird." It stands on a hill 285 meters above sea level, in a fertile area of Galilee halfway between the Mediterranean coast and the Sea of Galilee.

Archaeological finds reveal that the site's origins go back at least to 500 B.C., but the earliest written sources to mention it narrate events in the Hasmonean period, when the city was the capital of an administrative district. Sepphoris was involved in the series of disturbances that occurred throughout most of Judea soon after the death of Herod, with the result that it was destroyed and its inhabitants sold into slavery by Varus, the legate of Syria. Herod Antipas caused it to flourish again, making it, in the words of Josephus, "the ornament of all Galilee." Later on, at the time of the First Jewish Revolt, Sepphoris remained faithful to the empire: It flung open its gates to Vespasian's army and minted coins in which it styled itself "city of peace."

In Hadrian's time, and very probably before the outbreak of the Second Jewish Revolt, Sepphoris changed its name to Diocaesarea, which means "city of Zeus and the emperor." This change indicates that a pagan government had now taken over the city. It was only at the beginning of the third century that the Jewish element obtained local supremacy again, at a time when Sepphoris was reaching a period of extraordinary cultural growth. The presence here of the Jewish patriarch Judah ha Nasi (Judah the Prince) from 200 to 217 meant that Sepphoris could become a focal point for Jewish society. In all probability Judah ha Nasi drew up the Mishnah at Sepphoris. He is described in rabbinical sources as an eminent personality, as wise

Above: Roman theater from the first century A.D., with an auditorium capable of holding about 4,200 spectators

Below: Plan of ancient Sepphoris
1 *Theater*
2 *Palace from the early third century A.D., where the famous mosaic of the "Mona Lisa of Galilee" was found*
3 *Residential area*

as Solomon and a friend of the Roman emperor, who apparently went so far as to prostrate himself before the rabbi. This may well be an exaggeration, but it is nevertheless certain that at the time of Judah ha Nasi, relations between the Jews and the empire were very good. Notably, a coin minted at Sepphoris at the time of Caracalla commemorated a treaty of friendship between the senate and city of Rome on the one hand, and the holy *boule* (council) of Sepphoris on the other. Bearing in mind that the Talmud says that the Jews played an important role in the council of Sepphoris at the time of Rabbi Judah, we may deduce that this was a period of peace and fruitful collaboration between the Jewish and Greek populations as well.

There is sound evidence that culture and religion flourished at Sepphoris: Eighteen synagogues were built there, as well as a number of *batei midrash* (study houses). All this wealth was not dissipated after the death of Rabbi Judah. Even after the end of the third century, when the

patriarchate moved to Tiberias, Sepphoris remained a great center of learning, and many distinguished teachers lived there. But the life of the fourth-century city was disturbed by an important event: Various sources tell of a Jewish rebellion, led principally by Sepphoris, which was put down by Roman forces at the time of Gallus Caesar (351–352). Archaeologists have not been able to identify any destruction caused by this military intervention, but it has been possible to establish that the city was struck by the earthquake of 363, with the result that a number of luxury dwellings were abandoned.

By the end of the fourth century, earthquake damage had been repaired and Sepphoris began to flourish again, adding new private houses and a synagogue decorated with splendid mosaics. The majority of the population was still Jewish, but there is solid evidence of a Christian presence from the fifth century on, and archaeologists have been able to identify two churches.

From Roman times until the fourth century, the upper part of the city contained houses along a road leading into a square. The houses were certainly occupied by Jews, because as many as twenty-three ritual baths have been found in the area. But the discovery by archaeologists of objects such as two statuettes representing Prometheus and Pan is indicative of an interest in Hellenism. After the earthquake of 363, this whole area became an industrial site, especially for glassworking. Since manufactured goods dating to this period bear Christian symbols, and since a considerable proportion of the animal bones found in the postearthquake layer are those of pigs, we can conclude that the district was no longer inhabited by Jews.

The upper city also contains the theater, which was built in the first century A.D. on the steep northern side of the hill. It could hold about forty-two hundred people and enjoyed a magnificent view. On clear days, it is even possible to make out Mount Hermon in the Golan

Heights. To the south of the theater we find a luxury two-story house, built at the beginning of the third century A.D., with a large number of rooms, baths, and frescoed walls. It rapidly aroused the admiration of scholars and visitors because of a mosaic floor in the triclinium (dining room) with scenes from the life of Dionysos, processions, birds, fish, and masks. The panels depicting scenes from the life of Dionysos are framed with acanthus leaves, some of which form medallions, including one showing a fascinating woman who has come to be known as the Mona Lisa of Galilee. The mosaic dates to the early third century: in other words, to the time of Rabbi Judah. The dwelling was abandoned after the earthquake of 363.

Excavations carried out in the lower city have produced evidence of two broad, porticoed streets, a *cardo* and a *decumanus*, at the intersection of which three inscriptions with mosaics have been found, commemorating the re-laying of the pavements under the supervision of Bishop Eutropius. In the same area, opposite the intersection of the two roads, there is a church of elongate shape, with a nave, two wings, and side rooms. The apse faces east. Various pieces of evidence taken together suggest that the church was founded at the time of the work carried out by Eutropius, which can be dated to the late fifth or early sixth century. It seems natural to conclude, therefore, that he was responsible for having the church built at a time when that particular urban area was undergoing reconstruction.

Part of Sepphoris's appeal to visitors is its many buildings with rich mosaics, of which the Mona Lisa house is just one. In the lower city, at least three buildings decorated with mosaics have been unearthed. One of these, to the east of the *cardo*, is a large, porticoed basilican building with frescoed walls. The fact that it has mosaics depicting, among other things, birds and fish, has led scholars to suggest that this was the lower city market, mentioned in rabbinical writings.

Another very large building—the largest in Sepphoris—contains in its principal room a refined mosaic depicting scenes connected with the river Nile. A metric inscription in Greek, dating to the first half of the fifth century, records that the work was carried out by artists from Alexandria, a fact that bears witness to the sophisticated taste of the Sepphoris inhabitants. In a position of prominence in the mosaic is a Nilometer, a structure for measuring the height of the Nile and hence the level of tax to be paid by the inhabitants (the fertility of the land being related to Nile floods). The size of the building and its nature suggest that it was not a private house but a public building, perhaps a town basilica.

Another outstanding mosaic embellished the nave of a synagogue built in the early fifth century in the northern part of the city. The mosaic is arranged in seven horizontal bands of varying widths, subdivided in some cases into two or three panels; although some parts have been damaged and lost, it has come down to us in a generally good state of preservation. This complex mosaic begins at the entrance to the synagogue opposite the bema (the raised platform where the ark was placed and which was the focal point of Jewish ritual). First there is a representation of the angels visiting Sarah and Abraham, and then the Sacrifice of Isaac, the zodiac, the offering of bread and first fruits, the consecration of Aaron and his service in the Tabernacle, an architectural facade, and two menorahs flanked by Jewish symbols.

This elaborate work, according to Zeev Weiss, was intended to convey a very clear message about the promise God made to the people of Israel, guaranteeing them abundance and prosperity. It is very important to note that if the building depicted in the band nearest the most important part of the synagogue is the Temple, as seems likely, it shows that the Jews of the time were thereby expressing hope of redemption: They were looking forward to a time when the Temple would be rebuilt and the Jewish rite revived in order to restore prosperity to the world. Other mosaics found in late-antique synagogues in Israel express the same concept, but in no other case are these themes developed in such a complex way as at Sepphoris.

*The so-called Mona Lisa of
Galilee, detail of a floor
mosaic on a Dionysiac subject, found in the triclinium
of a palace from the third
century A.D.*

Above and opposite: Details of a mosaic found in a very large building. They show scenes on the banks of the Nile and date to the early fifth century A.D. Of particular interest is the Nilometer (opposite), a structure designed to measure the height of the river's floodwaters.

Hammat Gader

Fifth- to sixth-century synagogue at Hammat Gader

Opposite: The so-called Oval Hall in the baths complex at Hammat Gader

Hammat Gader lies east of the Jordan in the Yarmuk Valley, only 7 kilometers from Galilee as the crow flies. It takes its name from a Hebrew root meaning "hot" and from the town of Gadara, of which it was a dependency; the name therefore means "hot baths of Gadara." We know from literary sources, in fact, that Hammat Gader was one of the most famous thermal spa towns of imperial and late antique times, second only to the celebrated town of Baiae in the Gulf of Naples.

The water came from five different springs, each with its own characteristics and temperature, the hottest spring reaching fifty-one degrees Celsius.

It must have been the inhabitants of Gadara who first decided to turn their springs to advantage, but since we know that Antoninus Pius attached his name to the baths, we are bound to assume that he subsidized their construction. In the third century, Hammat Gader was a meeting place for the merchants and intellectuals of Jewish society. But its fame grew in late antiquity, and in the fifth century it was even visited by the empress Eudocia. In the second half of the sixth century, a special area of Hammat Gader was reserved for lepers, who were fed at public expense.

The bath complex had a number of rooms and formed part of a very large building on more than one floor—possibly as many as three, judging from a nineteenth-century drawing made by J. S. Buckingham, the first modern visitor to the site. One room that stands out in particular is the Oval Hall, which contained a pool and four baths, the latter being set up in the rounded corners of the room. The largest room was the Hall of the Fountains, which had a central area and two narrower extensions to north and south. The central area was 53 meters long and 13.4 meters wide. The large pool was surrounded by twenty-eight fountains.

The so-called Hall of the Fountains in the baths complex at Hammat Gader

The Hall of the Inscriptions is a room whose original pool was covered over in the mid-fifth century with a splendid marble floor, on which, over the course of time, inscriptions in Greek were incised with the names of donors. However, the most noteworthy inscriptions at the Hammat Gader complex are those found in the Hall of the Fountains: They contain a poem written by the empress Eudocia extolling the beauty of the building, and a text praising the benefactions of the emperor Anastasius.

The baths continued to be used even after the Arab conquest, but they were destroyed in an earthquake in 749.

In addition to the huge bath complex, Hammat Gader also had a pagan temple, a synagogue, and a theater. The synagogue was excavated in 1932 by the archaeologist E. L. Sukenik, who dated it to the fifth century and brought to light a number of inscriptions in Aramaic and Greek. These texts mention that construction of the synagogue was financed by the Jews of neighboring towns. The great bath complex was the subject of important excavation campaigns carried out between 1979 and 1982 under the direction of Yizhar Hirschfeld and Giora Solar.

Scythopolis
(Beth Shean)

Aerial view of the archaeological park at Beth Shean, the Scythopolis of Roman times

Opposite: Roman-period buildings at the foot of the acropolis

Scythopolis was almost certainly founded in the first half of the third century B.C. by the Hellenistic king Ptolemy Philadelphus. The complete name of the city as it appears in inscriptions and on coins was Nysa-Scythopolis, and the local tradition in sources from Roman times was that it had been founded by Dionysos, who apparently arranged for his nurse Nysa to be buried there. But we still do not know why the city was given the name Scythopolis, city of the Scythians, when it was refounded.

The city lies in a fertile spot where water is plentiful, thanks to the presence of a large number of springs. It stands at the intersection of two very important roads, one of which crosses the Jezreel Valley on its way from the coast, while the other crosses the Jordan Valley.

In 63 B.C., Pompey conquered Scythopolis, thereby removing it from Hasmonean dominion, and it became part of the Decapolis, a league of cities that defended the common Greek culture of its members. But Scythopolis continued to be a city with a mixed population in which the Jewish element was well represented. Many thousands of Jews were massacred by their fellow citizens at the time of the Great Revolt against Rome in A.D. 66, but in the second century A.D. the Jews were once again playing an important part in local life, as were the Samaritans.

In the first century A.D., Scythopolis was a fairly wealthy city and began to acquire a number of important monuments, but it was in the following century that its period of greatest development began—a fact that is confirmed by the choice of a new building material: a hard limestone instead of basalt.

Because of the uneven nature of the ground on which it was built, the city had an irregular shape. Dictating the development of Scythopolis were the mound on which the acropolis stood

and two riverbeds with steep banks. Only the flat central areas of the city could therefore have a regular layout with rectangular *insulae*. Main streets linked the city center to its gates, and there is evidence of the city's prosperity in the existence of at least four temples, a theater, a hippodrome, an *odeion* (which also served as a *bouleuterion*, that is, a meeting place for the local senate), a basilica, and at least two baths. There are numerous inscriptions that record how wealthy local citizens generously subsidized the construction of certain public buildings. One interesting work of art discovered at Scythopolis is a hexagonal

Dionysiac altar with decorated panels. It was donated to the city by a certain Seleucus at the time of the emperor Antoninus Pius and installed in the apse of the city's basilica.

Among the various city temples, we must mention that of Zeus Akraios (Zeus of the Heights), which stood on the acropolis and was reached by means of a monumental flight of steps. There was also a prominent temple in the city center, which may have been dedicated to Nysa.

Scholars think that toward the end of the third century, Scythopolis had a population of about fifteen to eighteen thousand, but in late antiquity it expanded considerably in all directions. It was given a surrounding wall to enclose recently built-up areas, and many buildings were also erected in areas outside the walls. In the western part of the city, near the theater, some new baths were also built to satisfy the needs of the increasing population. The city was famous for the manufacture of linen clothing, and the proliferation of commercial and industrial quarters bears witness to the particular character of the city in late antiquity: Here, as in other Near Eastern towns, practical and economic necessity supplanted aesthetics when it came to building. Literary sources show that toward the mid-fourth century a large proportion of the population must have been Christian, and archaeological investigations reveal that the pagan temples in the city fell into disuse at the end of that century or in the very early years of the next. By this time, therefore, Scythopolis had become solidly Christian.

Part of the city was destroyed or seriously damaged in the earthquake of 363, and later rebuilding was inferior to the original. Some of the public buildings that had embellished the city in early imperial times were never restored. This is exemplified by the fate of the city basilica, which was left in ruins until late in the fifth century, when an agora was created on the site. In the closing years of the fourth century, following the division of Palaestina into three administrative units, Scythopolis became the capital of Palaestina Secunda and the seat of its governor. The city soon recovered from the earthquake damage, and its economy and population grew throughout the fifth century and into the first decades of the sixth, when, it is reckoned, the population may have grown to thirty to thirty-eight thousand inhabitants.

A gradual decline followed the Samaritan revolt of 529 and the terrible plague of 541/42.

A visitor who today walks through the splendid Beth Shean archaeological park—fruit of the dedicated labors of the Israeli archaeologists Gideon Foerster, Yoram Tsafrir, and Gabi Mazor, who have uncovered many important parts of Scythopolis in recent years—will be particularly struck by the great colonnaded and porticoed streets with which it was embellished. Evidence of at least four important streets flanked by shops has been discovered, and scholars have called them North Street, Street of the Valley, Street of Palladius, and Street of Sylvanus.

The Street of Palladius is named after the governor responsible for its construction in the late fourth or early fifth century. It was probably laid on top of an earlier Roman street and led from the city temple esplanade to the theater. It had a portico and a row of shops, but it underwent a radical transformation in 506/7, when about ten shops were taken down to make way for a semicircular building that became, in effect, a commercial center. This alteration also involved the destruction of an important building at the back, one that had apparently served as a *bouleuterion* for meetings of the city senate. It seems likely that this change of use is a clue to a significant political and institutional change in the city: The senate must have ceded power to a small group of notables.

When it was built, in early imperial times, the Street of Sylvanus had a colonnaded portico decorated with statues and an ornamental pool, presumably intended to reflect the architectural features of the portico. The pool was restored after the earthquake of 363, but in 515/16 the street was completely remodeled. A new surface was laid at a higher level, the portico and pool were demolished, and a very large hall was built over them, probably for commercial use. Two inscriptions reveal that these important alterations were made possible by Sylvanus, an influential citizen of Scythopolis whose contacts at the imperial court had enabled him to obtain a subsidy from the emperor Anastasius. In the years immediately following, the street was extended as far as the amphitheater area; this is clearly confirmed by two inscriptions, which

The so-called Street of Sylvanus

record that the work was completed in 522, when Orestes was governor.

Three important inscriptions record that the city walls, which had probably been built in the fourth or fifth century, were rebuilt in the 520s. In this case, too, it is announced that a financial subsidy from the emperor was made possible by the intervention of an eminent citizen of Scythopolis, in this instance Arsenius, the son of Sylvanus. Literary sources tell us of the rise and fall of these two ambitious men of the Samaritan religion: Arsenius met his death in Alexandria, where he was impaled after being unjustly accused of supporting the bishop in demanding the torture of a deacon. Sylvanus, on the other hand, was burned alive at Scythopolis by his fellow citizens at the time of the Samaritan revolt.

The city theater underwent substantial reconstruction in the second century: Hard limestone was used for the seating, vaulting, and *scaenae frons*, which was decorated with reliefs, but granite was used for the columns. The building could hold about seven thousand spectators.

The hippodrome in the southern part of the city dates back to the second century and has been excavated only in part. It was adapted as an amphitheater in the second half of the fourth century, thanks to the construction of a semicircular wing inside the hippodrome arena. The area of the amphitheater is thus one-third that of the hippodrome. This alteration implies that from then on the structure was used for *venationes* (wild-animal spectacles) rather than chariot races. However, various pieces of evidence show that in the fifth century the amphitheater ceased to function, and archaeologists have also noted that at that time it was surrounded by private buildings.

One consequence of the christianization of the city was the rejection of pagan cults and statues representing mythological characters. We have already mentioned the fact that temples ceased to be used at the end of the fourth century. Excavations have also revealed that the temple in the city center had already been partly dismantled before 404. It must be emphasized that for many decades statues were regarded simply as works of art and therefore were valued as part of the city's cultural heritage, independently of their connection with paganism. This tolerant view must have given way later to an attitude of radical rejection, for archaeologists have found that many statues were buried under new buildings erected in the early sixth century, often after being mutilated. However, this does not mean that the antipagan fanaticism of the time rejected every kind of pagan artistic expression. In the early decades of the sixth century, the floors of public buildings were decorated with classicizing mosaics, including, we must remember, the very beautiful image of the city's Tyche (goddess of fortune) in the paving of a semicircular structure in the Street of Palladius. Nor is that all: images of the same type were used to decorate not only secular buildings but churches and synagogues as well. In the little synagogue inside the so-called House of Leontis, there were mosaics depicting Ulysses and the sirens, as well as images of a Nilotic variety.

By the sixth century the city had many churches, both inside and outside the walls, one of which had been built on top of the remains of the temple of Zeus Akraios on the acropolis, overlooking the city. In addition, excavations in the House of Leontis have brought to light a small late-antique Jewish synagogue, and a building outside the city walls is thought to be a Samaritan place of worship. But that is still only a hypothesis.

Mosaic of the local Tyche in
the paving of a semicircular
structure in the so-called
Street of Palladius

Samaria-Sebaste (Shomeron)

The west gate of ancient Samaria-Sebaste

Opposite: Roman street of the imperial period

Samaria, capital of the kingdom of Israel, was founded by Omri about 878 B.C. (1 Kings 16:23–24). It occupies a strategic position on a highland that overlooks the fertile hills of Samaria and two of the most important interregional communication links. It was therefore an object of interest for various conquerors operating in the region, whether Aramean, Assyrian, Persian, or Greek. After conquering the city in 332 B.C., Alexander the Great settled some of his Macedonian veterans there, thus adding a new ethnic group to a region that had already been colonized by the Assyrians; Samaria now became a Greek polis. As an object of contention between Ptolemies and Seleucids, it was destroyed on a number of occasions, and toward the end of the second century B.C. it was finally conquered and destroyed by the Hasmonean king John Hyrcanus. Pompey took the city from the Hasmoneans, and it was rebuilt on his orders by Gabinius, governor of Syria; from that time on, it was called Samaria Gabinia. Augustus gave it back to Herod, the heir of the Hasmoneans, who enlarged it, placing six thousand settlers there. Some of these were ex-soldiers and others inhabitants of the area, but evidently all were pagans. Herod renewed and extended the city walls; strengthened its defenses with large towers; embellished the city with splendid monuments, including a temple to Augustus and another to Kore; and changed its name to Sebaste (Greek for "Augusta") in honor of the emperor. In this way a new era began for the city in 28/27 B.C. Military units from Sebaste served as auxiliaries in the Roman army. In the struggle between the various claimants to the imperial throne after the death of Commodus, Sebaste sided with Septimius Severus, and when he prevailed over the other contenders and ascended the throne, he rewarded the city by making it a Roman colony and building or restoring many of its public buildings. Later on, however, the importance of Sebaste diminished as a result of competition from Neapolis (Nablus), which had been

Remains of the Roman civic basilica built by Herod and rebuilt in the late second century A.D.

pletely pagan city. It is certain, at any rate, that a bishop of Sebaste was present at the first ecumenical council (held at Nicea in 325). In the fourth century, the tomb of Saint John the Baptist was venerated at Sebaste, his body having apparently been placed by his followers in the tomb of the prophet Elisha. In 361–362, at the time of Julian the Apostate, the pagans in the city opened the tomb and burned the remains of Saint John, but monks managed to save some of the relics and a church was built over the venerated tomb. The head of Saint John had not been buried with his body, and from the fourth century onward various stories of its rediscovery began to circulate. In one version, it was found where Saint John had been imprisoned, and so there, too, a commemorative church was founded. When the crusaders arrived, both churches were in ruins and had to be rebuilt; after the withdrawal of the crusaders, the larger church, containing Saint John's tomb, became a mosque, while the other remained in the hands of Orthodox Greek Christians, who built a monastery beside it.

Excavations carried out in the city have revealed not only remains from earlier periods, such as the acropolis from the Israelite period and two fine towers from the Hellenistic walls, but also the layout of the city as rebuilt by Gabinius and enlarged by Herod, with a regular street plan and Roman-style houses with atria, and various public buildings. Outstanding among these is the Augusteum, a majestic temple (35 by 24 m) facing north, built on a hill overlooking the city from which the Mediterranean can be seen more than 30 kilometers away. The temple is raised on a 4.40-meter podium and has a monumental flight of steps leading down to a large rectangular courtyard built on the slope of the hill and supported by an artificial platform measuring 83 by 72 meters. The platform's supporting wall on the north side rose to a height of 15 meters, of which about 7 meters survive. The Augusteum was restored in the time of Septimius Severus, and the stairway and altar, which can be seen to this day, belong to that period. The torso of a colossal statue of Augustus has been found near the altar. North of the Augusteum stood a temple of Kore,

founded by Vespasian on the site of ancient Shechem.

Christianity came to Sebaste very early; indeed, it seems to have been the "city of Samaria" where the apostle Philip preached and established the first group of the faithful with the help of Peter and John (Acts 8:4–24). It was here that Simon Magus offered money to Saint Peter in exchange for supernatural powers (hence the word *simony* for the sin of buying or selling spiritual goods). The first bishop of Sebaste seems to have been Nicolas, one of the seven deacons ordained by Peter. But it is not clear whether this tradition is trustworthy, for the Acts of the Apostles place Philip's preaching before the conversion of Saint Paul, and at that time it was not usual for the apostles to evangelize the pagans, while Sebaste, as we have pointed out, was a com-

but only its foundations remain. It measured 36 by 15.50 meters and was surrounded by a temenos measuring 84 by 45 meters. Beneath the temple of Kore, the remains of a Hellenistic temple to Isis have been identified. East of these two temples, the remains of a theater dating to the early third century A.D. have been found. Still farther east, on an area of level ground, stood the forum (128 by 72.50 m), with porticoes on all sides. In the western colonnade, twenty-four column bases survive, and seven columns are still standing. Beyond the west side of the forum stood the basilica, 68 meters long and 32.50 meters wide, surrounded on three sides by monolithic columns with Corinthian capitals. Both forum and basilica were originally built by Herod but rebuilt in the late second century, and it is to that period that most of the visible remains belong. Along the south

side of the forum ran the city's main street, linking the east and west gates. Renovated under Septimius Severus, it measured more than 12 meters in width, was flanked by porticoes supported by monolithic columns 5.50 meters high, and had shops along its sides. In the northeast quarter of the city there is a stadium (230 by 60 m) built by Herod. It was surrounded by porticoes with Doric columns, but it was rebuilt toward the end of the second century, this time with Corinthian columns. Only one section of the city walls built by Herod remains. The rest were demolished to contribute to building work on the nearby city of Shechem, but one can still make out the line of the walls. They enclosed an irregular area whose east–west diameter is as much as a kilometer, and that from north to south only a little less. The city had no springs or wells, and in

Temple of Augustus

Below and opposite: Remains of an apsed Byzantine basilica

the Israelite period the inhabitants had to make do with rainwater collected in cisterns, but in Roman times an aqueduct was built to bring water from springs situated about 10 kilometers to the east. Its remains can be seen along the south side of the forum.

There are few Byzantine remains. The crusader church of Saint John the Baptist, which later became a mosque, is at the east end of the Roman city. It retains some of the original fifth-century columns and a marble floor, which may be Byzantine, in the tomb of the Baptist, now a vaulted underground chamber. The medieval church that commemorates the discovery of Saint John the Baptist's head lies to the south of the acropolis and includes the remains of an apsed Byzantine basilica. It seems that those who built the Byzantine church made use of architectural items from earlier pagan buildings.

Outside the city, to the east, there is a cemetery dating to Roman times. A second- or third-century mausoleum containing richly sculpted sarcophagi has been found there.

Neapolis

Roman theater at Neapolis

Opposite: Mosaic showing the face of a young person, found during excavations at Neapolis

Two arterial roads meet at the heart of the Samarian hills: one runs north–south and links Galilee to Judea and Jerusalem, while the other links the Mediterranean coast to the Jordan Valley. This natural crossroads was chosen for urban settlement as long ago as the Canaanite period. Here, at the north end of the saddle between Mount Ebal to the north and Mount Gerizim to the south, stood the city of Shechem, mentioned in the Bible. Shechem was finally abandoned toward the end of the second century B.C., and an urban settlement was revived in the area in A.D. 72/73, when Vespasian founded Flavia

Neapolis at the west end of the saddle, on the northern slopes of Mount Gerizim. This mountain was sacred to the Samaritan sect. Their religion was becoming increasingly distinct from Judaism in this period, and in the Persian and Hellenistic periods they had a place of worship enclosed in a temenos at the mountaintop. The Samaritan sanctuary was destroyed by the Hasmonean king John Hyrcanus toward the end of the second century B.C., but the Samaritans continued to climb the mountain to pray and make sacrifices. On at least two occasions—under Pontius Pilate in 35, and again in 67 during the war between Jews and Romans—a mass ascent by the Samaritans was interpreted by the authorities as an attempt at revolt, and the crowd was dispersed with a great deal of bloodshed. Perhaps it was to forestall this threat that the pagan city of Neapolis was founded at a point that controlled access to the mountain.

Some of the city's public buildings seem to have been erected in the first half of the second century, and a temple to Zeus Olympios was erected on one of the peaks of Mount Gerizim under Antoninus Pius. The temple and a grand flight of steps (as many as 1,300!) that led up from the city appear on Neapolitan coins from 160 onward. In this same period the city organized games involving athletes from all the provinces of the eastern Mediterranean.

During a power struggle between various claimants to the imperial throne on the death of

View of Mount Gerizim, the sacred mountain of the Samaritans

Commodus, Neapolis sided with Pescennius Niger against Septimius Severus; when the latter became emperor, the city was punished by losing some of its rights, including that of minting coins. However, the emperor's pardon was soon granted, perhaps because his son Caracalla intervened. In 244 Philip the Arab made Neapolis a Roman colony, calling it Colonia Flavia Julia Sergia Neapolis.

We do not know when Christianity arrived there. One of the earliest Christian apologists, the philosopher Justinus, was a native of Neapolis; he was martyred in Rome in 165, and it is not clear whether his conversion from paganism to the new religion took place at his native city or elsewhere. However that may be, Neapolis already had a bishop in the early years of the fourth century. Germanus of Neapolis took part in the synod of Ancyra (modern Ankara) and then in that of Neocaesarea in 314, and also in the ecumenical council of Nicea in 325. Most of the people in the Neapolis surroundings, however, were of the Samaritan religion, and in the Byzantine period many Samaritans lived in the city itself. From at least the fifth century on, Christians and Samaritans were often in conflict and blood was sometimes spilled, both because of animosity between the two communities and in an attempt to exert control over the sacred places. The Christians used violence against the Samaritans in depriving them of the well of Jacob, the tomb of Joseph, and finally even the sacred place at the top of the mountain, where the emperor Zeno built a church to Mary, Mother of God, in 484. For their part, the Samaritans attacked the Christians on a number of occasions. In the time of Zeno, they burst into the church during Mass and cut off the officiating bishop's fingers, and in 529, during a terrible revolt that spread throughout the region, they killed the

bishop and a number of priests. The authorities reacted with massacres and repressive laws, which tended to force the Samaritans to convert to Christianity. Although now much reduced, the Samaritan community continues to live at Neapolis and to pray on Mount Gerizim, but after a brief period of prosperity in crusader times, the Christians have now almost completely disappeared from the city, giving way to Muslims.

The modern city of Nablus preserves the old name and covers the area occupied in Roman and Byzantine times, which means that it has been possible to explore only a small proportion of the monuments from those periods. One outstanding monument is the theater, on whose north side a section of the main street has been discovered, crossing the city from east to west. It was about 11 meters wide and lined with columns. Under the street runs a tunnel that can be reached by descending a flight of fifty-six steps to a depth of 12 meters. This is, in fact, an aqueduct, which brought water to the city from a spring on its eastern periphery. Another conduit brought water from a spring to the southwest. There are numerous known springs inside the city, some of which are simply outlets from Roman aqueducts. A hippodrome was built in the northwest corner of Neapolis in the second century, but it ceased to be used in the third century when an amphitheater was fitted into the curve at its end—something that often happened in Roman cities in the region. In Byzantine times, Neapolis had a cathedral and probably another church as well. They can be identified in a vignette representing the city in the Madaba mosaic map, but no Byzantine church has been identified. It is likely that any remains lie hidden under the churches of crusader times, which have now been made into mosques. Outside the Roman and Byzantine city, cemeteries dating to various periods have been found on the slopes of Mount Ebal as well as on Mount Gerizim. There are some particularly noteworthy second- and third-century mausoleums with richly decorated sarcophagi.

At the foot of the mountain was a monumental propylaeum (gateway), the remains of which probably lie under the present-day Rijal el-ʿAmud

mosque. It gave access to steps that climbed up toward Tell er-Ras, the lower of the two peaks of Mount Gerizim. At the top of the steps stood a temple built by Antoninus Pius. It measured 14 by 21 meters and stood on a podium. Two stages of construction can be identified, one dating to the second century, and the other to the time of Caracalla (early third century). The temple was apparently restored during the reign of Julian the Apostate and remained in use into the second half of the fourth century.

As early as Persian times there was a temenos on the higher peak of the mountain, approached by means of a monumental stairway. This temenos was rebuilt in Hellenistic times, when there was actually a town around it. According to the archaeologist who recently excavated the area, there was a temple inside the temenos in both the Persian and Hellenistic periods: The earlier of the two was built to resemble the Jerusalem Temple, and the later was laid out on the model of Greek temples. Toward the end of the second century B.C. John Hyrcanus destroyed the town and sanctuary in an attempt to end Samaritan separatism and to force the Samaritans to recognize Jerusalem as the sole religious center. In the late Roman period, the Samaritans returned to build an enclosure and various structures in the sacred area, but these were destroyed in the late fifth century when Emperor Zeno had the Church of Mary, Mother of God erected on the site. A large number of inscriptions bear witness to the devotion of the Samaritans, who came to pray and make offerings. The earliest inscriptions are in the paleo-Hebrew alphabet, those of the Hellenistic period in Aramaic, and those of the late Roman period in Greek.

The church built by Zeno has an octagonal ground plan and was surrounded by fortifications built at a later stage by the emperor Anastasius, after the Samaritans attempted to reoccupy the mountain. These fortifications were subsequently extended and reinforced by Justinian after the Samaritan revolt of 520–530. A monastery was built beside the church. Even today, this is the sacred place where the Samaritans come to make their Passover sacrifices.

Coin showing Mount Gerizim

Jericho

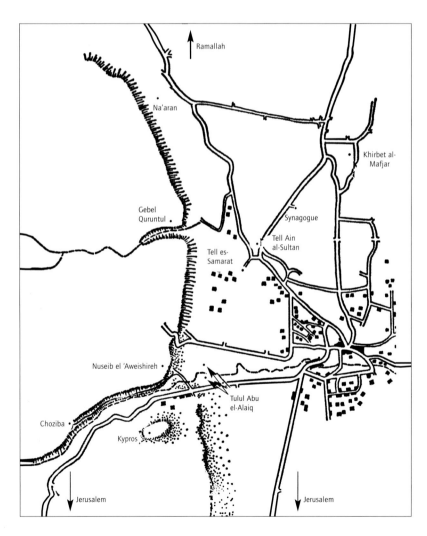

From the nineteenth century until recently it was thought that the Jericho of Hasmonean, Herodian, and Roman times lay to the south of the present-day city, near the ancient road down Wadi Qelt. In 1950 and 1951, American archaeologists found the remains of a splendid Herodian palace south of Wadi Qelt. Then for fifteen years or more, from 1973 on, a mission led by Ehud Netzer of the Hebrew University of Jerusalem investigated the area, making some extremely important discoveries. It was thus possible to ascertain that this was not the Jericho of Hellenistic and Roman times but a series of palaces and other dependent buildings. The location of the city of Jericho itself is therefore still unknown, and in any case it seems likely that the city's inhabited area was scattered rather than a compact nucleus.

Netzer's research has brought to light a series of splendid buildings dating to Hasmonean and Herodian times, which were used by the kings during the winter months. In winter, the average temperature is about ten degrees warmer in the valley of Jericho than in Jerusalem; hence it was possible to enjoy pleasant sojourns no more than about 25 kilometers from the capital. The first palace was built slightly above the plain, where Wadi Qelt emerged from the mountains. There was a first period of building about which we know very little. The palace dating to the time of King John Hyrcanus (135/134–104 B.C.) included a

tower in the southwest corner that must have risen to a height of 12 meters, a paved internal courtyard measuring 25 by 18 meters, and two areas to the north and south containing a number of rooms. The northern part was the larger: It had two stories and contained various dwelling and service rooms. Of particular significance were a room decorated with stucco panels and a mikvah (ritual bath) with two pools. The southern part was equipped for ceremonies and entertainments, and its focal point was a hall with frescoed walls. One important characteristic of this residence was the fact that it also had two pools for bathing and swimming, situated to the west of the palace itself.

Attached to the palace were vast grounds, irrigated by a system of pipes that brought water from springs in Wadi Qelt. This ambitious system made it possible not only to cultivate balsam and date palms on the arid land but also to bring water to the palace pools and rooms. Water supplies to the palace itself were provided by underground pipes, which fed off the conduit that brought water from Wadi Qelt for irrigation.

At the time of Alexander Jannaeus (103–76 B.C.), the life of the palace entered a new phase, characterized by the enlargement of the plantations and the addition of new pools. To supply the additional water required, new conduits were led in from four springs, three in the valley of Na'aran and one at Ein 'Auja. On the north side of the complex were added two large new pools, 3.5 meters deep and measuring 18 by 13 meters, the surrounding area being for the entertainment and recreation of guests. To the south of the pools was a pavilion measuring 23 by 17 meters, flanked by porticoes with Doric columns and decorated with frescoes and stuccoes. It stood on a raised platform and thus provided a view overlooking the pools. On the north side, in contrast, a large garden was laid out. It measured 70 by 60 meters and was surrounded by colonnades.

At a later stage in his reign, Alexander Jannaeus radically altered the character of the Jericho palace, evidently for reasons of security. A new building was erected on top of its predeces-

sor, which was packed in earth to form an artificial mound. The new raised palace was surrounded by a 7-meter-deep ditch and a 3-meter-high external wall. Any attackers who managed to scale the outer wall would have found a 10-meter drop at their feet, which they could not possibly negotiate. The only entrance, to the northeast, must have been heavily guarded. The palace itself was provided with towers, the tallest of which was to the northeast. It had been part of the earlier building but was now raised. Unfortunately, this building was made of mud bricks and therefore suffered from erosion, with the result that scholars have been unable to work out its plan.

At the time of Alexandra Salome (76–67 B.C.), an entirely new palace was built to the south of Alexander Jannaeus's pool complex.

These were the so-called twin palaces, erected for Alexandra's two sons, John Hyrcanus II and Aristobulus. Alongside each of these buildings was a garden with a pool. The original character of these palaces is quite striking. In the first place,

on p. 110: Map of the Jericho area

on p. 111: Tulul Abu el-Alaiq in Wadi Qelt, remains of Herod's third palace

Above: Baths at Herod's third palace

Opposite: View of Wadi Qelt near Saint George's monastery. In the top left-hand corner is a cave used as a dwelling by hermits in Byzantine times.

they were almost identical; and secondly, their construction took into consideration the fact that the area where they were to stand was not level, but sloped down toward the wadi. In order, therefore, to prevent a two-story building from obstructing the view toward the plain enjoyed by those using the pool complexes, the north side of the slope was dug out to create a level area for the new palaces, and high, robust supporting walls were provided. The twin palaces were rectangular, measuring 25.5 by 22.5 meters. At the center of each were an internal courtyard and a main hall for entertainments and ceremonies. There were other rooms with frescoes and stuccoes, as well as kitchens, mikvahs, and bathrooms whose interior included plastered baths.

Herod's first palace at Jericho was built around 35 B.C. to the south of Wadi Qelt; it was identified as a Herodian building as early as 1951 by the American archaeologist J. B. Pritchard. He thought it was a gymnasium, but Netzer's excavations have shown that it was in fact a rectangular palace measuring 87 by 46 meters, whose rooms— a reception hall and bedrooms for the king's courtiers and guests—were arranged around a large courtyard. The palace entrance was on the north side and was flanked by two structures, one of which was an elaborate bath complex decorated with geometric mosaics. The other was a mikvah. Water was supplied through pipes from springs in Wadi Qelt.

Herod's second palace replaced the Hasmonean complex, which was completely destroyed in the earthquake of 31 B.C. It made use of the two large pools, but they were now joined together in such a way as to form a single structure measuring 32 by 18 meters. The palace had two wings. The north wing was built around a courtyard and included a frescoed triclinium as well as bedrooms. On the south side of the triclinium was a terrace that enjoyed a splendid view over the wadi and plain. The south wing contained a covered courtyard, baths, and two more pools.

In building a third palace, Herod seems to have been trying to outdo himself, for it was an extraordinary undertaking. He created a complex divided into four different structures, one of which lay to the north of the wadi, and the other three to the south. The north and south buildings were connected by a bridge, which has now disappeared. The principal wing was to the north and included reception rooms of various sizes; bedrooms and service rooms; two courtyards, one of which had an exedra; an enormous triclinium paved with colored *opus sectile* stone slabs; and a long colonnade overlooking the wadi. The fact that the palace was built in *opus quadratum* and *opus reticulatum*, and the presence of elegant frescoes, some in the Third Pompeian Style, shows that the work was carried out by skilled foreign workers of Roman and Italic origin.

The other three parts of the complex, to the south of the wadi, consisted of a garden, a vast pool, and the so-called southern tell, or mound, Tel es-Samarat. The garden measured 145 by 40 meters and was surrounded by a wall that was sunk into the earth on the south side. There were niches in the wall, and at its center were *cavea*-shaped steps used as flowerbeds. The niches contained ornamental plants whose reflection could be admired in a water channel running between the wall and the garden. On its east and west sides, the garden had a colonnade decorated with frescoes and stuccoes. An enormous 90- by 42-meter pool was built to the east of the garden, while to the south, between the garden and the pool, was an artificial mound on top of which stood a building of outstanding originality and beauty. It measured 20.5 by 19.5 meters, contained a circular reception room, and had baths in the basement. Entry to the reception room was by means of a monumental flight of steps on the south side.

Less than 2 kilometers from Herod's winter palace rises Tel es-Samarat, an artificial mound on which a building with various rooms and courtyards was erected. A *cavea* stood on the tell, but it was not of the usual type, for it had no *scaenae frons*; a movable wooden stage must have been used for theatrical events. The *cavea* was provided with elongated sides, which formed a hippodrome measuring 320 by 80 meters, where chariot races were held.

Herodian Jericho reveals a development of tendencies already shown by the Hasmoneans, but now even more grandiose and colorful. The king and his guests could move about in an extraordinarily theatrical environment, with pools for swimming and another one large enough for boats, with baths, hippodromes, a theater, elegant halls, and an enchanting garden.

But these luxurious rooms witnessed dramatic events: It was here in the pool complex of the Hasmonean palace that Herod had his young brother-in-law Aristobulus drowned in 36 B.C., and in 4 B.C., five days before his own death, he ordered the execution of his son Antipater, who had been held prisoner in one of the palace rooms.

Herodion

Remains of columns at the so-called pool complex at lower Herodion

Opposite: The hill of Herodion, seen from the east

Herodion lies 6 kilometers southeast of Bethlehem, at the place where Herod defeated the men of Antigonus in battle in 40 B.C. At the time, Herod and his family were fleeing Jerusalem and found themselves in grave danger: Shortly before the battle, the vehicle carrying Herod's mother, Cypros, crashed, causing her serious injury. Herod was deeply upset, and, despairing of reaching safety from an enemy that was close at his heels, he even contemplated suicide. Nevertheless, he won the contest.

His plan to build Herodion was first put into effect in 23 B.C., many years after this fortunate victory, and its completion proved to be one of his grandest enterprises. Building took place in two distinct areas: A palace-fortress was built on a hill, and another complex was erected on the plain. The palace on the hill was surrounded by two concentric walls as much as 30 meters high. Within these walls, the palace was divided into two parts: an east wing containing a garden-courtyard embellished with exedras, and a western part containing living quarters, baths, and a triclinium. Three semicircular towers and a round tower were the dominating features of the building: The semicircular towers were 16 meters in diameter and had a number of stories, each of which was divided into storerooms and quarters for guests or servants. The round tower was 18 meters in diameter and still rises to this day to a height of 20 meters, but for various reasons it is thought to have been twice that high originally. It seems very likely that the upper floors were intended to house the king and his entourage. Netzer believes that in the summer months the heat would in fact have been intolerable in the west wing rooms, since they lay within a cylinder of walls, as we have seen. He therefore concludes that the most logical and

spectacular solution to the problem of providing pleasant conditions for the king and his family must have been precisely to furnish the upper rooms of the great tower as a royal residence. Since the tower rose above the cylindrical walls, those who occupied the upper rooms would enjoy plenty of fresh air, as well as a splendid view as far as Jerusalem.

At a later stage, after the building of the palace was completed, an enormous quantity of earth was piled up around the cylinder of walls, thus giving the hill the truncated-cone shape that is still so striking today. In this way Herodion took on an even more imposing and impregnable appearance. Access to the palace was by a flight of two hundred steps, and water supplies were assured by means of an aqueduct and a series of cisterns cut into the rock. These cisterns and some underground passages were used as a refuge by rebel Jews at the time of the Bar Kokhba revolt.

The lower part of Herodion included a huge building, very probably a palace, measuring 130 by 55–60 meters and now a total ruin. It was apparently not connected in any way to the other buildings in the plain. The so-called pool complex consisted of a pool within gardens surrounded on three sides by colonnades. The complex covered an area measuring 130 by 110 meters, and along its east and west sides were two long halls 10 meters wide. To the north of the complex a large number of rooms were built as living quarters and for storage and baths. Another bath, with mosaics, has been discovered to the west. Of particular interest among these mosaics are some in the tepidarium with geometric figures and pomegranates. The discovery of a basin fragment decorated with reliefs depicting sileni heads has been a cause of some amazement, because one would suppose that if Herod were a practicing Jew, as he always claimed to be, he would have observed the Jewish ban on the representation of the human figure.

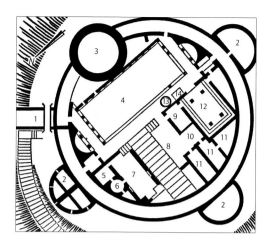

Plan of the palace-fortress of Herodion:
1 Original entrance
2 Semicircular tower
3 Main tower
4 Courtyard
5, 6, 7 Roman baths
8 Present entrance
9 Pantry
10 Round stones
11 Living quarters
12 Refectory/synagogue
13 Kiln
14 Ritual bath

Opposite: Aerial view of the palace-fortress of Herodion

Lower Herodion is dominated by a racecourse 350 meters long and 30 meters wide, which scholars originally thought to be a hippodrome. But now it seems that a suggestion that Netzer put forward is gaining support. According to him, the track was intended for a ceremonial procession leading to a monumental building at its west end, on the axis of the track itself. Josephus tells us that Herod's funeral took place at Herodion, and that he was buried there in accordance with his own specific instructions: His body was brought from Jericho on a golden litter studded with precious stones, the body being wrapped in a purple cloth and with a gold crown on the head. The procession, which included relatives, troops, and five hundred servants scattering perfume, reached its climax on the dramatic track at Herodion. We may well wonder whether Herod had perhaps already thought of being buried here on that distant day when he gained his unexpected victory over Antigonus. And finally, it should be noted that, in Netzer's opinion, some architectural remains found near the monumental building, which were reused in the construction of a late-antique monastery, originally belonged to Herod's now-vanished mausoleum.

Qumran

The Qumran area, by the Dead Sea

Opposite: Interior of man-made Cave 4, where about 500 manuscripts were found

Close to the Dead Sea—the deepest depression in the earth's crust at 418 meters below sea level—stood the ancient settlement of Khirbet Qumran. Its remains were first visited by a European explorer, Félicien de Saulcy, in 1850–51, but scholars paid no particular attention until the years immediately following the Second World War.

It was in 1947 that a Bedouin, searching for a lost sheep among the rocks near the site, came upon a cave, later called Cave 1, where he found twelve cylindrical jars. One of them contained a series of written scrolls on treated animal skins, which the Bedouin subsequently sold to a cobbler and antique dealer in Bethlehem. Four of the scrolls were bought by the Syriac Orthodox metropolitan of Jerusalem and the other three by E. K. Sukenik, professor of archaeology at the Hebrew University of Jerusalem. When the texts were deciphered and published, the name of Qumran immediately captured the attention of the scholarly community. The scrolls contained biblical texts, such as the Book of Isaiah, together with some unusual writings that were at first thought to relate to a community of a highly unusual type. Sukenik maintained that these writings were the work of the Essenes, a sect whose characteristics had been described by Josephus and other Greek and Latin writers. Over the next few years, up to 1956, new scrolls were discovered in another ten caves in the rocks surrounding the site, with the result that scholars now possessed about nine hundred scrolls. The investigation of the caves and excavation of the site of Khirbet Qumran were led by Father Roland de Vaux of the École Biblique in Jerusalem. His view was that the scrolls had been put in the caves by the people

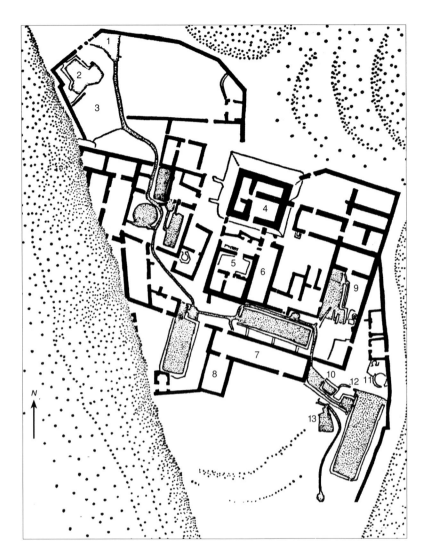

rumors that the Vatican was unwilling to reveal their contents.

Most of the nine hundred scrolls are made of treated animal skins, but some writings are on papyrus; one text (the so-called copper scroll) is on thin sheets of bronze. A great majority of the scrolls are written in Hebrew, with about twenty percent in Aramaic and just a few in Greek. All were written with reed pens and ink. The material found at Qumran includes various versions of the Hebrew Bible, apocryphal works, sectarian literature, biblical commentaries, and hymns of thanksgiving.

The writings show that the sect concerned broke away from the rest of the Jewish world—probably after the mid-second century B.C.—because it supported a more rigid observance of the Law than did the Hasmoneans. The members of the sect at Qumran, in opposition to the religious authorities of the time, refused to take part in the religious festivities and sacrifices at the Temple in Jerusalem, declaring that justice came from prayer alone. However, they prophesied that the power wielded by impious priests would come to an end, and they were certain that it was their destiny to restore purity to Temple worship. The sect was also apocalyptic, awaiting the end of days. Two messiahs would appear on earth—one a secular descendant of the house of David, and the other a priestly descendant of the house of Aaron—but the messianic age would be preceded by a war in which the "sons of light" would be pitted against the "sons of darkness." The term "sons of darkness" embraced the Jews as well as the Romans.

Many scholars have followed Roland de Vaux in maintaining that the scrolls were written by members of the Essene sect. One difficulty with this interpretation, however, lies in the fact that the name Essene never appears in the texts of the community, but supporters of this traditional theory have suggested that there is documentary evidence that a different term was used in Hebrew to indicate the Essenes. According to Josephus, the Essenes were essentially a community of unmarried men who lived a monastic life devoted to prayer and, obedient to rigid rules. A few mem-

who lived at Khirbet Qumran, that is to say, by an Essene monastic community.

Cave 4, unlike the others, is man-made and on its own yielded five hundred scrolls; they were found on the cave floor rather than in jars, which probably means that they were originally placed on wooden shelves. If that is indeed the case, it would suggest that this was the community library. The scrolls in Cave 4 were found to be in an extremely fragmentary condition, with the result that it was a long time before they could be published; and since they were in the safekeeping of the Jerusalem Dominicans, the delay fed

bers married and had children. They were a peaceful community, but Josephus tells us that one of the leaders of the Great Revolt was an Essene.

The American archaeologist Jodi Magness has modified some points in de Vaux's chronology, arguing that the Qumran community was founded around 100 B.C., and that the site was first destroyed at the time of the 31 B.C. earthquake and then damaged and abandoned in the closing years of Herod's reign or in the early years of that of Archelaus. It seems likely that this evidence of destruction is related to the serious internal conflicts in the Jewish world, which are reported in the sources. Within a short time, however, the community settled at Qumran again,

and continued to live there until the time of the Great Revolt, when it did not escape the violent repression of the Romans. Traces of destruction throughout the site and the presence of arrowheads are evidence of the dramatic destiny of the inhabitants of Khirbet Qumran. However, there are other scholars who do not accept the chronology that Magness established.

The Qumran settlement is divided into two sectors, the so-called main sector to the east and a secondary sector to the west. The main sector is overlooked by a tower in its northwest corner and includes rooms that have fascinated scholars and visitors ever since they were excavated by de Vaux such as a room for meetings, a refectory, and a scriptorium. It was possible to identify the largest

Aerial view of the Qumran settlement

Opposite: Plan of Qumran
1 *Decantation basin from the first century* A.D.
2 *Ritual bath*
3 *Original decantation basin*
4 *Tower with observation post*
5 *Assembly room*
6 *Room below scriptorium*
7 *Refectory*
8 *Pantry*
9 *Split caused by earthquake*
10 *Ritual bath*
11 *Kilns*
12 *Place for potter's wheel*
13 *Basin for preparing clay*

habitation but as meeting places for community members, or as kitchens, workshops for pottery production, tanneries, and stores. Magen Broshi and Hanan Eshel have concluded that people lived in the caves, as well as in tents and huts; indeed, they have found domestic crockery in some caves and remains of camps and tents close by. But other scholars support the theory that the sect lived within the settlement. They claim that members of the community used second-floor rooms in both sectors of the settlement, though Magness thinks these could not have held more than seventy people. The dimensions of the refectory are such that a communal meal could not be served to more than 150 people, though it seems to be the case that only full members of the community would have been allowed to partake of communal meals. Other scholars have put forward theories that are quite different from Magness's. In particular, the Israeli archaeologist Yizhar Hirschfeld has asserted that the Khirbet Qumran complex had dozens of rooms that could be used for habitation.

In recent years, various scholars have advanced theories that run counter to the traditional view that it was the denizens of the settlement who deposited the scrolls in the caves. Norman Golb has maintained that Qumran was really a fort; Robert Donceel and Pauline Donceel-Voûte identify Khirbet Qumran as a country villa; and Hirschfeld is convinced that what we really have here is a luxury dwelling similar to other buildings of the same type found in Samaria and Judea. The fact that the archaeologists Itzhak Magen and Yuval Peleg have found jewelry, containers for cosmetics, and fibulas seems proof that Khirbet Qumran was not just an isolated site inhabited by an ascetic sect but a place that belonged within the commercial dynamic of the time, and one whose inhabitants did not reject creature comforts. This last observation is further supported by the research of J.-B. Humbert, who has pointed out that the inhabitants paid a good deal of attention to the quality of their interior decoration.

The Dead Sea Scrolls, found in caves around the Qumran settlement. About 900 manuscripts were found, including various versions of the Bible, apocryphal works, sectarian literature, hymns of thanksgiving, and Bible commentaries.

room in the complex as a refectory because more than a thousand plates were found in an adjacent room, while the presence of inkwells in a room with tables and chairs made it possible to identify the scriptorium.

Magness has stressed that the inhabitants of Qumran were extremely strict about observing the rules of purity and consequently made their own jars and crockery, for fear of contamination from outside. She further argues that the members of the sect, or at least most of them, lived not within the settlement but in tents and huts, or even in the caves themselves. The buildings within the settlement were designed not for

If one accepts these assessments of the nature of the site, it follows that the inhabitants of Khirbet Qumran were not the ones who put the scrolls in the caves. It has therefore been claimed that the scrolls belonged to a Jerusalem library and that they were removed to the remote rocky caves of Qumran at the outbreak of the Jewish revolt against Rome.

Rocks near the Qumran site with caves where the so-called Dead Sea Scrolls were found. The exterior of Cave 4 can be seen in the middle.

Masada

The rocky spur of Masada near the Dead Sea

Opposite: Aerial view of the Masada site

"A rock of no slight circumference and lofty from end to end is abruptly terminated on every side by deep ravines, the precipices rising sheer from an invisible base and being inaccessible to the foot of any living creature, save in two places where the rock permits of no easy ascent. Of these tracks one leads from the Lake of Asphalt on the east, the other, by which the approach is easier, from the west" (*Jewish War* 7.280–81; trans. Thackeray). That

is how Josephus begins his description of Masada and the famous siege by the Roman army under Flavius Silva against the last pocket of Jewish resistance, a few years after the end of the First Revolt. Josephus is the only source for the episode, and he tells how a group of *sicarii* had taken over Masada at the beginning of the revolt, annihilating the Roman garrison stationed there. The year was A.D. 66, and the fortress remained in the hands of the *sicarii*, who had women and children with them, until a long time after the capture of Jerusalem and the destruction of the Temple brought the war to an end. Scholars think, in fact, that Masada fell in the spring of A.D. 73 or possibly 74.

Two figures stand out in the history of the siege of Masada: the Roman commander and governor of Syria, Flavius Silva, and the leader of the rebels, Eleazar ben Jair. Flavius Silva strikes us as a typical representative of the Roman military machine, based as it was on efficiency and determination in striving to achieve its aims. Josephus's narrative provides us with no personal details about him, but we know from an inscription that he was a native of Urbs Salvia—present-day Urbisaglia in the Marche region of Italy. Eleazar stands out, on the other hand, as an extraordinary personality. Josephus devotes considerable space to the speech that he made to his men, urging them to commit suicide rather than fall into the hands of the enemy.

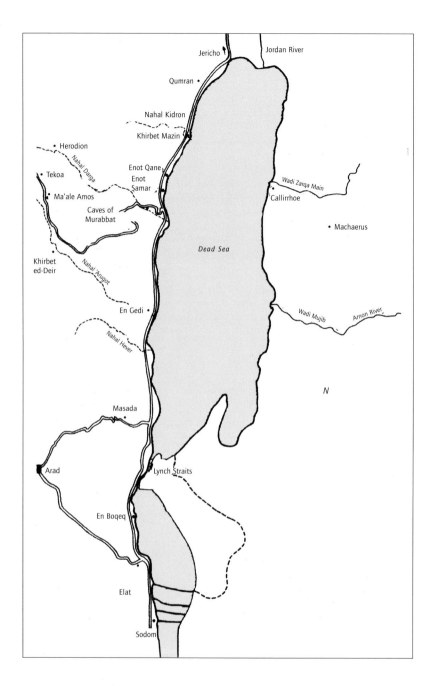

Above: Ancient sites around the Dead Sea

Right: Herodian storerooms and the upper terrace of Herod's northern palace

According to Josephus's narrative, which is confirmed in its essentials by archaeological data, Silva surrounded Masada with a wall to prevent the rebels from escaping. Having observed that the fortress was more accessible to the west thanks to an enormous rock that projected

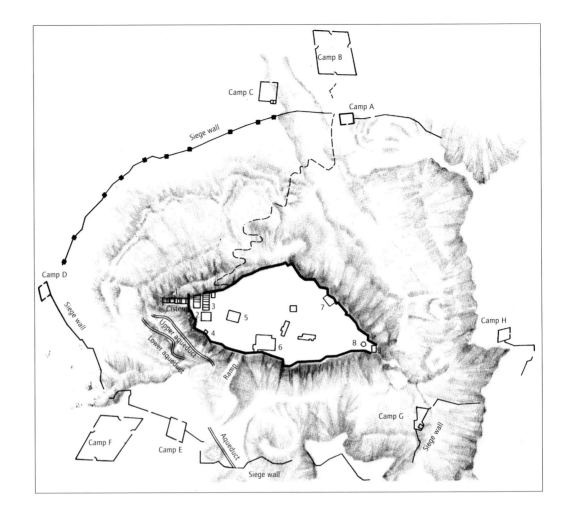

toward the summit of the ridge, he ordered the construction of earthworks there, on top of which he erected a platform. On this he raised an iron tower, and the artillery he positioned there soon drove back the rebels who were defending the wall. At the same time a battering ram succeeded in breaching but not demolishing the wall, for the *sicarii* had reinforced it by filling the casemates with earth containing wooden beams. Silva therefore decided to make use of incendiary torches, and the wall was soon engulfed in flames. As night approached, the Roman commander gave the order to wait for daybreak before entering the fortress. Meanwhile, in the fortress, Eleazar made the fateful decision to persuade his men to com-

mit collective suicide. It was nobler, he maintained, to sacrifice themselves for freedom than to fall into the hands of the Romans and be forced to witness the humiliation of their wives and children. When the Romans entered the fortress at dawn, they were amazed at the profound silence, and shortly afterward, two women who had hidden with five children to avoid Eleazar's suicide orders emerged from their hiding place. They explained what had happened and that the men had slain their loved ones before killing each other.

In Jewish tradition, the sacrifice of Eleazar and his men has been celebrated as an act of heroism aspiring to the status of myth, but it is

Above: The fortress of
Masada, seen from the north

Below: Herod's northern
palace, built around the
central terrace

was not a particularly hard task for the Romans.
As the American historian Jonathan Roth has ably
demonstrated, the siege did not last for years but
was over in less than two months—enough time,
that is to say, to build a siege wall and a ramp, and
to move artillery into position. All told, there were
about nine hundred *sicarii* in the fortress, including women and children, which means that their
defensive capability must have been slight in com-
parison with Roman military might. About eight
thousand soldiers had been brought up for the
siege, aided by slaves and the forced labor of civilian Jews for logistics and construction work.

Remains of the 4-kilometer siege wall and the
ramp, as well as of the eight camps that Silva set
up on the slopes of Masada, are still visible and
provide compelling evidence of the events.

One of the first Westerners to venture into
this inhospitable area was the American archaeologist and explorer Edward Robinson. As early
as 1838, he succeeded in identifying the siege
location as a rocky spur on which he trained his

clear that although Josephus admires the courage
of the men who defended Masada, he distances
himself from their tragic decision: He considers it
the inevitable result of the mistaken and over-
optimistic calculations of a group of bandits who
rebelled against the Romans, thinking they had a
real chance of victory.

It is important to note that, contrary to what
most scholars used to think, capturing Masada

Columbarium. The archaeologist Yigael Yadin thinks these niches were used to hold the funerary urns of non-Jewish staff at Herod's court.

binoculars from the En Gedi oasis. Then, four years later, S. W. Wolcott, a missionary and fellow American, actually set foot there. Thus the rediscovery of Masada began, and scientific research enjoyed moments of great excitement as a result of reconnaissance missions undertaken by two great experts in ancient military history, Alfred Von Domaszewki in 1897 and Adolf Schulten in 1932. After the Second World War, a group of enthusiastic young people from a kibbutz undertook some site studies and succeeded in identifying a number of water cisterns, and then in 1955 and 1956 a group of professional archaeologists—among whom Shemaryah Gutman was to play an important part then and later—carried out some important investigations. The great archaeological project that gave the Masada site explosive fame was that led by Yigael Yadin, the celebrated teacher of archaeology at the Hebrew University who had also been commander in chief of the Israeli army. From 1963 to 1965, thousands of

volunteers from all over the world took part in this enterprise, and their striking results were reported in a number of publications. Yadin's work has been followed up by other prominent archaeologists, such as Gideon Foerster and Ehud Netzer.

According to Josephus, the first person to build a fortress at Masada was Jonathan Maccabeus, in the second half of the second century B.C. Later on, Herod apparently carried out several grandiose schemes there, reinforcing the site with walls and providing it with several luxury palaces with an excellent water supply, thanks to some cisterns cut into the rock. Archaeological excavations, however, have not found any structures that can be safely attributed to the time of Jonathan or his Hasmonean successors, but they have confirmed the scope of Herod's ambitious plans.

Around the spur on which Masada stands, Herod built a casemate wall with a hundred towers, and inside the fortress he built two luxury palaces and three smaller ones. The first of the two large palaces was built to the west. It is a rectangular building with an internal open courtyard, giving onto various rooms, including a covered reception hall, rooms decorated with mosaics, a bathroom with a tub, and a mikvah. Of particular interest is a room in the eastern part of the palace, which scholars call the Mosaic Room because of its elaborate colored mosaic with geometric and floral patterns. Bedrooms were on the upper floor. The palace was considerably enlarged at a second and third stage of the Herodian period, acquiring two new wings: one to the north (fairly large and containing a number of rooms) and the other to the northwest, with four rooms on its south and west sides. When the building was complete it measured 66 by 48 meters. The casemate wall was built in this same period.

The three lesser palaces, not far from the west palace, also belong to the first stage of construction, as do three dovecote towers, a pool at the

south end of the mountain plateau, and some small baths in the north area.

The second Herodian phase saw the building of the second palace, one of the boldest constructions conceived by the king and his architects. It stood in the northern area of Masada, where the rock forms two successive terraces below the summit before it falls off in a precipice. The palace was arranged on three separate levels linked by a steep flight of steps: an upper terrace, a middle terrace 18 meters lower, and a lower terrace 12 meters below that. On all three terraces there were rooms for the king's family, reception rooms, and courtyards designed to give each terrace its own particular character. Thus the upper terrace had an open courtyard ending in a semicircle, the courtyard on the middle terrace contained a large round room, and the third terrace was almost square. The upper and lower terraces were surrounded by colonnades, as was the *tholos* of the middle terrace, but it stood within a larger space. Each of these courtyards offered a splendid view, but perhaps the most extraordinary prospect was reserved for guests in apartments on the lowest terrace, for these were perched on its precipitous edge. The lowest terrace also had a small bath establishment in the east wing.

At the top of Masada, opposite the entrance to the upper terrace, was a vast bath complex, richly decorated with mosaics and frescoes and provided with an exedra and a series of rooms for storing food and weapons. And there were more rooms beside the palace entrance for storage and services. A dam set in the wadi to the north of Masada made it possible to supply water to twelve reservoirs cut out of the rock.

The luxuriousness of the palace rooms and baths at Masada is striking. In the north palace in particular, the mosaics and frescoes in the bedrooms, corridors, and the hall between them on the upper terrace are fairly well preserved, and the porticoes and banqueting hall on the lower terrace also contain fresco remains. Archaeologist Gideon Foerster has examined the artistic styles at Masada in detail, identifying their Hellenistic and Roman components. He has reached the

conclusion that Herod employed skilled artisans from Italy to decorate the buildings at Masada. There is clear evidence that the king paid particular attention to the quality of the food provided for his court and guests, for amphorae have been found at Masada bearing inscriptions indicating their contents. Herod evidently provided himself with a fine cellar of wines specially brought from southern Italy, and he also imported *garum* (a rich fish sauce), honey, and apples from Cumae.

Of particular interest is a synagogue measuring 12 by 15 meters in the northwest area of the site. It originally had a vestibule and a hall with two rows of three columns supporting the roof. At a later stage, when Eleazar's *sicarii* occupied Masada, the appearance of the building was altered by removing the wall separating the hall from the vestibule. The wall was replaced by two pilasters, and at the same time another room was built in the north corner. Also dating to that second stage are some plastered seats along the main hall, made with stone taken from Herod's northern palace. Some Old Testament scrolls were found in holes dug out under the floor of the sec-

ond stage of occupation in the north room. This shows that the room had been used as a *genizah*, a place where documents written in Hebrew and considered sacred by Orthodox Jews were buried because they were no longer in use but could not be destroyed.

Archaeology has been able to prove that the *sicarii* built dwellings inside the casemate wall, but other parts of the site also show signs of occupation by the rebels.

At a later period, a monastic community settled at Masada. A small church with a side room decorated with mosaics was built in the fifth century, and some dwellings dating to that period have also been found.

Opposite: Thermal baths

The Masada synagogue—the earliest so far discovered

Bethlehem

Church of the Nativity

Opposite: Frescoed column in the Church of the Nativity

In Roman times, the birthplace of Jesus was no more than a village. It was inhabited by Jews until A.D. 135, when they were expelled on the orders of the emperor Hadrian during the suppression of the Bar Kokhba revolt. By the second century local Christians had identified the traditional birthplace of Jesus as a cave to the east of the village, where Hadrian ordered a grove sacred to the god Adonis-Tammuz to be planted. The develop-ment of the village began in the fourth century when Constantine, the first Christian emperor, had a church built on top of the Nativity grotto in 326. In the sixth century, Justinian had Constantine's church demolished because it was too small, and he sent an architect from the capi-tal to build a large basilica. Tradition has it that the emperor was dissatisfied with the architect's work and had him beheaded. The Church of the

Above: Plan of the Church of the Nativity

1 *Reinforcements*
2 *Sixth-century architrave*
3 *Entrance*
4 *Sixth-century architrave*
5 *Narthex*
6 *Armenian intaglios*
7 *Entrance to the Franciscan cloister*
8 *Closed end of side aisle*
9 *Saint Cataldus*
10 *Fourth-century mosaic floor*
11 *Saint Canute*
12 *Saint Olaf*
13 *Fourth-century baptismal font*
14 *Entrance to the Franciscan church*
15 *Entrance to the grottoes*
16 *Fourth-century mosaic floor*
17 *Entrance to the Grotto of the Nativity*
18 *Greek Orthodox altar*

Below, left: Reconstruction of the apse of the fourth-century Church of the Nativity
1 *Presbytery balustrade*
2 *Altar*

Below, right: Grottoes underneath the Church of the Nativity
1 *Saint Jerome's study*
2 *Entrance to the Franciscan church*
3 *Tomb of Eusebius of Cremona*
4 *Tomb of Saint Jerome*
5 *Tombs of Paula and Eustochium*
6 *Chapel of the Holy Innocents*
7 *Chapel of Saint Joseph*
8 *Grotto of the Nativity*
9 *Altar of the Manger*
10 *Altar of the Birth*
11 *Basilica entrances*
12 *Cistern*

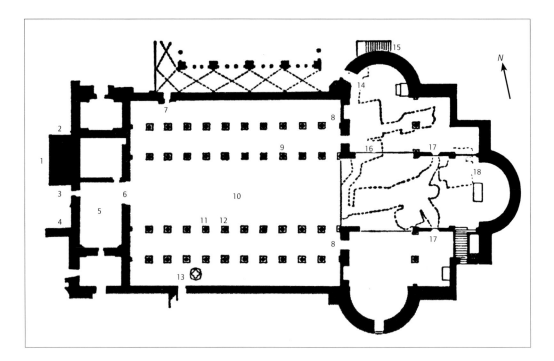

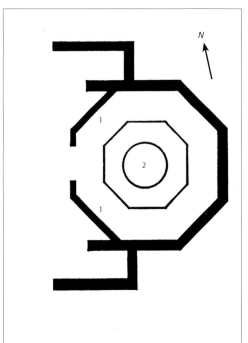

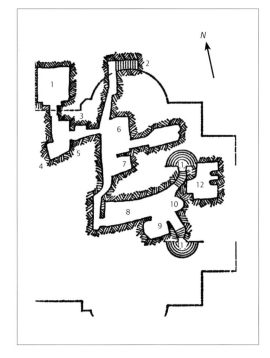

Church of the Nativity, grotto with the altar of the Holy Innocents. Early Christian burial niche

Nativity survived intact to the time of the Arab conquest and persisted until the arrival of the crusaders, who restored it.

Excavations carried out on the orders of the British mandatory authorities in the 1930s have clarified the history of the church. Constantine's building was a square basilica, each side measuring 26.5 meters, its nave and four aisles being separated by four rows of columns in local red stone with marble Corinthian capitals. Entry was through an entirely colonnaded square atrium on the west side. At the east end of the basilica was an octagonal structure, raised on two steps. It enclosed a smaller and higher platform, also octagonal, at the center of which was an opening, protected by a grille. Through this opening one could look down into the grotto, whose natural roof had been removed. Excavations underneath later flooring revealed that the floors of the atrium, basilica, and octagon were decorated with elegant mosaics in geometric, animal, and plant designs. They date to the fifth century and are therefore later than Constantine's building. In the sixth century, the nave was broadened at the expense of the aisles, and the church was extended westward, thereby becoming a rectangular basilica 33 meters long. The atrium was also modified: A narthex was constructed out of its east side, the west side was moved so as to lengthen the atrium and make it rectangular, and a defensive wall was built around it. In order to carry out these modifications, ten columns had to be added, together with four more at the corners. They were made in perfect imitation of the Constantinian columns and still support the church today. The early octagon was also transformed into the trefoil apse, which can still be seen. Before this solution was adopted, the sixth-century builders apparently tried to erect a dome on a circular base over the octagon, but they were unsuccessful because contemporary technology was not capable of spanning so large a gap. Perhaps the story of Justinian's anger at the unfortunate architect contains an echo of that failure.

Above: Interior of the Church
of the Nativity

Opposite: Constantinian
floor mosaic at the octagon
over the Crypt of the Nativity

a magnificent basilica. Hence the fifth-century church became an underground crypt and was adapted for use as a burial place. The basilica was destroyed in the seventh century, perhaps during the Persian invasion of 614, and was rebuilt on a more modest scale, becoming part of a monastery that was not abandoned until the tenth or eleventh century. Its ruins can be found today in the area of the Arab village of Beit Sahur.

Toward the end of the fourth century, Saint Jerome settled at Bethlehem, together with his disciple and protector, the Roman matron Paula. He built two convents there, one for men and one for women. Later on, other monasteries were established around Bethlehem. Of particular interest are two monasteries built in the sixth and seventh centuries by Georgian monks, as we learn from inscriptions in the Georgian script and language—among the earliest known examples of this script—that decorate the mosaic floors. One of the monasteries, at Bir el-Qutt, was excavated by the Franciscans in 1952–53; the other was discovered only last year by Israeli archaeologists.

An aqueduct built by Roman soldiers of the Tenth Legion passes close to Bethlehem, as we can tell from the fact that the names of centurions in charge of the various labor squads are engraved on sections of the conduits. This was one of the aqueducts that brought water to Jerusalem from the Pools of Solomon to the south of the city. It seems to have been built in the second century and probably brought water to the Pool of Hezekiah inside the old city, near the Jaffa Gate. The camp of the Roman legion was in this part of the city, and the soldiers either built the aqueduct to supply it with water or reactivated a Herodian aqueduct. An earlier aqueduct passed by Bethlehem in bringing water to the Temple Mount. A late-sixth-century inscription in Greek has been found between the two aqueducts, bearing an imperial edict that forbids tree planting or agricultural work within ten feet of the water pipes. The length of a foot (about 30 cm) is engraved underneath the text so that there will be no misunderstanding.

The crusaders restored the basilica, adding mosaics on the walls and paintings on the columns, but most of the paintings have now disappeared. They also built the convents attached to the church.

Another church connected with the Nativity story was built a short distance from Bethlehem, at the place where tradition has it that the angel appeared to the shepherds and announced the birth of the Messiah. The place was visited by pilgrims as early as the fourth century. A natural grotto at the spot was first given a mosaic floor, and then, toward the beginning of the fifth century, it was enlarged, stripped of its natural rock roof, and made into a church with a vaulted ceiling, still extant. A small chapel was built over the vault, and in Justinian's time this was replaced by

Hebron and Mamre

Above and opposite: Tomb of the Patriarchs

According to the Bible (Numbers 13:22), Hebron was one of the oldest cities in the world. This is where Abraham placed his tent "by the oaks of Mamre, which are at Hebron," and this is where he was visited by angels who told him of the future birth of his son Isaac (Genesis 13:18; 18:1–15); this is where Sarah died and Abraham bought the "double cave" as a tomb for his wife and himself (Genesis 23:1–20; 25:9–10). It was at Hebron that David was anointed king and there that he had his

capital before transferring it to Jerusalem (2 Samuel 2:3–4; 5:3–5). Hebron remained one of the principal fortresses of the kings of Judah until the Babylonian exile (sixth century B.C.), but in the second century B.C., when the Maccabees reestablished the independence of the Jews, Hebron was held by the Idumeans, who had migrated north from their original dwelling places in the Negev and southern Transjordan. About 163 B.C., Judas Maccabeus conquered Hebron, and toward the end of the second century John Hyrcanus, son of Simon, the last of the Maccabean brothers, completed the conquest of the region and forced the Idumeans to accept Judaism. It was from Idumea, in fact, that the family of Herod came, and by marrying Mariamme, the last of the Hasmoneans, he became king of the Jews. Herod was probably responsible for erecting the monumental building that the Arabs call Haram el-Khalil (sanctuary of the friend of God, that is, of Abraham) and the Jews call Me'arat hamach-pelah (double cave). The tombs of the three patriarchs and their wives are still venerated there today. Herod was also responsible for building the enclosure called Ramet el-Khalil, about 3 kilometers north of Hebron, which is thought to be Mamre, the site of Abraham's oak and well.

During the Great Jewish Revolt against the Romans, Vespasian destroyed Hebron by fire, but the town appears to have recovered rapidly, since a famous annual fair—one of the three most important in the country—was held by the oak (also

Mamre, the remains of a Byzantine basilica

referred to as the terebinth) of Mamre in the second century. It was a religious as well as a commercial event, and it brought visitors from neighboring provinces. Pagan rites were still celebrated there in the fourth century, according to Sozomen, a fifth-century religious writer. Because of these pagan festivities, the rabbis forbade the Jews to take part in the fair. Saint Jerome explains this prohibition differently, telling us that the Jewish prisoners captured during the Bar Kokhba revolt were sold as slaves by Hadrian at the fair of the terebinth, and the memory of this tragic episode caused the Jews to stay away from the fair for centuries. However, Sozomen tells us that in the fourth century the Jews did take part in the fair, alongside Christians and pagans, each group having its own reasons for doing so: the Jews were commemorating Abraham, the pagans were commemorating the three angels, and the Christians were commemorating Christ, who, according to some church fathers, was one of the three beings who appeared to Abraham. Each group prayed in its own way, and the pagans used to throw coins and lighted lamps into the well of Abraham.

In the third century, Hebron was a prosperous village, and at the beginning of the fourth it was already being visited by Christian pilgrims. Constantine's mother-in-law, Eutropia, chanced to visit the places sacred to Abraham while the fair was in progress, and she was scandalized to see pagan libations and sacrifices being made around the well of the patriarch. Consequently, she asked her son-in-law to purify the place. Constantine had a church built there, and a number of cells for monks and nuns were set up around it. Later on, the building containing the tombs of the patriarchs at Hebron was also turned into a church (a sixth-century pilgrim from Piacenza has described it for us). The Jews also came to visit the tombs of the patriarchs, so the church interior was divided into two by a partition: Christian pilgrims on one side, Jews on the other. After the Arab conquest, the Muslims took to venerating the tombs of the patriarchs as well, but it seems that the building did not become a mosque until after the crusader period. It is currently shared by Muslims and Jews.

Haram el-Khalil looks like a fortress. Its external walls are clearly Herodian, except for the highest part, which was added by the Arabs. Inside one can seen some large cenotaphs, which, according to tradition, contain the bodies of Abraham, Isaac, and Jacob and their wives, Sarah, Rebekah, and Leah. Muslims believe the body of Joseph is there as well, because in the Bible Hebron is also called Kiriath-arba, which means "city of the four": hence a fourth patriarch needed to be found buried here. A rabbinical tradition, of which Saint Jerome was aware, maintained that the fourth person was Adam. But since Christians prefer to place the tomb of Adam under Golgotha, Jerome suggests that the fourth person was Caleb, the head of the tribe of Judah sent by Moses to explore the Promised Land (Numbers 13:6). A different tradition spoke of Joseph, but his tomb was venerated by the Samaritans at Shechem and was converted into a church in the fifth century. Hence only the Muslims, starting around the tenth century, have embraced the tradition that the fourth patriarch buried here was Joseph. Beneath the rooms adapted as mosques are some underground chambers to which the Muslims have disallowed access. The few investigations that have been made since 1967, however, have revealed the existence of tombs belonging to the Middle Bronze Age and perhaps the Israelite periods. It appears that the house of David, transformed into a church, was also venerated at Hebron in the fourth century, as was a cave in which the eleven sons of Jacob, except for Joseph, were supposed to be buried.

Ramet el-Khalil is a rectangular enclosure measuring 49 by 65 meters, surrounded by a wall made of huge stone blocks (some are almost 5 m long and more than 1 m high). The wall has survived up to a height of almost 6 meters. The entrance is on the west side. In the southwest corner of the enclosure is a well: It is probably the traditional well of Abraham, since a number of coins of the Constantinian period have been found in it. An oak tree was venerated inside the enclosure until the fourth century, when the tree died; but another must have been planted, because it was described by a seventh-century pilgrim. In the Middle Ages, an oak was planted outside the enclosure, but there is no trace of this one either. The stone floor whose remains can be seen today is later than the Herodian floor, which was removed; it may date to the Byzantine period. The

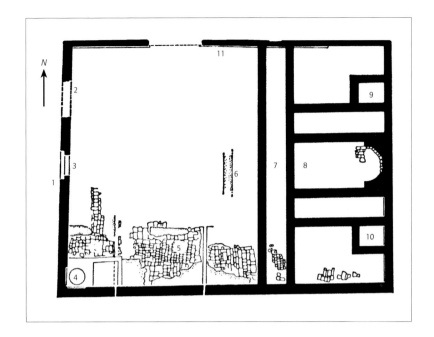

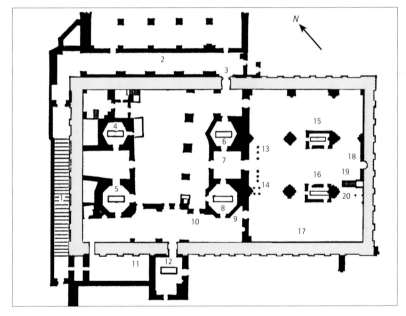

remains of a church have been found in the eastern part of the enclosure, but it is not clear whether this was the Constantinian church or, more likely, the one built by the crusaders and dedicated to the Trinity.

Caesarea

Aerial view of Caesarea, the city built by Herod the Great

Opposite: The Roman theater at Caesarea

Caesarea lies on the sandy shore of the Mediterranean, about halfway between the modern cities of Tel Aviv and Haifa, at a place where the coastline best affords the creation of a port. The hinterland is the Plain of Sharon, certainly the most fertile area of ancient Judea/Palestine. The origins of what became the great metropolis of Roman and late-antique Judea and Palestine are to be found in Hellenistic times, in the third century B.C. Josephus tells us that Herod the Great founded Caesarea at a place previously called Strato's Tower, and there is indeed a papyrus dat-

ing to 259 B.C. bearing witness to the fact that Strato's Tower was already in existence at that time. The most recent archaeological excavations confirm that the origins of the site must be linked to the energetic activities of King Ptolemy II Philadelphus. Strato may have been one of his officials.

The discovery of quantities of Hellenistic pottery suggests that Strato's Tower must have been a vibrant city. It was surrounded by walls, though we do not know their exact position relative to those built later by Herod. Strato's Tower may have been not so much a port as a group of landing places.

During the first century B.C., the city declined after an earthquake, so we can assume that when Herod turned his attention to the site, it was more or less deserted and the harbor silted up and unusable. But Herod realized the enormous potential of Strato's Tower and built a city there. He called it Caesarea and gave it a very modern structure, with an artificial port called Sebastos (Greek for "Augustus"). Josephus provides us with a fairly detailed description of this grandiose undertaking, which produced "a bigger port than Piraeus." He tells us that stone blocks up to 15 meters long were dropped into the water to a depth of up to 37 meters in order to build jetties out into the sea, complete with towers and walls. Structures with vaulted ceilings were also set up for merchants who stopped in the city with their

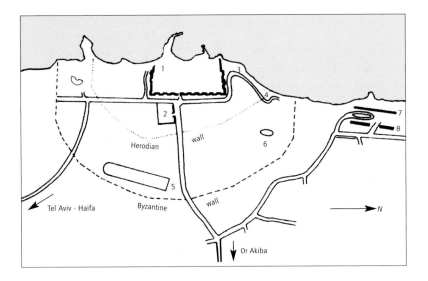

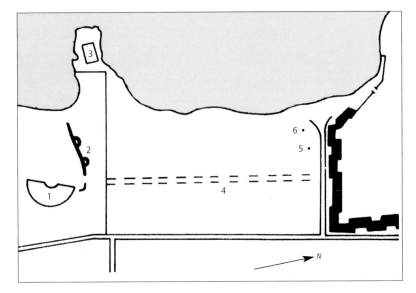

may have been simply a transcription error on the part of a copyist.

Houses in the city were built of white stone, and the streets were arranged in a regular pattern. The temple of Augustus and the goddess Rome was an imposing and very beautiful building, which stood on a mound not far from the southern jetty of the port. Caesarea also had an amphitheater, a theater, and several squares; Herod instituted games, held every five years, with valuable prizes to enhance the city's prestige.

The construction of the port and city with its monuments was a central event in Herod's reign. He must have spent enormous sums of money on the project, but he had probably worked out the benefits likely to accrue: Goods produced in his kingdom could circulate more easily by sea, and this emporium would produce wealth and income from taxes on trade. Augustus, for his part, was bound to increase his appreciation of this Jewish king, who had founded a port able to guarantee an increase in trade in this part of the Mediterranean. The very names that Herod gave to the port and the city—and the dedication of the temple to Augustus and the goddess Rome—were emblematic of Herod's firm allegiance to an all-powerful Rome and its leader.

In this way, Caesarea effectively became a polis, complete with a senate and magistrates, and with a mixed population of Jews and Greeks. When Herod's successor, Archelaus, was removed from power and exiled by the Romans (A.D. 6), the territories over which he had ruled passed into direct Roman administration, and the governor of Judea established his headquarters in Herod's former palace on the promontory at Caesarea.

In their narratives of important events, literary sources mention some of the principal monuments in the city. In his *Jewish Antiquities*, Josephus tells how King Agrippa I was present in the year 64 at games arranged in honor of the emperor Claudius. On the second day, Agrippa came to the theater dressed in a wonderful garment woven entirely out of silver, and shouts of acclaim rose from the audience. But the king was suddenly struck with severe pain. He was swiftly removed to his palace, where he died five days

goods. The entrance to the port was dominated by three colossal statues mounted on columns.

Building operations must have involved thousands of slaves and other workers, for construction proceeded at a considerable pace and was completed in the dozen years between 20 and 9 B.C. It should be noted that one statement made by Josephus has proved to be wrong: modern studies have shown that far from being 37 meters deep as Josephus suggests, the harbor was just 5.5 meters deep in Roman times. This mistake

later. The Acts of the Apostles also tell us that in the year 58 Saint Paul was brought as a prisoner to Caesarea and was kept under guard in the Roman governor's palace for almost two years before leaving for Rome.

In the context of events leading up to the Great Jewish Revolt of 66–70, terrible clashes in Caesarea between two groups of inhabitants—the Jews and the pagan Syrian Greeks—played an important part. The clashes led to a massacre of the Jews, about ten thousand of whom probably lost their lives.

The city was raised to the rank of Flavian colony by Vespasian and continued to flourish up to the sixth century. The discovery of numerous houses and suburban villas with mosaic floors shows that the area outside the walls was densely inhabited and cultivated by a wealthy local aristocracy. A series of warehouses and *horrea* (granaries) found during recent excavations in the southwest area of the city, by the shore, indicate that the import and export of goods played an important part in city life. The warehouses had enormous storage spaces with large oil containers (*dolia*), while grain was kept in thick-walled underground rooms. Important modernizing work was carried out at the port under the emperor Anastasius.

The Jews still constituted an important part of the population. One rabbinical source tells us that Rabbi Akiba, a leading figure in the opposition to the Romans at the time of Hadrian, was cruelly put to death by the imperial power and was buried at Caesarea by his fellow Jews: "And they carried him all night until they reached the *tetrapylon* of Caesarea. When they got there, they ascended three steps and then descended and the cave opened before them and they saw a chair, some seats, a table, and a menorah. They set Rabbi Akiba on a bed and left. Then the cave was sealed, and a candle was burning on the menorah." Since archaeologists have indeed found a *tetrapylon* (a quadruple monumental arch) at Caesarea, and Jewish burial areas have been identified in the area, it is likely that this story is more than just a fable.

In the third century and the early years of the fourth, a Jewish academy led by Rabbi Oshaiah and then by Rabbi Abbahu enjoyed a prominent position at Caesarea. Also in the third century, Origen, one of the great fathers of the Christian church, founded his famous school of Christian theology there. At the request of the local bishop, Origen delivered sermons at least once daily. He composed many of his most important works at Caesarea and the fame of the school echoed throughout the Christian world, to the extent that Caesarea was considered one of the greatest intellectual centers of early Christianity. Origen's school, it should be remembered, offered a vast range of teaching, from grammar and rhetoric to physics, mathematics, geometry, and astronomy, and on to philosophy and biblical and theological studies. In other words, this was no less than an ancient university, with an important library embracing various areas of knowledge. At the time of the persecutions under the emperor Decius, Origen was imprisoned and tortured, and he died shortly afterward, probably as a result of his sufferings.

Another outstanding Christian figure, the historian and intellectual Eusebius, was born at Caesarea. He was a friend of the emperor Constantine and was bishop of Caesarea from about 315 until his death in 340. Yet another son of Caesarea was the great sixth-century lay historian Procopius, who described the wars of Justinian.

Some sources provide us with interesting information about fourth-century Caesarea. There were evidently a great many Samaritans in the city, as many as the Jews, Christians, and pagans put together. The office of the provincial governor was apparently almost exclusively staffed by Samaritans.

In this context, it is not surprising that imperial laws restricting the rights of the Samaritans caused considerable turmoil at Caesarea. A series of Samaritan rebellions against the authorities proved a serious blow to the city. The first rebellion occurred in 484, but it must have been the other two, in 529–530 and 555, that affected the city most profoundly. Together with an outbreak of plague and a general economic crisis in the

Opposite, above: Northern and eastern areas
1 *Area revealed by the excavations*
2 *Byzantine street*
3 *Synagogue area*
4 *Herodian wall*
5 *Hippodrome*
6 *Amphitheater*
7 *Upper aqueduct*
8 *Lower aqueduct*

Opposite, below: Southern area
1 *Roman theater*
2 *Byzantine wall*
3 *Pool*
4 *Cardo maximus*
5 *Byzantine baths*
6 *Mithraeum*

Roman Empire, they set in motion a gradual decline. The final blows to the prosperity of Caesarea came with the Persian conquest of 614 and then the Arab conquest of 640 or 641. In Islamic times Caesarea was no more than a small town with an abandoned harbor.

There have been numerous archaeological missions to Caesarea, and research activity at the site continues unabated. Discoveries show that it was a very important urban center, with a population estimated at between thirty-five and one hundred thousand. Many typical Roman city buildings have been brought to light, and Caesarea and its archaeological park provide an outstanding example of urban organization in imperial and late-antique times.

At least three buildings dating to the time of Herod the Great's activities at Caesarea have been identified. One is the royal palace, which stood at the end of the promontory. It is thus called the lower palace, in order to distinguish it from the upper palace, which was in all probability built at a later stage, when a Roman administration replaced that of the Jewish kings. The lower palace is on two floors and is built around a peristyle with various rooms leading off it. A pool hewn out of the rock lies at its center. On the west side it had a large curved balcony offering a splendid view toward the open sea. The upper palace is a good example of a *praetorium*, the public building used by the representatives of Roman power for administrative and judicial purposes. It consisted of a very large courtyard for the public and rich private rooms with painted walls and mosaic floors; it also had warm baths. The most representative part of the private area was a large room for dining and entertainment.

Herod's amphitheater, mentioned by Josephus, has recently been discovered in the shore area between the port and the palace. Its nature and dimensions are very surprising, however, because it really most resembles a hippodrome, but on a reduced scale; in size it is more like a stadium (its length, at 290 m, is much greater than what one would expect of a normal amphitheater). There are various indications that this was a multifunctional structure, intended not

*Opposite: Colossal statue in
red porphyry, perhaps representing the emperor Hadrian*

only for chariot races—though of a different type
than the typical Roman races normally held in
much longer hippodromes—but also for athletic
competitions, gladiatorial games, and wild-
animals fights. In referring to it as an amphitheater, Josephus was evidently not trying to specify
a particular type of structure but simply indicating in a general way that it was different from a
theater in form.

It has been known for some time, thanks to
aerial photography, that there was also a proper
amphitheater. It is situated to the northeast,
beyond the Herodian walls. It seems to date to the
same period as the hippodrome in the southeast
area of the city, which was excavated in the 1970s
and has been dated to the second century. This
hippodrome was deliberately demolished in late
antiquity, probably in the early sixth century.

Also deserving mention is a theater that has
been discovered in the southernmost part of the
city. It could hold an audience of four thousand
and is certainly the Herodian building mentioned
by Josephus. It is a particular attraction for visitors because it was here, on an internal stairway,
that Italian archaeologists in 1961 discovered the
now famous Pontius Pilate inscription carved on
a piece of stone that had been reused in fourth-
century restoration work on the theater. The
inscription is unfortunately incomplete, but it
unequivocally reminds us of the part that the prefect of Judea played in the Gospels. It appears to
commemorate the fact that he had a temple built
or decorated in honor of Emperor Tiberius. A
different interpretation of the text has recently
been suggested, however, by Geza Alföldy: In his
opinion, Pontius Pilate had arranged for a new
tower to be built at the port and named after
Tiberius. In other words, this was a structure similar to the one that Josephus says was built in
honor of Drusus.

Among the most recent and significant
archaeological discoveries, we must particularly
mention a second *praetorium*, built toward the
end of the first century for the procurator, whose
job was to assist the Roman governor as representative of the imperial power in the province. This
building stood in the first city *insula* to the south

of the port and comprised a whole administrative
complex, with gardens, halls, and baths. In late
antiquity, however, it was used as a palace by the
provincial governor. We can glimpse the kind of
life that people led in this seat of imperial power
in late antiquity from the fact that it boasts a
series of inscriptions in mosaic medallions on the
floors of some of the seven rooms of the building.
These rooms are arranged around a central hall,
which scholars have identified as an archive. In
the inscriptions, the heads of various different
administrative offices call on the aid of God and
give their names, whereas officials of lower rank
are mentioned only collectively and anony-
mously. Another medallion contains a passage
from the epistle of Saint Paul to the Romans: "Do
you wish to have no fear of authority? Then do
what is good and you will receive its approval."

Herodian Caesarea had a surrounding wall
and was also thought to have an aqueduct, but
more recent studies have suggested that this
aqueduct, which brought water from the Shuni
spring, was not built until the first century A.D.,
before the reign of Vespasian. As the city grew
in subsequent decades, the need for water
increased, and the emperor Hadrian doubled the
capacity of the aqueduct by adding a second
channel. Some inscriptions show that the work
was carried out by a detachment of the VI Ferrata
Legion. This aqueduct is referred to by scholars
as the high-level aqueduct to distinguish it from
a later low-level aqueduct, which was probably
built in the early fourth century and brought
water from other springs to the north of the city.

On the other hand, new walls were not built
until the fifth century, which confirms that in
the glorious days of *pax romana*, such walls were
thought to be unnecessary. The new city now
covered a large area that included the amphitheater and the hippodrome, as well as roads and
monumental installations of more recent construction. And late-antique Caesarea must have
expanded still further as its population grew. It
is interesting to note in this connection that during late antiquity a third aqueduct was built, to
bring water from the al-Asal spring to the south
of the city.

In the sixth century, the area south of the south-central part of the city—the area around the theater—was enclosed in fortifications known as the *kastron*. That fits what is known in the case of other cities in the Roman East, in which a particular district came to assume the functions of a citadel. The *praetorium* on the promontory was partially dismantled and scholars suggest that in its reduced form it was used as headquarters by the *dux*, who was the military commander for the province.

The most significant pagan religious building at Caesarea is the temple of Augustus and the goddess Rome, which was built on a platform and thus dominated the city and the port. The cult of the emperor was also practiced in a temple dedicated to Hadrian, but we know of it only from written sources. In all probability the Hadrianeum originally housed a colossal statue of the emperor in red porphyry (2.45 m high), which can now be seen in a different location, at the border of a late-antique monumental quarter of the city. The statue is missing its head, hands, and feet, which must have been made of some other material— probably marble.

One very interesting discovery has been that of a Mithraeum, founded in the second or third century in an underground room in the procurator's *praetorium*. This was a vaulted room with benches cut out to serve as seats for members of the congregation. The vaults were painted with scenes from the deeds of Mithras and with representations of converts as they went through the various stages of ritual initiation. There were two slits in the vault, one to let light into the room and the other for some highly symbolic purpose, for on the day of the summer solstice a ray of light fell close to the altar, illuminating it at noon.

The presence of Jewish worship at Caesarea is shown by the remains of one synagogue found in the northern part of the city, where most of the Jews lived; but judging from the evidence of written sources, there must have been others. Excavation of the synagogue has brought to light some inscriptions in Hebrew and Greek and some Corinthian capitals with menorah symbols. It has

been possible to establish that the synagogue was destroyed in a fire during the fourth century and rebuilt in the fifth.

Late-antique literary sources mention various churches in Caesarea, but only one has been identified with certainty by archaeological missions: an octagonal building with an imposing flight of entrance steps, which was built between 525 and 550 on top of the temple of Augustus and Rome.

Ashkelon (Ascalon)

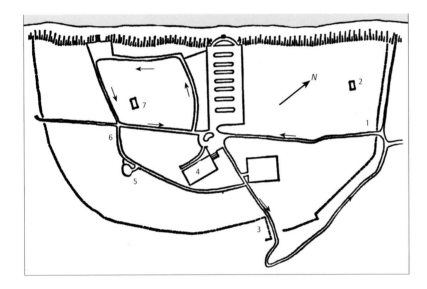

Plan of the ancient city of Ashkelon

1 *Jaffa Gate*
2 *Crusader church*
3 *Jerusalem Gate*
4 *Basilica*
5 *"Well of peace"*
6 *Crusader church*
7 *Byzantine church*

Opposite: Remains of Roman columns in a crusader wall by the sea

Ashkelon is a port on the Mediterranean coast, 63 kilometers south of Jaffa (Tel Aviv) and 15 kilometers north of Gaza, with a history going back at least to Chalcolithic times. It was well known to the Egyptian pharaohs. It was also famous in the Greek world as early as the seventh century B.C., when the poet Alcaeus of Mytilene included it among the fabulous eastern cities visited by his brother Antimenides during his wanderings as a mercenary soldier. Herodotus speaks of the temple of Aphrodite Urania in Ashkelon—the earliest

temple to the goddess, whose sacred doves still flocked undisturbed on the roofs of the city in Roman times and even came down to peck at people's dining tables. Later on, Ashkelon's principal god was Derketo or Atargatis, a fusion of Aphrodite and the Phoenician goddess Astarte, represented as half woman and half fish. Other important local deities were Isis "the omnipotent," Apollo, and Asclepius "with the lion."

During the Philistine period, Ashkelon was a city-state, and after being sacked by the Babylonian king Nebuchadnezzar (604 B.C.), it came under Phoenician influence and prospered through trade. In the Hellenistic period it was an independent polis with its own coinage and developed as a Greek cultural center, the home of philosophers and illustrious scholars. Even when the Hasmonean dynasty was at its period of maximum expansion, Ashkelon did not fall into the hands of the Jews; Pompey did not annex it to the province of Syria, nor did Augustus incorporate it into Herod's kingdom. It seems instead to have enjoyed the status of ally of the Roman people, since cohorts of Ashkelonite soldiers served as auxiliaries in the Roman army as early as the Augustan age. It is known that there was a body of Ashkelonite archers in imperial times, and their skill was in fact proverbial in the sixth century.

Ashkelon's territory was vast, stretching as far east as Idumea, a region conquered and judaized by the Hasmonean kings. Herod's family, which

came from Idumea, maintained friendly relations with Ashkelon, to the extent that there is a tradition, recorded by the earliest third- and fourth-century Christian historians, that Herod's father was the son of an Ashkelonite slave at the temple of Apollo. This legend was born of the hostility between Christians of Jewish origin and Herod, and of the traditional hostility between Jews and Ashkelonites. It was probably also encouraged by the fact that Herod heaped benefits upon the city of Ashkelon and enriched it with monuments: baths, splendid fountains, and porticoes, not to mention a royal palace for Augustus, which the emperor later gave to Herod's sister Salome.

In Roman times, a substantial Jewish community lived at Ashkelon, but as in other pagan cities, there was hostility between Greeks and Jews. When the Great Revolt against the Romans began and the pagans in Caesarea massacred the local Jews, Judean Jews took their revenge by attacking various pagan cities and villages, including Ashkelon, which was set on fire. The Ashkelonites

nificent basilica whose remains can be admired to this day. Ashkelon was also host to sporting competitions involving athletes from the whole of the Mediterranean basin. The wrestling was particularly famous.

Christianity reached Ashkelon no later than the end of the third century. Its most famous local martyrs, venerated in Byzantine times at a sanctuary outside the walls, were not citizens of Ashkelon but three visiting members of the Egyptian clergy who were arrested at the city gates and interrogated; they confessed to being Christians and were put to death on the spot. The bishops of Ashkelon took part in the ecumenical councils, including the first, held at Nicea in 325. Ashkelon continued to flourish not only throughout the Byzantine period but also after the Arab conquest and in crusader times, when it acquired as many as five churches: four for the Latins and one for the Greeks (Santa Maria Viridis, or St. Mary the Green). The medieval port was blocked by Saladin's soldiers in 1191 to prevent the crusaders from using it. Today, broken columns and other Roman and Byzantine architectural elements, which the Muslim soldiers threw into the harbor, lie scattered underwater and on the beach.

In the Hellenistic and Roman periods, the sailors, merchants, and bankers of Ashkelon were active throughout the eastern Mediterranean, in Greece, Thessaly, and Macedonia—and also in southern Italy, as we can tell from inscriptions. Since it stood in a fertile and well-watered area, Ashkelon was famous for its fruit and vegetable plantations, vineyards, and gardens, as well as for its agricultural exports, especially henna, figs, wine, and onions. There was one particular highly flavored Ashkelon variety of onion that was much admired by the ancients and eventually acquired a name in various European languages (*scalogno* in Italian, *eschaloigne* in French, *escalonia* in Spanish, and *scallion* in English). Some goods were exported in locally manufactured amphorae, known as Ashkelon amphorae, which have turned up in archaeological excavations throughout the Mediterranean basin and elsewhere in Europe. The area around Ashkelon is to this day scattered with

in their turn killed twenty-five hundred Jews living in the city. A further rebel attack was repulsed by the Roman soldiers garrisoned there.

When the province of Judea was reorganized after the revolt, Ashkelon was incorporated into it, though it preserved a certain measure of self-government as a polis and later as a colony. It enjoyed a period of particular prosperity under the Severan emperors, who were apparently responsible for restructuring the city on Roman town-planning lines, and for building a mag-

Detail of a Roman sarcophagus lid

Opposite: Pilaster with a statue of Winged Victory standing on a globe supported by Atlas

the remains of potters' workshops with their characteristic kilns and the shards of production rejects. They effectively constituted an industrial belt around the city. Winepresses dating to Roman and Byzantine times are also common in the Ashkelon surroundings. The city was famous not only for its maritime and export trade but also for its fairs, which attracted visitors from the whole of Palestine and the surrounding provinces. The wealth accumulated through these various activities is evident in the splendor of the numerous late-Roman painted tombs that have been found near Ashkelon.

Ashkelon was one of the very first sites in Palestine to attract European archaeologists. Lady Hester Stanhope, a somewhat eccentric Englishwoman, led an expedition to Ashkelon in 1815, discovering there a peristylar building and a statue of an emperor. Lady Stanhope's personal physician made a sketch of the statue, after which it was quickly smashed in order not to offend the religious sensibilities of Muslims. The building that Lady Stanhope discovered has not been identified, but a splendid basilica was later exca-

vated by English archaeologists after the First World War. They thought it was Herod's porticoed building, but more recent studies have suggested that it was probably built at the time of Septimius Severus (late second–early third century), though there were some first-century honorific inscriptions on its walls. It is thought that these probably came from an earlier basilica or *bouleuterion*.

The basilica consists of a rectangular hall, 110 meters long and about 35 meters wide, surrounded by a portico of Corinthian columns: twenty-four on the long sides and six on the short. Some of the columns, up to 8 meters in height, have survived. At the south end of the basilica there was an apse 15 meters in diameter, flanked by two rectangular rooms. Just inside the entrance to the apse were sculpted pilasters: Three of these have Winged Victories, of which the only complete one stands on a globe held aloft by Atlas. A fourth pilaster shows Isis accompanied by a small figure who may be her son Horus or a priest of her cult. Other statues found at Ashkelon representing various gods and an emperor (probably a Severan) seem to have come from the same basilica, in whose apse the imperial cult was practiced.

Excavations at Ashkelon have also revealed some Hellenistic *insulae* with villas, some of which were inhabited in the Roman period but destroyed in the fourth century when a bath complex was built on the site. This complex was in its turn replaced in the sixth century by a large building with an apse. The drains from the baths, which were no longer used after the construction of the Byzantine building, were found to be obstructed by the skeletons of more than a hundred newborn babies—evidently unwanted children who were drowned at birth.

Nothing remains of the Roman theater, except for some seat fragments and the circular depression on which the seating rested. During the Byzantine period, it was shown to pilgrims as a "well of peace" or "well of Abraham." There are some late-Roman tombs with frescoes, among which the most noteworthy are the Tomb of the Nymphs, in which the frescoes represent nymphs and cupids in a Nilotic landscape, a grape harvest scene, and other mythological and naturalistic subjects; the Tomb of the Niches, with frescoes of human figures in the niches; and the Tomb of the Peacock.

Ashkelon increased in size in the Byzantine period, spreading northward into a suburb now called Ashkelon Barnea, where two basilican churches with mosaic floors have been excavated. The date of one of these churches has been established as late fifth century by means of two Greek inscriptions bearing a date reckoned from the start of the Ashkelon era (that is, from A.D. 104). Within the old city walls, near the gate known as the Jerusalem Gate, there was a third church, probably built in the fifth century as well. It was a basilica whose gallery and sloping roof were supported on columns of Aswan granite. The earlier marble floor also contained a cruciform baptismal basin with water supplied through a lead pipe. The church was made into a mosque in the tenth century by the Fatimid caliphs and then restored as a church (Santa Maria Viridis) in the crusader period. In the Byzantine period, Ashkelon also had a synagogue (perhaps more

than one), of which only fragments have survived: bits of a marble balustrade decorated with a menorah; the base of a column also decorated with menorah, shofar (a ram's horn sounded on the occasion of solemn feasts), and ethrog (a citron, mostly used to celebrate Sukkoth); a fragment of a dedicatory inscription in Aramaic; a fragment containing a list of the priestly families who served in the Temple (various copies of this list have been found in Israel and elsewhere); the shaft of a column with an incised inscription in Greek naming the family that donated the column (its members have Jewish names); and a fragmentary stone inscription commemorating an offering made to a synagogue by a group of people. This latter inscription also bears a date expressed in the Ashkelon era, corresponding to A.D. 605/6.

Gaza

The ancient Philistine city of Gaza stood on the southern coast of Palestine. Later on it became a Persian fortress and was subsequently destroyed by Alexander the Great in 332 B.C. It rose again, however, and became an object of contention between the Ptolemaic kings of Egypt and the Seleucid kings of Syria, until the time came when it was captured and destroyed by the Hasmonean king Alexander Jannaeus around 90 B.C. Pompey took it from the Hasmoneans in 61/60 B.C., and Gabinius, the Roman governor of Syria, had it rebuilt. Roman Gaza is some way south of the ancient Philistine city, about 5 kilometers inland from the coast, and has been identified as Tell 'Azza. When did the move take place? Some modern historians think Gabinius was responsible for refounding Gaza at the new site, but according to an ancient tradition, the site of ancient Gaza was deserted after the time of Alexander the Great, which would mean that the new city moved south as early as Hellenistic times. The matter cannot be resolved without carrying out excavations, however, and that is impossible at present, since the modern city covers the whole area, forming one of the most densely populated places in the world.

The city of Gaza calculated its era from the time of its foundation by Gabinius. It rapidly became one of the most important cities in the region, thanks in part to its position on the Via Maris linking Egypt and Syria, but principally because it was a port. In 30 B.C. Gaza was incorporated into the kingdom of Herod, and on his death it was annexed to the province of Syria. In A.D. 66, when the Jewish revolt against the Romans began, Gaza was attacked by the rebels and destroyed; and when the province of Judea was reorganized after the revolt, Gaza became part of it, though it retained its status as an autonomous polis. Emperor Hadrian visited it in 129/30 and conferred certain privileges upon it, one of which was the right to hold an annual fair, the Hadrian *panegyris*. This was one of the three most important fairs in the country, along with those of Mamre and Accho. It may have been at the time of the fair that games were held at Gaza, attracting athletes from all parts of the Mediterranean. In the second half of the third century, the city became a Roman colony.

Christianity must have reached Gaza very early, if one is to believe a tradition that says the first bishop of the city was Philemon, one of the seventy-two disciples of Jesus and the recipient of an epistle from Saint Paul. A number of local martyrs, including Bishop Sylvanus, were condemned to torture and impalement during the persecution of Maximinus (307–10). It seems, however, that although the new religion was embraced by a majority of those who lived at the port, it was slow to spread among the inhabitants

of the city itself, especially the aristocracy. As
a result, Constantine decided to separate the
two places and make the port an independent
municipality called Neapolis ("new city") and
Constantia in honor of the emperor's sister.
Later on, the emperor Julian the Apostate
revoked the separation. The port was now
called Maiumas (a term that simply means
"port") and formed a single unit with the city,
but it kept its own bishop, in spite of repeated
attempts by the bishops of Gaza to absorb the
diocese of Maiumas. The christianization of
Gaza proceeded slowly, not only because of the
strength of pagan tradition, and especially the
cult of the local god Marnas, but also because
of competition from Manichaeism. But at the
beginning of the fifth century, Bishop Porphyrius
acted energetically against the Manichaean mis-
sionaries and succeeded in expelling them from
the city; at the same time he pressured the
emperor Arcadius, through his wife Eudoxia, to
abolish paganism at Gaza by force. In the end
the emperor was persuaded. He sent soldiers to
Gaza, and under their protection the bishop and
Christians of the city destroyed the temple of
Marnas and erected in its place a church, which
took the name Eudoxiana in honor of the
empress. Paganism survived at Gaza for at least
two centuries, however, influencing the local
Christian culture through its philosophical, literary, and artistic traditions.

In the summer of 541, bubonic plague entered
Palestine through the port of Gaza, brought by
ships plying their trade with Egypt, where the
terrible disease had arrived from India. From
Gaza the epidemic spread to the whole of
Palestine and the province of Arabia, and thence
to Syria and Asia Minor. It decimated the population throughout the provinces of the eastern
Roman Empire. An epitaph dated June 541 records
the death of a whole family at Gaza, and during
the autumn and winter we can follow the advance
of the plague inland through the surviving funerary inscriptions with dates. The Arab invasion, on
the other hand, brought no great upheaval. After
a battle near Gaza in 635, the city surrendered

and became the seat of the governor of southern
Palestine. At the time of the conquest, sixty
Byzantine soldiers who had been taken prisoner
were urged to accept Islam and died as martyrs
when they refused. But apart from this episode,
the Christians continued to live in peace under
Muslim rule, together with the Jewish and
Samaritan communities, until the crusader
conquest.

In both the Roman period and that of the
Byzantines that followed, Gaza was a center of
Greek culture and the birthplace of many outstanding figures, especially in the field of rhetoric
and philosophy. The city boasted splendid temples: to Zeus, Helios, Aphrodite, Apollo, the local
Tyche, and especially Marnas. In the Byzantine
period, a mosaic school flourished there, its
splendid products embellishing churches and
public buildings at Gaza and throughout the surrounding area. Unfortunately, however, scarcely
anything remains of these monuments and works
of art except for a few descriptions by contemporary writers. The famous Eudoxiana church, completed about 408, was a magnificent cruciform
building, its interior embellished with thirty-two
monolithic columns of Euboian marble; not a
trace of the Byzantine church remains. In the
twelfth century, a crusader church of Saint John
the Baptist was erected on the site, and this later
became a mosque, now called Djami el-Kabir (the
Great Mosque). Inside one can see that ancient
columns have been reused: One of them, in fact,
once bore an inscription in Aramaic and Greek,
which read "Ananias, son of Jacob," and above it
was a relief with menorah, shofar, lulab, and
ethrog, surrounded by a wreath. The relief, which
was destroyed by Muslims a few years ago, showed
that the column came from a synagogue of the
late-Roman period. This detail adds a final touch
to the history of the building as an epitome of
both mutual tolerance and friction between the
three monotheistic religions in the country.

The rhetorician Choricius of Gaza provides
us with a description of two city churches built in
the early sixth century, as well as a list of secular
buildings, including a covered market built by

Bishop Marcianus during the reign of Justinian. From Choricius's description we learn that the churches, dedicated to Saint Sergius and Saint Stephen, were decorated with wall mosaics like those in the churches in Ravenna. Saint Sergius was a basilica with a square atrium surrounded by porticoes, with a baptistery and other annexes. Over the nave was a dome resting on an octagonal base and decorated with figures of prophets. On the church walls were scenes from the Gospels: the Annunciation, the Birth of Christ, the Presentation in the Temple, Christ's various miracles, and then the Last Supper, the Crucifixion, the Resurrection, and the Ascension. In the apse was a mosaic of the Virgin and Child flanked by Saint Sergius and Saint Stephen on a gold ground. The monumental entrance was decorated with sculptures and medallions with the symbols of the Passion. The Church of Saint Stephen was attached to the bishop's palace, and a monumental flight of steps led up to the entrance in the splendidly decorated western facade. This in turn gave on to an atrium surrounded by porticoes and then the church itself. There were Nilotic scenes on the walls, and high up, above the matronea (married women's gallery), was a row of wild animals. In the apse was the figure of Saint Stephen holding a model of the church in his hand, with Saint John beside him and Christ above him. Four porphyry columns separated the nave from the presbytery.

The rhetorician John of Gaza describes another sixth-century building: a winter bath complex, in the dome of which was an allegorical representation of the cosmos, with a cross at its center, surrounded by three heavens divided into quadrants by the arms of the cross. Inside each quadrant were depicted personifications of the primordial features of the universe and time: Atlas with the globe of the sun, the hours of the day, the seasons, the constellations, the earth, the sea, and so on. It appears that another dome with the same type of decoration representing the cosmos was created—quite certainly by artists of the Gaza school—at a public building at Beersheba in

the Negev, around the year 520. What is certain is that splendid mosaics can still be seen today in various sixth-century churches in the Negev; they bear witness to the very high artistic achievements of the Gaza school.

At Gaza itself, or rather at Maiumas, a single mosaic has survived, in the only building that it has been possible to explore archaeologically. The mosaic is in the floor of a basilica with a nave and four aisles, measuring 30 by 26 meters, but has survived only in part. In the nave we see King David playing the lyre, surrounded by wild animals; the name David is written in Aramaic in the vignette. This identifies the building as a synagogue. The side-aisle floors were decorated with medallions made of vine tendrils and containing figures of animals. In one of the medallions, a Greek inscription tells us both the date of the mosaic, Loos (July–August) 509, and the names of two benefactors—Menahem and Joshua, sons of Jesse—who were timber merchants. The synagogue was built not far from the fortified wall at the port, on top of an earlier building—apparently a dyehouse, which was destroyed in a fire in the fourth century. The remains of another building, also destroyed by fire, have been excavated beside the dyehouse. Among the objects found in the ruins were an anchor and needles for repairing nets, which suggest that this was a fisherman's house or store. A damaged statue of the Good Shepherd has also been found in the Maiumas area.

We know from literary sources that the poor in Gaza spoke Aramaic, but all the inscriptions discovered in the city—except for the two from synagogues mentioned above—are in Greek. They are almost all epitaphs, and very few commemorate building activity. Of particular interest among the latter is an inscription apparently dating to the early seventh century, which records the restoration of the city walls by two private enterprises. It is possible that the work was commissioned by the local authority in view of the threat of the first Arab incursions, before the conquest of Gaza by Islamic forces in 635.

Towns of the Negev

Shivta, remains of the late-fourth-century southern church

Opposite: View of the Negev

It would be difficult for visitors not to be enchanted with the ruins of what are commonly known as "the Byzantine towns of the Negev": Haluza (Elusa), Mamshit (Mampsis or Kurnub), Shivta, Avdat, Nizzana (Nessana), Sa'adon, and Rehoboth. One must remember, however, that these "towns" were never more than simple villages, except for Elusa, which acquired the official status of polis in late antiquity. As we shall see, the history of these sites and their surrounding territory is fascinating because it is punctuated by economic, demographic, and religious developments that successively altered their nature. What is extraordinary about these settlements is that they managed to develop in a terrain that was environmentally hostile, namely the arid zone of

the central Negev, where the annual rainfall varies between 100 and 150 millimeters (3.9–5.9 in.). In such conditions it is difficult for agriculture to flourish, and the land can be profitably cultivated only by applying special techniques.

The central Negev was part of the Nabataean kingdom until the Romans abolished the monarchy and reorganized the entire realm as the province of Arabia (A.D. 106). The Nabataeans were a trading people who had become rich thanks to their control over a large part of the spice road, along which incense and other luxury goods were transported from southern Arabia to the Mediterranean port of Gaza. Their capital was Petra: a central hub on the spice road, which, by the time of Augustus, had become a city rich in splendid monuments, much enamored of Greek culture, and much visited by foreigners.

As far as the Negev towns are concerned, we have to remember that Avdat (Oboda) and

Haluza (Elusa) were situated on the last stretch of the spice road—but in Nabataean times they must have been little more than caravan stations. Shivta (Sobata) and Sa'adon (Sudanon) were small settlements away from the region's main roads. Rehoboth (ancient Bethomolachon?) and Nizzana were on the road that led from the north into Sinai, while Mamshit (Kurnub) lies farther north at an important intersection of roads from Judea, the Dead Sea, the lands beyond the Jordan, and also—via Beersheba—the Mediterranean coast. Scholarly research has not succeeded in finding substantial traces of a Nabataean settlement at Rehoboth, and all the structures found at Sa'adon belong to late antiquity. Nizzana, on the other hand, already had a certain importance at the time of the Nabataean king Aretas IV (a contemporary of Augustus), as we can tell from the large number of pottery and coin finds, and from various glass objects datable to his time. Remains of buildings from the first and second centuries A.D. have also been found there, both in the lower part of the town and on the acropolis. Some buildings dating to Nabataean times have also been found at Mamshit, but in this case, too, it seems likely that at the time it was no more than just a stopping place along the road.

We have mentioned that the Nabataeans earned a great deal from trade, but it must also be stressed that their agriculture in this arid land was very fruitful. We are sure of this, because what the Greek natural historian Strabo tells us is supported by the results of various archaeological investigations. Scholarly research has been able to prove that in that part of their land now in Jordan—especially around Petra—the Nabataeans had water channels and collection systems that allowed them to irrigate fairly substantial tracts of land. A few clues from recently initiated research seem to suggest that even in small Negev settlements, the Nabataeans had begun to use agriculture, though on a very small scale.

The town of Avdat (Oboda) in the Negev had a rather special role. Uranius, a late-antique historian, says that the town took its name from an

ancient Nabataean king who was buried and subsequently venerated there. The Israeli archaeologist Avraham Negev thinks he has identified the
temple dedicated to King Obodas in a building
on the acropolis that can be dated to the time of
Aretas IV, one of Obodas's successors. Avdat
must have been a place of some importance for
the Nabataeans, and, significantly, recent excavations have revealed the existence of a large
dwelling in the northern sector datable to the
first century A.D.

An important stage in the history of the
region was reached when the Nabataean kingdom
was incorporated into the Roman Empire in A.D.
106. Exactly why this should have happened is
unclear, but it seems that economic and political
considerations led the Romans to annex what had
been an allied kingdom and one that in practice
was already subordinate to the imperial power.
Let us not forget that this was the time of

Emperor Trajan, who had strong imperialist lean-
ings. The whole kingdom was organized as a
Roman province and given the name Arabia, but
life went on there much as usual and the basic
economic characteristics of town and country
remained substantially unchanged.

In the third century, the Roman Empire went
through a profound political, economic, and military crisis. Regarding the province of Arabia, it
has been possible to establish that as early as the
reign of Caracalla, some minor stopping-places
along the spice road between Petra and Avdat had
ceased to be active. At about the same time, Petra
ceased to manufacture its characteristic unguen-
taria for perfumes and ointments. Traces of abandonment have also been found at a house at
Avdat. But life there soon picked up again, as is
clear from a series of inscriptions, the first dating
to 267, which commemorate the completion of
some restoration work on the acropolis.

*Opposite: View of the Avdat
site*

*Avdat, gate of the Byzantine
"citadel"*

The collapse of the great land-based trade in goods from southern Arabia marked a real change in the life of Petra and the Negev, for that was to a large extent the basis of their economy. However, the fact that agriculture had been practiced in the past provided the impulse for an extraordinary rebirth. From the late fourth and early fifth century on, the Negev enjoyed an unequaled economic acceleration, which lasted until the time of the Arab conquest. All the preexisting sites grew, many new villages and settlements appeared, and the arid land in the countryside was systematically put under cultivation, thanks to the application of hydraulic systems similar to those that the Nabataeans had devised on a small scale. We know that agriculture was based largely on the cultivation of vines, and so we can imagine the

striking spectacle offered by the Negev desert, with the wadis and surrounding land carpeted with vineyards. It was in this context of economic expansion, and not later than the mid-fourth century, that Haluza acquired the status of polis.

The Negev underwent an administrative change at the time of Diocletian (A.D. 284–305), when it was transferred from the province of Arabia to that of Syria, and when Palaestina was subsequently (385/86–390/92) divided into three parts by Emperor Theodosius I, the Negev became part of Palaestina III, or Palaestina Salutaris.

Christianity spread through the region thanks largely to the missionary zeal of Hilarion, a monk who was active around the middle of the fourth century. Such was the

impulse created by his extraordinary personality that many hermits settled in the lands of the Negev and took to cultivating the vine. In Saint Jerome's "Life of Hilarion," we are told that he built the first church at Haluza, setting in motion a process that was soon followed up in other Negev towns.

Avdat (Oboda) is certainly the most striking of the Negev towns, situated as it is on a hill 655 meters above sea level and about 80 meters above the surrounding area. Two sectors enclosed by a wall stand out on the summit of a rocky spur to form the acropolis. The first of these, on the west side, is often called the ecclesiastical sector or acropolis, whereas the other is commonly called the citadel. In the northwest corner of the acropolis, a Nabataean temple was

built at the end of the first century B.C.; it has been identified as the temple of King Obodas, previously mentioned. It was probably more extensive than is suggested by the visible remains today, which consist only of a tower measuring 8.75 by 13 meters. This tower was divided into a number of areas (a portico, a large hall, and an adytum or sacred enclosure, which was itself divided into two). For a num-ber of reasons, the archaeologist Avraham Negev thinks that King Obodas was deified and worshipped in the smaller part of the adytum, and that the larger area was reserved for the worship of the two most important gods in the Nabataean pantheon: Dusares and Allat. There are also two churches on the acropolis: one on the north side and one dedicated to Saint Theodore on the south side. They date respectively to the second half of the fourth and the second half of the fifth century, but with a large margin of uncertainty.

As for the citadel, it was probably built in the fifth century as a refuge for the population in case of danger. The area looks like a military fort, but it lacks any internal buildings, except for one room, a chapel, and two cisterns that stored water drained from the large courtyard and, by means of channels, from the surrounding area.

Some inhabited areas of Oboda have been identified: an elegant quarter of twenty or thirty houses was built to the south of the acropolis, probably in the late third century; and a complex of about four hundred houses grew up on the west slope from the fifth century onward, each one beside a cave that served as storeroom, workshop, and wine cellar.

That the cultivation of the vine was of great importance is shown by the presence of various installations for pressing grapes, as well as very large vats. These installations are usually found outside the settlement, but in recent years one was found associated with a farm beside the southern district.

Another very interesting discovery was that of a thermal bath building to the west of the village. It was built in late antiquity and has all the facilities normally found in Roman buildings of this kind.

Scholars who visited the Negev in the early years of the twentieth century were tentatively aware of the line of a surrounding wall, and this has now been thoroughly established, thanks to excavations carried out by Peter Fabian. Some small towers have been discovered in the system of walls, and a date of the fifth century has been suggested for the whole.

Avdat, acropolis, southern church or church of Saint Theodore, second half of the fifth century

Mamshit, third-century Roman fresco with Eros and Psyche, found in a Nabataean dwelling

One of the great attractions of Avdat is a military fort measuring about 100 meters square and lying 300 meters northeast of the acropolis. This fort has been variously dated by scholars, who have been unable to reach a consensus even after several excavation campaigns. The theory that it was a Nabataean fort has been completely discarded, and it is now thought to have been founded in the years immediately following the conquest of the Nabataean kingdom by the forces of Trajan. Tali Erickson-Gini, on the other hand, thinks it was built at the time of Diocletian. It must have been able to accommodate a military unit of about five hundred men.

Haluza (Elusa) lies about 21 kilometers southwest of modern Beersheba, at an elevation of about 230 meters. Because it is so near modern towns such as Gaza, the site has been extensively looted over the course of time: Even the stonework from its houses has been taken for use as building material.

As we have noted, Haluza is the only Negev town to have acquired the status of city, in late antiquity. Although situated in an arid place and surrounded by desert, Haluza grew in the course of the centuries from a small trading station to a town of some importance, with a population estimated at about 10,500. A number of rhetoricians who were friends of the famous intellectual Libanius of Antioch taught in this town, which even acquired a small theater in the southwest quarter: Excavations have revealed its remains. An inscription records that new surfacing work was carried out on the road leading to the theater in 454/55 under the supervision of an eminent citizen named Zenobius Abramius, who was probably a descendant of the Zenobius of Elusa who was Libanius's teacher.

At least four churches were built at Elusa, but only the cathedral, in the southwest quarter of the town, has been excavated. It is the largest church in the whole of the Negev. It has a basilican ground plan with a nave and two side aisles, and columns forming arches stretched the whole length of the building. Wooden beams set above the arches served as a base for the gallery floor. The gallery ceiling was supported by a row of columns that were slimmer than the columns below. The building was very richly ornamented: It was paved and its aisles were faced with imported marble, as were the columns supporting Corinthian capitals, while the aisles themselves had a white mosaic pavement.

It still remains to be proved whether the town was surrounded by a proper wall, but some four-room towers have been found along the city perimeter. One of these towers still stands today to a height of 10 meters.

Mamshit (also called Mampsis or Kurnub) is situated 5 kilometers southwest of the modern town of Dimona. In antiquity it was at the intersection of several important roads, one of them leading from the coast via Beersheba to Mamshit and then on to the Dead Sea. Anyone traveling north or south between Judea and Arabah also had to pass through Mamshit. The town came into being as a caravan station in the first century A.D. Some buildings attributable to this period have been found, but it was only after the Roman conquest that the town developed to significant size, even acquiring some luxury dwellings with a

central courtyard and a number of rooms, and often a tower with an internal staircase as well. In all, Mamshit had twelve *insulae* containing thirty dwellings. The discovery of a military cemetery with tombs of soldiers of the III Cyrenaica legion and the I Augusta Thracum cohort shows that the Roman army must have had a garrison at Mamshit, at least for a while. Furthermore, it was almost certainly the army that in the second or third century built a system of three dams in the wadi to the west of the town. Two churches were built in late antiquity: a larger one in the southeast corner of the village, and a smaller one in the southwest. Both have single apses and mosaic paving. They may well have been built in the second half of the fourth century.

Shivta (Sobata) lies about 40 kilometers southwest of Beersheba at an elevation of 360 meters. The site is relatively well preserved, with recognizable streets and outer limits. It is an outstanding example of a late-antique village built with an irregular urban plan. The alignment of the streets was planned before construction of the various houses in the inhabited area, with the efficient collection of rainwater in mind. Water was channeled along the streets, within the courtyards, and off the roofs of houses. Shivta has a main street crossing the village from south to north, and three churches: one for each area of the village. The northern and southern churches have been dated to the end of the fourth century, while the central church is a much later building, dating to the late sixth or early seventh century.

Nizzana (Nessana) is situated 52 kilometers southwest of Beersheba, at a height of 250 meters above sea level, on the road that links the central Negev and the Sinai. The site extends over a flat eastern area and a western area that rises rapidly from the banks of Wadi Azouz until it forms what is effectively an acropolis. A fort can be seen on the acropolis, as well as two churches: one to the north and the other to the south. The northern church is dedicated to Saints Sergius and Bacchus. It has a single apse and is paved with polychrome marble fragments; it is surrounded by chapels, a baptistery, and various rooms and must have been founded before 464, because it contains an inscription with that date. The southern church, dedicated to Mary, is smaller and of later date. It has three apses and was built toward the end of the period of Roman

View of the Mamshit site

On p. 174: Mamshit, northern church, baptistery

On p. 175, above: Mamshit, southern church, apse

On p. 175, below: Mamshit, remains of a Nabataean dwelling

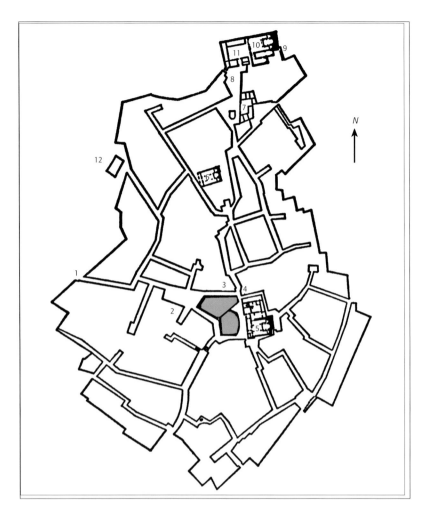

Plan of Shivta

1 *Modern entry*

2 *House*

3 *Double cistern*

4 *Cistern*

5 *Southern church*

6 *Central church*

7 *Winepress*

8 *Square*

9 *Water-distribution hut*

10 *Northern church*

11 *Atrium*

12 *Winepress*

*Opposite: Shivta, southern
church, cross-shaped
baptismal font*

occupation. The fort is a rectangular structure measuring 35 by 85 meters. It has five square towers with various rooms along their east and west sides. During the closing stage of its occupation, when the military unit stationed at Nizzana left, the building must have been used for habitation.

The lower part of the village was badly damaged by the Turks at the beginning of the twentieth century, and as far as one can gather from the reports of scholars who were working at that time, it must have consisted primarily of dwellings; but churches were also found. In 1989, thanks to new excavations supported by Ben Gurion University of the Negev, a church with a nave and two side aisles was found. Researchers established that the acropolis and lower town were linked by a flight of steps, and that houses had been built along the slope.

Nessana must have been a caravan station for the Sinai desert, and although it already existed in late Hellenistic times, it only really developed in late antiquity, especially from the fifth century onward. The site is famous above all because it was the subject of a research mission led by H. D. Colt in 1935–37, during which numerous papyri were discovered, mostly in Greek and dating to between 512 and 689. The papyri represent various kinds of documents, such as deeds of marriage, divorce, inheritance, and sale, as well as tax receipts and also literary texts, including fragments of Virgil's *Aeneid*. In addition, some of the papyri contain documents relating to Arab administration.

It seems likely that Rehoboth began life as a simple stopping place between Haluza and Nizzana on the road to Sinai. In late antiquity it became a fairly extensive village with a population calculated at about thirty-five hundred, based on the size of the inhabited area. Rehoboth therefore must have been second in size only to Haluza.

The village gradually spread out from a nucleus that included what is known as the central church. There is no sign of a regular plan in this early center, but in the new quarters into which the population spread, there are signs of aligned streets, with intersections at right angles.

Except for the central church, all churches were built in the village outskirts or even beyond the inhabited area. The central church has a single apse and dates to the late fourth or early fifth century. Archaeological excavations carried out in the 1970s concentrated on the northern church, which is three-apsed, contains chapels, and has a very large atrium at the front. It was built in the second half of the fifth century.

Sa'adon is situated nine kilometers southwest of Haluza. It is the smallest village we know of in the Negev, but it is also the one in which the street alignment is most nearly regular throughout the inhabited area. It has not been much studied by archaeologists, but they have noted the existence of two churches, which are smaller than those in other Negev towns. A building discovered to the south of the southern church seems to be a basilica, whose atrium is larger than those of the two churches.

Synagogues, Churches, and Monasteries

Remains of the Gamla synagogue

Opposite: Entrance to the Baram synagogue

Synagogues

The Jewish synagogue, or "place of assembly," already existed in the Hellenistic period, as we can tell from archaeological discoveries in Egypt, among other places. In Second Temple times, we find mention of synagogues in Palestine and beyond, with the New Testament being one of our richest sources of information. It should be remembered that in those days the purpose of the synagogue was different from what it was later. As long as the Temple existed, specifically religious functions—especially sacrifice and prayer—could

take place only in the Temple, while the synagogue served for public readings from the Torah and the prophets, and for study.

Of the many synagogues in existence in Second Temple times, only five have been identified with certainty as a result of archaeological excavations. One of these, dating to the first century B.C., forms part of the Hasmonean complex at Jericho; another has been excavated at Gamla, a small town in southern Golan that was destroyed during the Great Revolt; and two more have been identified in the fortresses of Masada and Herodion, where the Zealots made their last stand after the fall of Jerusalem. A fifth has recently been discovered, at Modiin. These synagogues have several characteristics in common: They are rectangular, peristylar halls with steps along three or four sides for use as seats. A flat roof rested on columns, and in some cases it is possible to identify a niche used for storing Torah scrolls. Other rooms were attached to the halls, but the whole structure did not have the monumental appearance that later synagogues do, nor was there any special orientation relative to the cardinal directions. One characteristic feature was the water supply for an attached ritual bath or a bath for ablutions. In the case of Masada and Herodion, the halls used as synagogues originally had some other purpose (as a triclinium at Herodion, and probably a stable at Masada) and were altered by adding whatever was required:

benches, a ritual bath (at Herodion), or a storage place for Torah scrolls. At Masada, it was possible to identify the hall as a synagogue thanks to the discovery of a *genizah* (a storage place for religious books that are no longer in use) under the floor.

However, most of the synagogues discovered in Palestine belong to the late-Roman or Byzantine period, or in some cases the proto-Islamic period. Their geographical distribution clearly reflects the distribution of the Jewish population in the late-antique period, which we know partly from literary sources. The greatest number of synagogues is found in eastern Galilee (whereas western Galilee is almost exclusively occupied by churches, and all traces of the Jewish population that lived there in the early centuries A.D. have disappeared), throughout Lower Galilee, in Golan, the Jordan Valley, southern Judea, the coastal plain, and the northern Negev. A number of Samaritan synagogues have been discovered in recent years in Samaria: at the border between Samaria and Judea and on Mount Carmel. They appeared toward the end of the third or fourth century, and do not seem to have

survived beyond the sixth. During this last period, the Samaritans were cruelly persecuted by the Byzantine authorities and lost a large proportion of their rural population in various revolts. For later periods, there are traces of Samaritan places of assembly and worship only in the Shechem area and on Mount Gerizim, where a small Samaritan community lives to this day.

The first monumental synagogues appear in the late-Roman period, around the third century. Scholars do not concur on the initial date or origins of what is apparently the earliest synagogue type and the most widespread in Galilee and Golan: a rectangular building, divided into aisles by two rows of columns, or three rows in the larger buildings (in the latter case, the third row is parallel to the back wall of the synagogue). The facade has three entrances, is richly decorated with architectural features, and usually faces toward Jerusalem. The buildings have two stories, and the rows of columns support galleries used as a matroneum (married women's area). Among the most splendid examples of this type of synagogue are those at Capernaum (see revelant chapter), Chorazin, and Meron. Later on, a syna-

gogue type develops with a basilican ground plan, much like a church's. As with churches, these synagogues have an apse, a narthex, and an atrium and floors richly decorated with mosaics. The apse, often separated from the nave by a balustrade, faces toward Jerusalem; it serves as a focal point for readings from the Torah and the recital of prayers, which have now become part of the liturgy. In synagogues with a basilican ground plan, the columns support upper-story galleries for the use of women. Among the most beautiful examples of this type of synagogue are the one at Gaza (see revelant chapter), whose mosaic floor bears the date "Loos [July–August] 509"; that of Beth Alpha at Beth Shean, where the floor can be dated from an inscription belonging to the reign of Justinus (probably Justinus I, 518–527, rather than Justinus II, 565–578); and the one at Jericho, built in the late sixth or early seventh century. Various transitional forms between the Galilean and basilican types can be found that are coeval with the other types.

One type of synagogue that is more common in the south of Judea also has a rectangular ground plan but is arranged "sideways": that is, with the long side—often with an apse—facing Jerusalem. In this case, too, the building has something resembling a narthex on the side opposite the apse, and occasionally an atrium as well, also arranged sideways. The floors are decorated with mosaics.

Synagogues were usually very richly decorated. In Galilee and Golan we see an abundance of sculpted architraves with plant motifs or animal figures (lions or eagles), as well as cornices in low relief, shells above the windows, and very ornate capitals and other architectural features. In Byzantine synagogues, one also finds balustrades decorated in relief with vine tendrils and Jewish cultic motifs, and dedicatory inscriptions as well. All these are features that can also be found in contemporary churches, mutatis mutandis (i.e., with crosses instead of Jewish motifs). The floor mosaics—commonest toward the south of Lower Galilee—make much use of geometric and vegetable motifs and garlands, but they also often have favorite subjects, especially the *aron haqodesh* (cupboard for sacred scrolls), portrayed to resemble the Temple facade, with a triangular tympanum supported on columns, and a tied

Opposite: Facade of the Baram synagogue

Remains of the Chorazin synagogue

Detail of a floor mosaic in the En Gedi synagogue

Opposite: Floor mosaic in the Beth Alpha synagogue. The mosaic is divided into three panels: the first shows the Tabernacle of the Torah, the second shows the wheel of the zodiac, and the third, nearest the entrance, shows the Sacrifice of Isaac.

curtain to protect the door. At the side are representations of two menorahs and various cultic objects, especially the shofar (ram's horn), the lulab (palm branch), and the ethrog (citron), used particularly during Sukkoth ceremonies. Sometimes two facing lions are shown beside the *aron haqodesh*. Sometimes the menorah appears on it own (not only in mosaics, but also engraved on door jambs and capitals), and examples have been found of menorahs sculpted in the round. Another favorite subject is the zodiac with Helios at the center. This was seen not as a pagan motif but as a symbol of time, the seasons, and the eternal movement of the heavens, and therefore as a symbol of divine power. In the Byzantine period, the prohibition against the representation of images was largely abandoned, so biblical scenes could also be represented on synagogue floors. At Beth Alpha one finds the Sacrifice of Isaac; David appears at both Gaza and Meroth in Galilee; Noah's Ark is at Gerasa in Jordan; and Daniel is represented at Khirbet Suseya in southern Judea and at Na'aran near Jericho. In the synagogue discovered a few years ago at Sepphoris there is an entire cycle of Bible stories: the consecration of Aaron in the service of the Tabernacle and the daily sacrifice; the offering of loaves and first fruits; the Sacrifice of Isaac; and the angels visiting Abraham and Sarah to announce the birth of Isaac. Also depicted are the zodiac with the chariot of the sun at the center, surrounded by human figures representing the astrological signs and the seasons; lions; *aron haqodesh*; and so on. It appears that the taste for figurative art—once it was permitted—went beyond biblical scenes, for there is a building at Beth Shean, which functioned at least in part as a synagogue, with a mosaic floor portraying Ulysses and the sirens, and a Nilotic landscape. As in the case of the Orpheus in a Christian chapel at Jerusalem, the pagan subject was reinterpreted to convey a moral message (in the case of Ulysses, the human spirit resisting the temptations of physical pleasure), making it suitable for a religious setting.

Inscriptions are frequently found in synagogues, as in churches. In synagogues they are expressed in Greek or Aramaic, and for the most part they commemorate donors' offerings or community involvement in the construction, decoration, or restoration of the building concerned. However, we need to take note of two unusual inscriptions, both in Aramaic. In the synagogue at Rehov, south of Beth Shean, there is an early-seventh-century mosaic floor with a long quotation from the Jerusalem Talmud about rules for a sabbatical year. During such a year, which came around every seven years, the Jews were forbidden to cultivate the land and eat the fruits that it produced. However, this rule applied only within the borders of the land of Israel reoccupied after the Babylonian exile, and then only in the areas effectively occupied by Jews. It was therefore necessary to draw up a detailed list of "permitted" areas (those occupied by non-Jews, whose fruits could be eaten during a sabbatical year) and "forbidden" areas (that is, Jewish areas, whose fruits could not be eaten). The inscription thus served to remind the members of the community where they could and could not obtain supplies of food, without having to consult books. The text of this inscription is extremely important, because it preserves some passages not included in the Talmud, and it supplies the correct spelling of a large number of geographical names that have come down to us in distorted forms through the long textual tradition of the Talmud.

There is another particularly interesting inscription in the synagogue at En Gedi. This village lies in a little oasis on the shore of the Dead Sea. It was inhabited solely by Jews, who applied themselves to the cultivation of the resin *opobalsamon* (balsam), a basic ingredient in the preparation of medicines and perfumes. The village was apparently destroyed and abandoned around the mid-sixth century, and the secret of how to cultivate this precious plant—known only to the local Jews—was lost, together with the plant itself, which is now extinct. An inscription in Aramaic in the synagogue contains a curse on anyone who "causes dissension in the community, provides false information about his neighbor to the Gentiles, robs his neighbor, or reveals the secrets of the town." This last phrase may refer to the secret of the manufacture of

opobalsamon, on which the prosperity of the village depended.

The Samaritan synagogues mentioned above have been identified as such only in recent years, and almost solely because of their geographical position, since they have so many points in common with Jewish synagogues. They, too, have rectangular halls with seating steps along the walls, and they, too, have mosaic floors with cultic motifs well known among the Jews: menorahs, *aron haqodesh*, the shofar, the "bread table" on which offerings were made in the sanctuary, and the incense shovel. But there are no human or animal figures, because the Samaritans observed the prohibition against images far more strictly than the Jews. In the Samaritan synagogues, too, we find dedicatory inscriptions in Greek. Judging from the buildings that have been investigated so far, it appears that they were oriented toward Mount Gerizim. It also appears that the

Samaritans preferred to situate their synagogues outside the urban area, or at least on its edges, unlike the Jews, who usually chose a central site and, whenever possible, the highest point in the village. Perhaps this preference was due to the strict observance of the commandments by the Samaritans, which led them to choose for their synagogues places that were protected as much as possible from contact with daily activities. The two best-explored synagogues are those at el-Khirbe, near Samaria-Sebaste, and at Khirbet Samara, a few kilometers farther northwest.

Churches and monasteries

The first Christians certainly had places where they assembled (*ecclesiae*), but archaeology has not found any traces of them, except perhaps for the so-called House of Saint Peter at Capernaum (see above). It is not clear what these primitive churches looked like, and how they were

The Mar Saba monastery in
the Kidron Valley

different from other buildings. There is a story told by Epiphanius, a monk of Jewish origin who came from southern Judea and subsequently became bishop of Salamina in Cyprus, which illustrates this difficulty. In the second half of the fourth century—a time when there were already many conventional churches in Palestine— Epiphanius was on his way to Jerusalem when he stopped one evening at a village. He saw the light of a lamp, and when he asked what it meant, he was told it was a church. Epiphanius went in to pray and was greatly scandalized to find a curtain there on which was painted an image of Christ and a saint. Being very conscious of the fact that making images was forbidden, he rushed to tear down the curtain, ignoring the protests of the villagers, who insisted that he buy them another one. It is clear from this story that the "church" was just like an ordinary house except for the lighted lamp and the curtain protecting the altar, and indeed in mosaic representations of sacred buildings on church floors in subsequent centuries, a constant feature is the lamp glimpsed through a window, sometimes with the corner of a curtain waving in the breeze.

The earliest monumental churches in Palestine were built in the time of Constantine. As we pointed out above, it was he who had the Anastasis and the Martyrium built on the site of the Holy Sepulcher, the Church of the Nativity at Bethlehem, and another church at Mambre, on the spot where the oak and well of Abraham were venerated. And other churches were built at Jerusalem during the time of the Constantinian dynasty (see relevant chapter). Even at this early stage we find two types of ecclesiastical buildings: the basilica and the martyrium. The Christian basilica derives from the Roman civic basilica, a rectangular building divided into three aisles by two rows of columns, with an apse on one of the short sides. The Christian basilica normally had the apse at the east end and the entrance (usually a central door with others on either side of it) at the opposite end; in front of the doors was an atrium, usually colonnaded and with an underground cistern. The basic basilican ground plan gradually acquired new

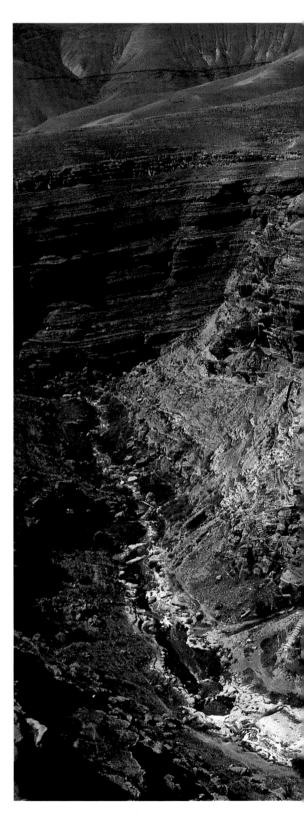

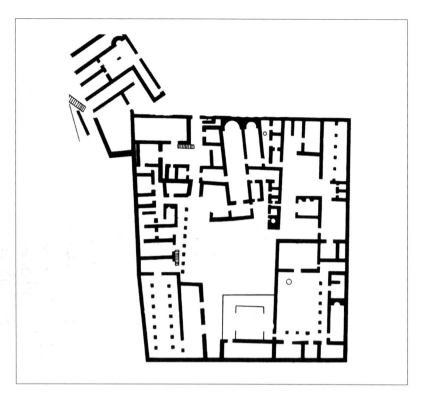

known Western type of basilica with a transept is very rare in Palestine. As a narthex or side rooms were introduced, the position of the entrance sometimes changed, and it might now appear in the north or south side, depending on the topography of the site and how the building fitted into the local urban framework.

A martyrium is a church with a central plan. It may be round or hexagonal, and it is built around a focal point that is some sort of venerated site. The name "martyrium" derives from the fact that such a site was usually a tomb: the sepulcher of Christ, or the tomb of a martyr. A number of churches with this ground plan were built in the fifth century, the earliest being the Cathisma Church between Jerusalem and Bethlehem. It was built around the rock where Mary allegedly sat to rest on her way to Bethlehem: In the middle of the church a piece of rock has been left bare to indicate the venerated spot. The same principle was applied in the construction of the Church of the Ascension (now a mosque) on the Mount of Olives, and it is interesting to note that the Muslim Dome of the Rock, built on the Temple esplanade at the spot where Mohammad rose to heaven, is constructed in the same way, having a polygonal ground plan around a piece of bare rock. A hexagonal ground plan was also chosen for the late-fifth-century Church of Mary Mother of God on Mount Gerizim, though there was no spot venerated by Christians on the mountain.

The churches that have been explored archaeologically are rarely preserved above the level of their foundations. This is because once the building was abandoned, the walls were systematically dismantled and the blocks of stone reused for other buildings. Only in parts of the country with a low population density, such as the Negev desert, or in fairly remote areas of the Galilee mountains, does one find churches whose walls have survived up to a certain height, despite the fact that the frequent earthquakes in the region have caused a good deal of destruction. But even where walls have been destroyed to below floor level, it is possible to identify the ground plan of the church thanks to its mosaic floors. The custom of paving floors with mosaics

features: a narthex separated the atrium from the church; spaces were introduced on each side of the apse, later developing into two side apses of smaller dimensions than the central apse; chapels and service rooms were introduced, as well as a baptistery and a burial crypt. The well-

was very widespread in the Byzantine period, and there were numerous flourishing schools in Palestine for artists who worked in a particular area. Their styles can be recognized in the various monuments. It is also worth pointing out that the same artists worked in both churches and synagogues, and many of the decorative motifs found in churches can also be found in synagogues.

A church floor was usually divided into a number of "carpets": one or more in the nave, one or more in the aisles, and smaller panels between columns. The narthex was often floored with mosaics as well, but less richly, while the floor of the atrium was usually made of stone slabs. Each of the various mosaic "carpets" had a different motif. Geometric patterns are commonest in aisles and narthex (though figurative panels may also be found, as at the Kissufim church). More elaborate patterns are often found in the nave. The commonest of these is a vine emerging from an amphora, often near the central entrance to the church, with its tendrils forming medallions in which figures of all kinds are inserted: vignettes with scenes of the hunt or the grape harvest, animals, and various objects. There is a fine example in the church at Horvat Beer Shema in the northwest Negev: One of the medallions here contains the figure of a woman and child thought to represent Hagar and Ishmael, who, according to the Bible story, were sent away by Abraham into the desert in this very area.

Hundreds of Byzantine churches have been found in the region between the Mediterranean and the river Jordan. The only areas that are relatively poor in that respect are eastern Galilee and Golan, where settlements were primarily Jewish, and Samaria. The population here was Samaritan, especially in rural areas, and Christianity only penetrated into cities with bishops (Samaria-Sebaste and Neapolis), along the edges of the territory and along the main roads, where we find monasteries rather than village churches.

There are a great many monasteries in Palestine. The most important city churches had attached monasteries whose members saw to the daily liturgy. There were also many monasteries in outlying areas and in some villages. Country monasteries seem to have been much less plentiful in Palestine than in Syria, for example: In the fifth century, Christians were still not the majority of the population, and even in the sixth century the non-Christians—Jews, Samaritans, Manicheans, and others—were numerous. But the majority of monastic foundations were in the Judean desert and along the Jordan; many pilgrims came to this region to worship at the holy places and decided to settle there to live a life of prayer. In the desert to the south, east, and northeast of Jerusalem, more than seventy monasteries are attested. Many of them have been identified, in that we know the names of their founders and many of the circumstances surrounding their history, thanks both to various hagiographic sources and to the narratives of pilgrims who visited them for centuries, up to and beyond the Middle Ages.

We know of two types of monasteries in the desert: the cenoby and the laura. In a cenoby, the monks lived together and observed a rule established by their founder, which generally involved seven hours of daily prayer: midnight prayer; morning prayer at dawn; tierce, sext, and nones (at about 9 a.m., noon, and 3 p.m., respectively); vespers before dinner; and compline after sunset, before retiring to bed. The monks ate their one or two meals a day together and devoted many hours to physical labor, both in running the monastery and in the various activities by which they made a living. (Most monasteries were not self-sufficient, depending in part on offerings from pilgrims and assets brought by the monks themselves when they entered the community.) The monastery itself was a compact complex, generally consisting of a building surrounded by a wall, often with a tower, and having an internal courtyard from which one reached the church, the refectory, and various service buildings. Monastery churches were different from others in that they usually had a single nave without columns, and no narthex. In a number of cases a monastery church was built inside a natural cave, which could be roughly adapted for liturgical use by cutting into the rock, building a wall or two, and laying a mosaic floor. The monks' dormitories were usually on the second floor and have

Opposite, above: Plan of the monastery of Martyrius
1 Refectory
2 Kitchen
3 Bathroom
4 Eighth-century animal enclosure
5 Portico
6 Chapel
7 Courtyard
8 Courtyard
9 Burial cave
10 Chapel
11 Burial chamber
12 Chapel
13 Storeroom
14 Blocked entry
15 Chapel
16 Church
17 Niche for rolling stone
18 Chapel

Opposite, below: Remains of the monastery of Saint Martyrius

therefore not survived. One of the most important structures in a cenoby was the system for
collecting and saving rainwater, for most of these
monasteries did not have springs available. Desert
monks became so skilled in this art that they had
water available not just for drinking but also for
irrigating kitchen gardens and orchards.

A laura, on the other hand, was a monastery
of hermits. Each monk lived in his cell for five or
six days a week, working and praying on his own.
Prayer times were announced acoustically: A
length of wood was struck by the monk whose job
it was to supervise the liturgy. Only on Sundays—
and on Saturdays or part of Saturdays as well in
some lauras—did the monks gather in church to
listen to Mass and receive Communion, after
which they had a communal meal. Each year, a
few monks were chosen to carry out the tasks
necessary for the survival of the community: A
bursar took charge of hospitality and cooking,
and a muleteer made necessary purchases and
sold the fruits of the monks' labors (usually rope
or baskets made of woven palm leaves). All these
positions—except for that of the hegumen, or
head—were temporary, however, so that they did
not interfere overly with the life of isolation that
the monks had chosen. The physical structure of a
laura was quite different from that of a cenoby. Its
nucleus was a church and a few service buildings,
and the rest was a scattering of cells anywhere
from a few dozen to a few hundred meters apart.
The cells were linked by paths; in fact, the word
laura apparently derives from the Greek word for
"path." Each cell or group of cells had a cistern for
collecting rainwater. Lauras were generally
founded in inaccessible gorges, partly by making
use of natural caves and partly by building cells,
which were usually fairly spacious, consisting of
at least two rooms. Every slope available between
the cells was terraced and cultivated as a kitchen
garden by the individual monks.

The first monasteries in the Judean desert
were three lauras founded in the first half of the
fourth century by Saint Chariton. According to
legend, Saint Chariton came to Jerusalem on a
pilgrimage from Iconium (Konya in southern
Turkey) and was kidnapped by bandits near

Pharan, on the way to Jericho. But being miracu-
lously freed and left in possession of his captors'
treasure, he used this wealth to build a church in
the bandits' own cave. Here he settled and began
preaching. He converted the local population to
Christianity, gathered together a group of disciples, and taught them the basic rules of life in
a laura. Later on Saint Chariton left En Farah
(Pharan) and founded two more lauras: one on a
ridge of the mountains overlooking Jericho (the
Laura of Douka), and the second, called the
Souka Laura or Old Laura, in the gorge near
Teqoa, now called Wadi Khareitun.

In the first half of the fifth century, another
pilgrim came to En Farah. This was Euthymius,
who came from Melitene in eastern Turkey. After
spending a few years here, he and his friend
Theoctistus founded a cenoby in the wild gorge
of Wadi Mukellik, to the south of the road to
Jericho. Later on, Euthymius founded two more
monasteries, a cenoby and a laura, and he trained
a generation of disciples who went on to found
other monasteries. The most famous of these disciples was Sabbas, another Cappodocian, who
founded a great number of cenobies and lauras
not only in the Judean desert but in other parts of
Palestine as well. The most important of his foundations is the Great Laura, now called Mar Saba,
in the Kidron Valley, which has continued to be
inhabited with few interruptions to this day. Its
present appearance reflects the reconstruction
and rebuilding work of later centuries, but the
original sixth-century cells can still be seen in the
surrounding gorge.

Only a few of the desert monasteries have been
the subject of archaeological exploration. One of
the most splendid is the cenoby of Martyrius, now
in the little town of Meale Adummim. Martyrius
was a disciple of Euthymius and founded his
monastery after leaving Euthymius's laura, whose
cells were too cramped and uncomfortable for
him. After becoming patriarch of Jerusalem some
years later, Martyrius evidently devoted a great deal
of care and money to enlarging and embellishing
his foundation, making it one of the principal
cenobies in the Jerusalem area. The monastery has
three churches and a large refectory (all decorated

with splendid mosaics), baths, stables and service rooms, enormous water cisterns, and a hostel annex for pilgrims. The building had two floors, and the monks' living quarters were on the upper floor.

Another important monastery in the area is that of Saint George in Wadi Qelt, which, like Mar Saba, is still inhabited today. This monastery embodies a particular type, of which there are various examples in the desert near the river Jordan. In the center was a cenoby that housed the novices and the monks who performed various services, as well as others who preferred the cenobite life, and near the cenoby was a laura where the more experienced monks lived in solitude, joining the cenobites on Sundays for Mass and a communal meal. The Wadi Qelt laura was abandoned as early as the time of the Persian invasion in the early seventh century, when it became dangerous for the hermits to live beyond the protection of the cenoby walls. Today only the nucleus of the monastery is inhabited, but a few dozen years ago hermits lived for a time in the isolated cells. Here, too, as at Mar Saba, the current appearance of the monastery reflects modern reconstruction work, but the original Byzantine structures can easily be identified in various parts of the building.

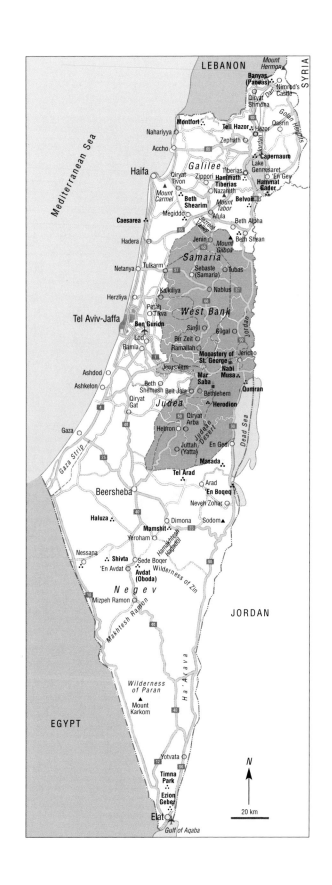

Bibliography

Abbreviations

ANRW = *Aufstieg und Niedergang der römischen Welt* (Berlin and New York)

BASOR = *Bulletin of the American Schools of Oriental Research*

IEJ = *Israel Exploration Journal*

JRA = *Journal of Roman Archaeology*

JRS =*Journal of Roman Studies*

NEAEHL = E. Stern, ed., *The New Encyclopedia of Archaeological Excavations in the Holy Land*, 4 vols. (Jerusalem, 1993)

SCI = *Scripta Classica Israelica*

TIR = Y. Tsafrir, L. Di Segni, and J. Green, *Tabula Imperii Romani. Judaea-Palaestina. Maps and Gazetteer* (Jerusalem, 1994)

ZPE = *Zeitschrift für Papyrologie und Epigraphik*

Jewish Origins

Dever, W. G., *What Did the Biblical Authors Know and When Did They Know It?* (Grand Rapids, MI, 2001).

Freedman, D. N., ed., *The Anchor Bible Dictionary* (New York, 1992).

Friedman, R. E., *Who Wrote the Bible?* (New York, 1987).

Hayes, J. H., and J. M. Miller, eds., *Israelite and Judaean History* (London, 1977).

Roman Judea and Palestine

On the Jews and their land

Abel, F. M., *Géographie de la Palestine* (Paris, 1933–38).

Alon, G., *The Jews in Their Land in the Talmudic Age* (Jerusalem, 1980).

Avi-Yonah, M., *The Jews of Palestine: A Political History from the Bar Kokhba War to the Arab Conquest* (Oxford, 1976).

Boccaccini, G., *Middle Judaism: Jewish Thought 300 B.C.E.–200 C.E.* (Minneapolis, 1991).

Cohen, S., *The Beginning of Jewishness* (Berkeley, 1999).

Horbury, W., W. D. Davies, and J. Sturdy, eds., *The Cambridge History of Judaism. 3: The Early Roman Period* (Cambridge, 1999).

Kuhnen, H. P., *Palästina in griechisch-römischen Zeit* (Munich, 1990).

Sacchi, P., *Storia del secondo Tempio, Israele tra VI secolo a.C. e I secolo d.C.* (Turin, 1994).

Safrai, S., and M. Stern, eds., *The Jewish People in the First Century* (Assen, 1974–76).

Schäfer, P., *The History of the Jews in Antiquity: The Jews of Palestine from Alexander the Great to the Arab Conquest* (Luxembourg, 1995).

Schürer, E., *The History of the Jewish People in the Age of Jesus Christ*, rev. and ed. by G. Vermes, M. Black, and F. Millar (Edinburgh, 1973).

Schwartz, S., *Imperialism and Jewish Society, 200 B.C.E. to 640 A.D.* (Princeton and Oxford, 2001).

Smallwood, E. M., *The Jews under Roman Rule* (Leiden, 1976).

Sperber, D., *The City in Roman Palestine* (Oxford, 1998).

On Jewish rights within the imperial framework, and cultural relations between Judaism and Hellenism

Baltrusch, E., *Die Juden und das Römische Reich* (Darmstadt, 2002).

Belayche, N., *Iudaea-Palaestina: The Pagan Cults in Roman Palestine (2nd to 4th Century)* (Tübingen, 2001).

Ben Zeev, M., *Jewish Rights in the Roman World* (Tübingen, 1998).

Bickerman, E., *The Jews in the Greek Age* (London, 1988).

Edwards, D. R., *Religion and Society in Roman Palestine: Old Questions, New Approaches* (London and New York, 2003).

Feldman, L., *Jew and Gentile in the Ancient World: Attitudes and Interactions from Alexander to Justinian* (Princeton, 1993).

Geiger, J., "Local Patriotism in the Hellenistic Cities of Palestine," in A. Kasher, U. Rappaport, and G. Fuks, eds., *Greece and Rome in Eretz Israel* (Jerusalem, 1990), pp. 141–50.

Gruen, E. S., *Heritage and Hellenism: The Reinvention of Jewish Tradition* (Berkeley, 1998).

Hengel, M., *Judaism and Hellenism: Studies in Their Encounter in Palestine during the Early Hellenistic Period* (London, 1974).

Juster, J., *Les Juifs dans l'empire romain* (Paris, 1914).

Rabello, A. M., "The Legal Condition of the Jews in the Roman Empire," *ANRW* 2, 13 (Berlin and New York, 1980), pp. 662–762.

Tcherikover, V., *Hellenistic Civilization and the Jews*, 2d ed. (New York, 1982).

An indispensable work on literary sources about the Jews

Stern, M., *Greek and Latin Authors on Jews and Judaism*, 3 vols. (Jerusalem, 1974–84).

Commentary on the most important inscription sources

Boffo, L., *Iscrizioni greche e latine per lo studio della Bibbia* (Brescia, 1994).

On the Maccabees and Hasmoneans

Bar Kochva, B., *Judas Maccabeus: The Jewish Struggle against the Seleucids* (Cambridge, 1989).

Bickerman, E. J., *Der Gott der Makkabäer* (Berlin, 1937).

Derfler, S. L., *Hasmonean Revolt: Rebellion or Revolution* (Lewiston, ME, 1990).

Efron, J., *Studies on the Asmonean Period* (Leiden, 1987).

Gera, D., *Judaea and Mediterranean Politics: 219–162 B.C.* (Leiden, 1997).

Millar, F., "The Background to the Maccabean Revolution," *Journal of Jewish Studies* 29 (1978), pp. 1–21.

Sievers, J., *The Hasmoneans and Their Supporters* (Atlanta, 1990).

On the arrival of the Romans in Judea
Shatzman, I., "The Integration of Judaea into the Roman Empire," *SCI* 18 (1999), pp. 49–84.

On Herod the Great and his descendants
Gabba, E., "The Finances of King Herod," in A. Kasher, U. Rappaport, and G. Fuks, eds., *Greece and Rome in Eretz Israel* (Jerusalem, 1990), pp. 160–68.

Hoehner, H. W., *Herodes Antipas* (Cambridge, 1972).

Kokkinos, N., *The Herodian Dynasty* (Sheffield, 1998); "Justus, Josephus, Agrippa II and His Coins," *SCI* 22 (2003), pp. 163–80.

Kushnir-Stein, A., "Agrippa I in Josephus," *SCI* 22 (2003), pp. 153–61.

Perowne, S., *The Life and Times of Herod the Great* (London, 1956).

Schalit, A., *König Herodes: Der Mann und sein Werk* (Berlin, 1969).

Schwartz, D. R., *Agrippa I: The Last King of Judaea* (Tübingen, 1990).

On the position of the client kings within the Roman world
Braund, D. C., *Rome and the Friendly King* (London and Canberra, 1984).

Cimma, M. R., *Reges socii et amici populi romani* (Milan, 1976).

Sullivan, R. D., *Near Eastern Royalty and Rome, 100–30 B.C.* (Toronto, 1990).

On Herod's grandiose buildings in general
Japp, S., *Die Baupolitik Herode's des Grossen. Die Bedeutung des Architectur für die Herrschaftslegitimation eines römischen Klientelkönigs* (Rahden, 2000).

Lichtenberger, A., *Die Baupolitik Herodes des Grossen* (Wiesbaden, 1999).

Netzer, E., *The Palaces of the Hasmoneans and Herod the Great* (Jerusalem, 2001).

Roller, D. W., *The Building Program of Herod the Great* (Berkeley, 1998).

On the age of Herod
Fittschen, K., and G. Foerster, eds., *Judaea and the Graeco-Roman World in the Time of Herod the Great in Light of Archaeological Evidence* (Göttingen, 1996).

On Roman administration
Momigliano, A., *Ricerche sull'organizzazione della Giudea sotto il dominio romano 63. a.C.–70 d.C.* (Bologna, 1934).

On the Pontius Pilate inscription
Alföldy, G., "Pontius Pilatus und das Tiberieum von Caesarea Maritima," *SCI* 18 (1999), pp. 85–108; "Nochmals: Pontius Pilatus und das Tiberieum von Caesarea Maritima," *SCI* 21 (2002), pp. 133–48.

Frova, A., "L'iscrizione di Ponzio Pilato a Cesarea," *Rendiconti dell'Istituto lombardo* 95 (1961), pp. 419–34.

Prandi, L., "Una nuova ipotesi sull'iscrizione di Ponzio Pilato," *Civiltà Classica e Cristiana* 2 (1981), pp. 25–35.

On Pontius Pilate
Bond, H. K., *Pontius Pilatus in History and Interpretation* (Cambridge, 1998).

Firpo, G., "Erennio Capitone e Ponzio Pilato: Due personalità a confronto," *Quadrifluus amnis. Studi di letteratura, storia, filosofia e arte offerti a Mons. C. Vona* (Chieti, 1987), pp. 235–58.

Lémonon, J. P., *Pilate et le gouvernement de la Judée. Textes et monuments* (Paris, 1981).

On John the Baptist
Lupieri, E., *Giovanni Battista fra storia e leggenda* (Brescia, 1988).

On the trial of Jesus
Amarelli, F., and F. Lucrezi, eds., *Il processo contro Gesù* (Naples, 1999).

Millar, F., "Reflections on the Trial of Jesus," *A Tribute to Geza Vermes: Essays on Jewish and Christian Literature and History*, P. R. Davies and P. T. White, eds. (Sheffield, 1990), pp. 355–81.

Winter, P., *On the Trial of Jesus*, rev. by T. A. Burkill and G. Vermes (Berlin and New York, 1974).

On the date of the Crucifixion
Kokkinos, N., "Crucifixion in A.D. 36: The Keystone for Dating the Birth of Jesus," *Chronos, Chairos, Christos: Nativity and Chronological Studies Presented to Jack Finegan*, J. Vardaman and E. M. Yamauchi, eds. (Winona Lake, IN, 1989), pp. 133–63.

On the environment in which Jesus grew up
Sanders, E. P., *Jesus and Judaism* (London, 1985).

Vermes, G., *Jesus the Jew* (London, 1973).

On Jewish society in Judea from Herod to the outbreak of the Great Revolt, relations with the Roman authorities, and internal feuding
Firpo, G., "La terminologia della resistenza giudaica antiromana in Giuseppe Flavio," *Rendiconti dell'Accademia dei Lincei*, ser. 9, 8 (1997), pp. 675–714.

Goodman, M., *The Ruling Class of Judaea* (Cambridge, 1987).

Horsley, R. A., and J. S. Hanson, *Bandits, Prophets and Messiahs: Popular Movements at the Time of Jesus* (San Francisco, 1985).

Jossa, G., *Gesù e i movimenti di liberazione della Palestina* (Brescia, 1980).

Rhoads, D. M., *Israel in Revolution: 6–74 C.E.* (Philadelphia, 1976).

On the Jewish sects
Hengel, M., *Die Zeloten* (Leiden, 1976).

Mason, S., *Flavius Josephus on the Pharisees: A Composition Critical Study* (Leiden, 1991).

Neusner, J., *The Rabbinic Traditions about the Pharisees before 70* (Leiden, 1971); *From Politics to Piety: The Emergence of Pharisaic Judaism* (Englewood Cliffs, NJ, 1973).

Saldarini, A. J., *Pharisees, Scribes and Sadducees in Palestinian Society* (Edinburgh, 1981).

Stemberger, G., *Pharisäer, Sadduzäer, Essener* (Stuttgart, 1991).

On the armies of the Herodian kings

Gracey, M., "The Armies of the Judaean Client Kings," *The Defence of the Roman and Byzantine East*, P. Freeman and D. Kennedy, eds. (Oxford, 1986), pp. 311–23.

On the Roman army in Judea

Isaac, B., and I. Roll, "Legio II Traiana in Judaea," *ZPE* 33 (1979), pp. 149–56 (republished in B. Isaac, *The Near East under Roman Rule* [Leiden, 1998], pp. 198–207).

Mor, M., "The Roman Army in Eretz Israel in the Years 70–132," *The Defence of the Roman and Byzantine East*, op. cit., pp. 575–602.

Speidel, M. P., "The Roman Army in Judaea under the Procurators," *Ancient Society* 13/14 (1982/83), pp. 233–40.

For the Great Revolt and the personality of Flavius Josephus

Berlin, A., and J. Overman, eds., *The First Jewish Revolt: Archaeology, History and Ideology* (London and New York, 2002).

Cohen, S. J. D., *Josephus in Galilee and Rome: His Vita and Development as a Historian* (Leiden, 1979).

Mason, S., ed., *Understanding Josephus* (Sheffield, 1998).

McLaren, J. S., *Power and Politics in Palestine: The Jews and the Governing of Judaea 100 B.C.–A.D. 70* (Sheffield, 1991).

Parente, F., and J. Sievers, eds., *Josephus and the History of the Greco-Roman Period: Essays in Memory of Morton Smith* (Leiden, 1994).

Price, J., *Jerusalem under Siege: The Collapse of the Jewish State, 66–70 C.E.* (Leiden, 1992).

Rajak, T., *Josephus: The Historian and His Society* (London, 1983).

Rappaport, U., "John of Gischala: From Galilee to Jerusalem," *Journal of Jewish Studies* 33 (1982), pp. 81–95.

Schwartz, S., *Josephus and Judaean Politics* (Leiden, 1990).

Troiani, L., *Commento storico al "Contro Apione"* (Pisa, 1977).

Vidal-Naquet, P., "Du bon usage de la trahison," *Josephus, De Bello Judaico*, trans. P. Savinel (Paris, 1977).

On the battle of Beth Horon

Gichon, M., "Cestius Gallus' Campaign in Judaea," *Palestine Exploration Quarterly* 113 (1981), pp. 39–62.

On the siege of Masada

Richmond, I. A., "The Roman Siege Works of Masada, Israel," *JRS* 52 (1962).

Roth, J., "The Length of the Siege of Masada," *SCI* 14 (1995), pp. 87–110.

Schulten, A., "Masada: Die Burg des Herodes und die Römischen Lager," *Zeitschrift des deutschen Palästina-Vereins* 56 (1933).

Yadin Y., *Masada: Herod's Fortress and the Zealots' Last Stand* (London, 1966).

On the world of the rabbis in imperial times and late antiquity and their contribution to the religious and political debate

Cohen, S., "The Significance of Yavneh: Pharisees, Rabbis and the End of Jewish Sectarianism," *Hebrew Union College Annuary* 55 (1984), pp. 27–53.

Hezser, C., *The Social Structure of the Rabbinic Movement in Roman Palestine* (Tübingen, 1998).

Kalmin, R., *The Sage in Jewish Society in Late Antiquity* (London and New York, 1998).

Levine, L. I., "The Jewish Patriarch (Nasi) in Third Century Palestine," *ANRW* 2, 19, 2 (Berlin and New York, 1979); *The Rabbinic Class of Roman Palestine in Late Antiquity* (Jerusalem, 1989).

Neusner, J., *From Politics to Piety*, op. cit.; *Judaism: The Evidence of the Mishnah* (Chicago, 1981).

Urbach, E. U., *The Sages: The World and Wisdom of the Rabbis of the Talmud* (Cambridge, MA, 1975).

On the monuments built in Rome after victory in the Jewish War

Alföldy, G., "Ein Bauinschrift aus dem Colosseum," *ZPE* 109 (1995), pp. 195–226.

Pfanner, M., *Der Titusbogen* (Mainz, 1983).

Yarden, L., *The Spoils of Jerusalem on the Arch of Titus: A Re-investigation* (Stockholm, 1991).

On the *fiscus iudaicus*

Goodman, M., "Nerva, the *fiscus iudaicus* and Jewish Identity," *JRS* 79 (1989), 40–44.

On the Second Jewish Revolt

Applebaum, S., *Prolegomena to the Study of the Second Jewish Revolt* (Oxford, 1976).

Eck, W., "The Bar Kokhba Revolt: The Roman Point of View" *JRS* 89 (1999), pp. 76–89.

Isaac, B., and A. Oppenheimer, "The Revolt of Bar Kokhba, Scholarship and Ideology," *Journal of Jewish Studies* 36 (1985), pp. 33–60 (republished in B. Isaac, *The Near East under Roman Rule* [Leiden, 1998], pp. 220–56).

Mildenberg, L., *The Coinage of the Bar Kochva War* (Frankfurt, 1984).

Schäfer, P., *Der Bar Kokhba-Aufstand. Studien zum zweiten jüdischen Krieg gegen Rom* (Tübingen, 1981).

———, ed., *The Bar Kokhba War Reconsidered* (Tübingen, 2003).

Yadin, Y., *Bar-Kochba: The Rediscovery of the Legendary Hero of the Last Jewish Revolt against Imperial Rome* (London and Tel Aviv, 1971).

On documents of the Trajan and Hadrian periods found in Dead Sea caves

Aramaic, Greek and Hebrew Documentary Texts from Nahal Hever and Other Sites, H. M. Cotton and A. Yardeni, eds. (Oxford, 1997).

Benoit, P., J. T. Milik, and R. de Vaux, *Les grottes de Murabba'at* (Oxford, 1960).

Judean Desert Studies, *The Documents from the Bar Kochva Period in the Cave of Letters*: N. Lewis, ed., *Greek Papyri* (Jerusalem, 1989); Y. Yadin, J. C. Greenfield, A. Yardeni, and B. A. Levine, eds., *Hebrew, Aramaic and Nabataean-Aramaic Papyri* (Jerusalem, 2002).

On Roman administration

Cotton, H. M., "Some Aspects of the Roman Administration of Judaea/Syria-Palaestina," *Lokale Autonomie und romische*

Ordnungsmacht in den kaiserzeitlichen Provinzen vom 1–3 Jahrhundert, W. Eck, ed. (Munich, 1979), pp. 75–89.

Eck, W., "Zum konsularern Status von Iudaea im fruhen 2. Jh.," *Bulletin of the American Society of Papyrologists* 21 (1984), pp. 55–67.

On the position of the patriarch

Jacobs, M., *Die Institution des jüdischen Patriarchen* (Tübingen, 1995).

On the economy of Palestine

Bar, D., "Was There a 3rd-c. Economic Crisis in Palestine?" *The Roman and Byzantine Near East* 3, J. H. Humphrey, ed. (Portsmouth, RI, 2002), pp. 43–54.

Lapin, H., *Economy, Geography, and Provincial History in Later Roman Palestine* (Tübingen, 2001).

Safrai, Z., *The Economy of Roman Palestine* (London and New York, 1994).

Sperber, D., *Roman Palestine 200–400: The Land* (Ramat-Gan, 1978).

On the administrative reorganization in late-antique *Palaestina*

Mayerson, P., "Libanius and the Administration of Palestine," *ZPE* 69 (1987), pp. 251–60; "Justinian's Novel 103 and the Reorganization of Palestine," *BASOR* 269 (1988), pp. 65–71; both republished in P. Mayerson, *Monks, Martyrs, Soldiers and Saracens* (Jerusalem, 1994), pp. 284–93; 294–300.

On Christianity in Palestine

Binns, J., *Ascetics and Ambassadors of Christ: The Monasteries of Palestine, 314–631* (Oxford, 1994).

Hunt, E. D., *Holy Land Pilgrimage in the Later Roman Empire A.D. 312–460* (Oxford, 1982).

Taylor, J. E., *Christians and the Holy Places: The Myth of the Jewish-Christian Origins* (Oxford, 1993).

On the Finding of the True Cross

Dijvers, J. W., *Helena Augusta: The Mother of Constantine the Great and the Legend of Her Finding of the True Cross* (Leiden, 1992).

Walraff, M., "La croce negli storici ecclesiastici," *Mediterraneo antico* 5 (2002), pp. 469–71.

On the decline of paganism

Hohlfelder, R. L., "A Twilight of Paganism in the Holy Land," *City, Town and Countryside in the Early Byzantine Era,* R. L. Hohlfelder, ed. (New York, 1982), pp. 75–113.

Tsafrir, Y., "The Fate of Pagan Cult Places in Palestine: The Archaeological Evidence with Emphasis on Beth Shean," *Religious and Ethnic Communities in Later Roman Palestine,* H. Lapin, ed. (Bethesda, MD, 1998), pp. 197–218.

On relations between the various communities

Stemberger, G., *Juden und Christen im Heiligen Land. Palästina unter Konstantin und Theodosius* (Munich, 1987).

Stroumsa, G., "Religious Contacts in Byzantine Palestine," *Numen* 36 (1989), pp. 16–42.

On the Roman army in Palestine in late antiquity

Isaac, B. "The Army in the Late Roman East: The Persian Wars and the Defence of the Byzantine Provinces," *The Byzantine and Early Islamic Near East: 3. States, Resources and Armies,* A. Cameron, L. Conrad, and G. King, eds. (Princeton, 1995), pp. 125–55 (republished in B. Isaac, *The Roman Near East* [Leiden, 1998], pp. 437–69).

For the Samaritans and their revolts

Di Segni, L., "The Samaritans in Roman-Byzantine Palestine: Some Misapprehensions," *Religious and Ethnic Communities in Later Roman Palestine,* H. Lapin, ed. (Bethesda, MD, 1998), pp. 51–66.

Holum, K. G., "Identity and the Late Antique City: The Case of Caesarea," ibid., pp. 172–77.

Montgomery, J. A., *The Samaritans* (Philadelphia, 1907; New York, 1968).

Pummer, R., *Early Christian Authors on Samaritans and Samaritanism* (Tübingen, 2002).

The Samaritans, A. D. Crown, ed. (Tübingen, 1989).

On the Jews in the Christian emperors' legislation

Linder, A., *The Jews in Roman Imperial Legislation* (Detroit and Jerusalem, 1987).

Rabello, A. M., *Giustiniano, ebrei e samaritani* (Milan, 1987).

On Christian-Jewish relations in the seventh century

Olster, D. M., *Roman Defeat, Christian Response, and the Literary Construction of the Jew* (Philadelphia, 1994); "Letteratura apocalittica ebraica e cristiana nel VII secolo: Un raro caso di 'dialogo' ebraico-cristiano," *Gli ebrei nell'impero romano,* A. Lewin, ed. (Florence, 2001), pp. 279–93.

On the Roman-Persian wars under Heraclius, and the Arab conquest

Kaegi, W. E., *Byzantium and the Early Islamic Conquests* (Cambridge, 1992); *Heraclius, Emperor of Byzantium* (Cambridge, 2003).

The Sites

Excellent points of departure for individual sites

Archaeological Encyclopedia of the Holy Land (rev. and updated), A. Negev and S. Gibson, eds. (New York and London, 2001).

The New Encyclopedia of Archaeological Excavations in the Holy Land, E. Stern, ed. (New York, 1993).

Tsafrir, Y., L. Di Segni, and J. Green, *Tabula Imperii Romani (TIR). Iudaea-Palaestina* (Jerusalem, 1994).

Jerusalem

It is impossible to provide a detailed bibliography of Jerusalem in the Roman and Byzantine periods. The following list contains only general works, including some of the earliest modern research carried out in Jerusalem before the urban development of the late nineteenth century. For details on individual subjects or monuments, see the articles in *Reallexikon zur byzantinischen Kunst;* Ovadiah, *Corpus; NEAEHL; TIR;* Tsafrir and Safrai, *The History of Jerusalem;* and their bibliographical lists. Finally, www.archpark.org.il is a website devoted to the archaeology of Jerusalem from the time of David to the Crusades; the post-70 Roman period and the Crusade period are in course of preparation. The site also includes a panoramic view of the virtual model of the Second Temple in the Davidson Center in the archaeological park to the south of the Temple Mount in Jerusalem.

Abel, F. M., s.v. "Jérusalem," *Dictionnaire d'archéologie chrétienne et de liturgie* 7 (Paris, 1927), cols. 2304–74.

Amit, D., "New Data for Dating the High-Level Aqueduct and the Wadi el Biyar Aqueduct, and the Herodion Aqueduct," *The Aqueducts of Palestine*, D. Amit, J. Patrich, and Y. Hirschfeld, eds., *JRA* Supplementary ser. 46 (Portsmouth, RI, 2002), pp. 253–66.

Avigad, N., *Discovering Jerusalem* (Nashville, 1983).

Avi-Yonah, M., and H. Geva, s.v. "Jerusalem: The Byzantine Period," *NEAEHL* 2, pp. 768–85.

Ben Dov, M., *The Dig at the Temple Mount* (Jerusalem, 1982).

Biddle, M., *The Tomb of Christ* (London, 1999).

Bieberstein, K., and H. Bloedhorn, *Jerusalem, Grundzüge der Baugeschichte: Vom Chalkolithikum bis zur Frühzeit des osmanichen Herrschaft*, 3 vols., Beihefte zum Tübinger Atlas des Vorderen Orients, Reihe B, Geisteswissenschaften 100 (Wiesbaden, 1994).

Billig, Y., "The Low-Level Aqueduct to Jerusalem: Recent Discoveries," *Aqueducts of Palestine*, op. cit., pp. 245–52.

Bliss, F. J., and A. C. Dickie, *Excavation at Jerusalem 1894–1897* (London, 1898).

Geva, H., ed., *Ancient Jerusalem Revealed* (Jerusalem, 1994; 2000).

Geva, H., and N. Avigad, s.v. "Jerusalem: The Second Temple Period," *NEAEHL* 2, pp. 717–57.

Geva, H., and M. Avi-Yonah, s.v. "Jerusalem: The Second Roman Period," *NEAEHL* 2, pp. 758–67.

Kenyon, K. M., *Excavating 3000 Years of History* (London, 1967); *Digging up Jerusalem* (London, 1974).

Levine, L. I., *Jerusalem: A Portrait of the City in the Second Temple Period (538 B.C.E.–70 C.E.)* (Philadelphia, 2002).

Martin, G., *Jerusalem: Illustrated Historical Atlas* (London, 1994).

Mayer, L. A., and M. Avi-Yonah, "Concise Bibliography of Excavations in Palestine," *Quarterly of the Department of Antiquities in Palestine* 1 (1932), pp. 163–93.

Mazar, A., "A Survey of the Aqueducts of Jerusalem," *Aqueducts of Palestine*, op. cit., pp. 210–43.

Mazar, B., *The Excavations in the Old City of Jerusalem near the Temple Mount* 1–2 (Jerusalem, 1971).

Meiron, E., ed., *Jerusalem, a Walk through Time*, 2 vols. (Jerusalem, 1999).

Milik, J. T., "La topographie de Jérusalem vers la fin de l'époque Byzantine," *Mélanges de l'Université Saint Joseph de Beyrouth* 37 (1960–61), pp. 127–89.

Olivas, V., *The Holy City of Jerusalem: A Bibliography with Indexes* (Huntington, NY, 2001).

Ovadiah, A., *Corpus of the Byzantine Churches in the Holy Land* (Bonn, 1970), pp. 75–98, nos. 65–89.

Ovadiah, A., and C. Gomez de Silva, "Supplementum to the Corpus of the Byzantine Churches in the Holy Land (Part I)," *Levant* 13 (1981), pp. 221–25, nos. 23–28 (204–9); "Supplementum (Part II)," *Levant* 14 (1982), pp. 134–43, nos. 19–27; "Supplementum (Part III)," *Levant* 16 (1984), pp. 136–38, nos. 17–21.

Purvis, J. D., *Jerusalem, the Holy City: A Bibliography* (Metuchen, NJ, 1988).

Shiloh, Y., *Excavations at the City of David: 1. 1978–1982: Interim Report of the First Five Seasons* (*Qedem* 19) (Jerusalem, 1984).

Thomsen, P., "Die lateinischen und griechischen Inschriften der Stadt Jerusalem und ihre nächsten Umgebung," *Zeitschrift des deutschen Palästina Vereins* 43 (1920), pp. 138–58; 44 (1921), pp. 1–61, 90–168; "Nachtrag," ibid. 64 (1941), pp. 203–50.

TIR, s.v. "Hierosolyma, Ierusalem, Aelia Capitolina," pp. 145–46.

Tsafrir, Y., s.v. "Jerusalem," *Reallexikon zur byzantinischen Kunst* 3 (Stuttgart, 1975), pp. 526–615.

Tsafrir, Y., and S. Safrai, eds., *The History of Jerusalem: The Roman and Byzantine periods (70–638 C.E.)* (Jerusalem, 1999) (in Hebrew).

Tushingham, A. D., *Excavations in Jerusalem, 1961–1967* (Toronto, 1985).

Vincent, L. H., and F. M. Abel, *Jérusalem. Recherches de topographie, d'archéologie et d'histoire: 2. Jérusalem nouvelle*, 4 vols. (Paris, 1914–26).

Warren, C., *Underground Jerusalem* (London, 1876).

Warren, C., and C. R. Conder, *The Survey of Western Palestine: Jerusalem* (London, 1884).

Wilkinson, J., *Jerusalem as Jesus Knew It* (London, 1978).

Wilson, C., and C. Warren, *Recovery of Jerusalem* (London, 1871).

Yadin, Y. ed., *Jerusalem Revealed* (New Haven and Jerusalem, 1976).

Capernaum

Corbo, V., S. Loffreda, A. Spijkerman, and E. Testa, *Cafarnao*, Studium Biblicum Franciscanum, Collectio maior 19, 4 vols. (Jerusalem, 1975).

Guérin, V., *Description géographique, historique et archéologique de la Palestine: Galilée* 1 (Paris, 1880), pp. 226–39.

Loffreda, S., *Recovering Capharnaum* (Jerusalem, 1985); *Cafarnao* (Jerusalem, 1995).

Loffreda, S., and V. Tzaferis, s.v. "Capernaum," *NEAEHL* 1, pp. 291–96.

Orfali, G., *Capharnaüm et ses ruines* (Paris, 1922).

TIR, p. 97.

Tzapheres, V., et al., *Excavations at Capernaum* 1 (Winona Lake, IN, 1989).

Tiberias

Bagatti, B., *Antichi villaggi cristiani di Galilea*, Studium Biblicum Franciscanum, Collectio minor 13 (Jerusalem, 1971), pp. 48–61.

Di Segni, L., "Tiberiade romano-bizantina attraverso le sue iscrizioni," *Hebraica. Miscellanea di studi in onore di Sergio J. Sierra*, F. Israel, A. M. Rabello, and A. M. Somekh, eds. (Turin, 1998), pp. 115–63.

Dothan, M., *Hammath Tiberias* (Jerusalem, 1983); s.v. "Hammath Tiberias," *NEAEHL* 2, pp. 573–77.

Guérin, V., *Description géographique: Galilée* 1, op. cit., pp. 250–63, 270–73.

Hirschfeld, Y., *A Guide to Antiquity Sites in Tiberias* (Jerusalem, 1992); "The Anchor Church at the Summit of Mt. Berenice, Tiberias," *Biblical Archaeologist* 57, 3 (1994), pp. 122–34; "Imperial Building Activity during the Reign of Justinian and Pilgrimage to the Holy

Land in Light of the Excavations on Mt. Berenice, Tiberias," *Revue biblique* 106 (1999), pp. 236–49.

———, ed., *Tiberias* ('Idan 11) (Jerusalem, 1988) (in Hebrew).

Hirschfeld, Y., G. Foerster, and F. Vitto, *NEAEHL* 4, pp. 1464–73.

Hoehner, H. W., *Herod Antipas* (Cambridge, 1972), pp. 91–100.

TIR, pp. 138–39; 249–50.

Winogradov, Z. S., "The Aqueducts of Tiberias," *Aqueducts of Palestine*, op. cit., pp. 295–304.

Sepphoris

Di Segni, L., "Appendix: Greek Inscriptions in the Nile Festival Building," *From Dura to Sepphoris: Studies in Jewish Art and Society in Late Antiquity* (Portsmouth, RI, 2000), pp. 91–100.

Kessler, H. L., "The Sepphoris Mosaic and Christian Art," ibid., pp. 65–72.

Kühnel, B., "The Synagogue Floor Mosaic in Sepphoris: Between Paganism and Christianity," ibid., pp. 31–44.

Meyers, E. M., "Roman Sepphoris in Light of New Archaeological Evidence and Recent Research," *The Galilee in Late Antiquity*, L. I. Levine, ed. (Cambridge, MA, 1992), pp. 321–38; "Aspects of Roman Sepphoris in the Light of Recent Archaeology," *Early Christianity in Context: Monuments and Documents*, F. Manns and E. Alliata, eds. (Jerusalem, 1993).

Meyers, E. M., E. Netzer, and C. L. Meyers, *Sepphoris* (Winona Lake, IN, 1992).

Miller, S. S., *Studies in the History and Traditions of Sepphoris* (Leiden, 1984).

Rayna, G. S., "A Missing Link: Some Thoughts on the Sepphoris Mosaic," *From Dura to Sepphoris*, op. cit., pp. 45–51.

Sepphoris in Galilee: Crosscurrents of Culture, exh. cat., R. M. Nagy, ed. (Raleigh, NC, 1996).

Strange, J., "Six Campaigns at Sepphoris: The University of South Florida Excavations, 1983–1989," *The Galilee in Late Antiquity*, L. I. Levine, ed. (Cambridge, MA, 1992), pp. 339–55.

Waterman, L., *Preliminary Report on the University of Michigan Excavations at Sepphoris, Palestine* (Ann Arbor, 1937).

Weiss, Z., "The Sepphoris Synagogue Mosaic and the Role of Talmudic Literature in Its Iconographical Study," *From Dura to Sepphoris*, op. cit., pp. 15–30.

Weiss, Z., and E. Netzer, "New Evidence for Late-Roman and Byzantine Sepphoris," *The Roman and Byzantine Near East: Some Recent Archaeological Research* (Ann Arbor, 1995), pp. 162–76; *Promise and Redemption: A Synagogue Mosaic from Sepphoris* (Jerusalem, 1996).

Weiss, Z., and R. Talgam, "The Nile Festival Buildings and Its Mosaics: Mythological Representations in Early Byzantine Sepphoris," *The Roman and Byzantine Near East* 3, J. H. Humphrey, ed. (Portsmouth, RI, 2002), pp. 55–90.

Hammat Gader

Buckingham, J. S., *Travels in the Countries of Bashan and Gilead* (London, 1821).

Di Segni, L., "Greek Inscriptions of the Bath-House in Hammat Gader," *ARAM* (Society for Syro-Mesopotamian Studies) 4 (1992), pp. 307–28.

Di Segni, L., and Y. Hirschfeld, "Four Greek Inscriptions from Hammat Gader," *IEJ* 36 (1986), pp. 251–68.

Green, J., and Y. Tsafrir, "Greek Inscriptions from Hammat Gader: A Poem by the Empress Eudocia and Two Building Inscriptions," *IEJ* 32 (1982), pp. 77–96.

Habas (Rubin), E., "A Poem by the Empress Eudocia: A Note on the Patriarch," *IEJ* 46 (1996), pp. 108–19.

Hirschfeld, Y., *The Roman Baths of Hammat Gader* (Jerusalem, 1997).

Sukenik, E. L., "The Ancient Synagogue of El-Hammeh," *Journal of the Palestinian Oriental Society* 15 (1935), pp. 101–80.

Scythopolis (Beth Shean)

Agady, S., et al., "Byzantine Shops in the Street of the Monuments at Bet Shean (Scythopolis)," *What Athens Has to Do with Jerusalem*, L. V. Rutgers, ed. (Leuven, 2002), pp. 423–506.

Applebaum, S., "The Roman Theatre of Scythopolis," *SCI* 4 (1978), pp. 77–97.

Di Segni, L., G. Foerster, and Y. Tsafrir, "The Basilica and an Altar to Dionysos at Nysa-Scythopolis," *The Roman and Byzantine Near East* 2, J. H. Humphrey, ed. (Portsmouth, RI, 1999), pp. 59–75.

Fitzgerald, G. M., *Beth-Shan Excavations 1921–1923: The Arab and Byzantine Levels* (Philadelphia, 1931); *A Sixth Century Monastery at Beth-Shan* (Philadelphia, 1939).

Foerster, G., and Y. Tsafrir, "Nysa-Scythopolis: A New Inscription and the Titles of the City in Its Coins," *Israel Numismatic Journal* 9 (1986), pp. 53–58.

Fuchs, G., *Scythopolis: A Greek City in Eretz Israel* (Jerusalem, 1983) (in Hebrew).

Lifschitz, B., "Scythopolis: L'histoire, les institutions et les cultes de la ville à l'époque hellénistique et impériale," *ANRW* 2, 8 (Berlin and New York, 1977), pp. 262–94.

Mazor, G., *Public Baths in Roman and Byzantine Nysa-Scythopolis, Roman Baths and Bathing: 2. Design and Context* (Portsmouth, RI, 2000).

Mazor, G., and R. Bar Nathan, "Scythopolis—Capital of Palaestina Secunda," *Qadmoniot* 107–8 (1994), pp. 117–37 (in Hebrew).

Ovadiah, A., and J. Turnheim, *"Peopled" Scrolls in Roman Architectural Decoration in Israel: The Roman Theatre at Beth Shean, Scythopolis* (Rome, 1994).

Rowe, A., *The Topography and History of Beth-Shan* (Philadelphia, 1930).

Tsafrir, Y., "Further Evidence for the Cult of Zeus Akraios at Beth Shean (Scythopolis)," *IEJ* 39 (1989), pp. 76–78; "The Fate of Pagan Places in Palestine: The Archaeological Evidence with Emphasis on Beth Shean," *Religious and Ethnic Communities in Later Roman Palestine*, H. Lapin, ed. (Bethesda, MD, 1998), pp. 197–218.

Tsafrir, Y., and G. Foerster, "From Scythopolis to Baysan: Changing Concepts of Urbanism," *The Byzantine and Early Islamic Near East: 2. G. R. D. King and A. Cameron, eds., Land Use and Settlement Patterns* (Princeton, 1994), pp. 95–115; "Urbanism at Scythopolis–Beth Shean in the Fourth–Seventh Centuries," *Dumbarton Oaks Papers* 51 (1997), pp. 85–146.

Zori, N., "The House of Kyrios Leontis at Beth Shean," *IEJ* 16 (1966), pp. 123–34; "The Ancient Synagogue at Beth Shean," *Eretz Israel* 8 (Jerusalem, 1967), pp. 149–67.

Samaria-Sebaste

Avigad, N., s.v. "Samaria," *NEAEHL* 4, pp. 1300–1310.

Bagatti, B., *Antichi villaggi cristiani di Samaria*, Studium Biblicum Franciscanum, Collectio minor 19 (Jerusalem, 1979), pp. 60–72.

Crowfoot, J. W., *Churches at Bostra and Samaria-Sebaste* (London, 1937).

Crowfoot, J. W., K. M. Kenyon, and E. L. Sukenik, *The Buildings at Samaria* (London, 1942).

Frumkin, A., "The Water-Supply Network of Samaria-Sebaste," *Aqueducts of Palestine*, op. cit., pp. 267–77.

Guérin, V., *Description géographique, historique et archéologique de la Palestine*: Samarie 2 (Paris, 1875), pp. 188–209.

Hamilton, R. W., *Guide to Samaria-Sebaste* (Jerusalem, 1944).

Reisner, G. A., C. S. Fisher, and D. G. Lyon, *Harvard Excavations at Samaria (1908–1910)*, 2 vols. (Cambridge, MA, 1924).

TIR, pp. 220–21.

Neapolis

Bagatti, B., *Antichi villaggi cristiani di Samaria*, op. cit., pp. 45–58.

Guérin, V., *Description géographique: Samarie* 1, op. cit. (Paris, 1874), pp. 389–423.

Magen, Y., "The Roman Theatre at Shechem," *Vilnay Jubilee Volume* (Jerusalem, 1984), pp. 269–77; "The Western Mausoleum at Neapolis," *Eretz Israel* 19 (1987), pp. 72–91 (in Hebrew); "The Church of Mary Theotokos on Mount Gerizim," *Christian Archaeology in the Holy Land: New Discoveries*, Studium Biblicum Franciscanum, Collectio Maior 36, G. C. Bottini, L. Di Segni, and E. Alliata eds. (Jerusalem, 1990), pp. 333–42; s.v. "Shechem-Neapolis," *NEAEHL* 4 (1993), pp. 1354–59; "Mount Gerizim and the Samaritans," *Early Christianity in Context: Monuments and Documents*, Studium Biblicum Franciscanum, Collectio Maior 38, F. Manns, ed. (Jerusalem, 1993), pp. 91–147.

TIR, p. 195.

Jericho

Bar-Nathan, R., *Hasmonean and Herodian Palaces at Jericho*: 3. *The Pottery* (Jerusalem, 2003).

Gleason, K., "Garden Excavations at the Herodian Winter Palace in Jericho," *Bulletin of the Anglo-Israel Archaeological Society* 7 (1987–88), pp. 21–39.

Kelso, J. L., and D. C. Baramki, "Excavations at New Testament Jericho and Khirbet en-Nitla," *Annual of the American Schools of Oriental Research* 29–30 (1955), pp. 29–30.

Meshel, Z., "A New Interpretation of the Finds at Herodian Jericho," *Eretz Israel* 11 (1973), pp. 194–196 (in Hebrew).

Netzer, E., "The Hippodrome That Herod Built at Jericho," *Qadmoniot* 13 (1980), pp. 104–7; "The Herodian Theatre, Amphitheatre and Hippodrome at Tell es-Samarat in the Plain of Jericho," *Judea and Samaria Research Studies. Proceedings of the Fifth Annual Meeting 1995*, Y. Eshel, ed. (Ariel, 1996), pp. 135–41; "A Synagogue from the Hasmonean Period Recently Exposed in the Western Plain of Jericho," *IEJ* 49 (1999), pp. 203–21; *Hasmonean and Herodian Palaces at Jericho* 1 (Jerusalem, 2001).

Netzer, E., and G. Garbrecht, "Water Channels and a Royal Estate of the Late Hellenistic Period in Jericho's Western Plains," *Aqueducts of Israel*, D. Amit, J. Patrich, and Y. Hirschfeld, eds. (Portsmouth, RI, 2002), p. 380.

Pritchard, J. B., "The Excavations at Herodian Jericho, 1951," *Annual of the American Schools of Oriental Research* 32–33 (1958).

Rozenberg, S., *The Wall Paintings of the Herodian Palace at Jericho, Judaea and the Greco-Roman World in the Time of Herod in the Light of Archaeological Evidence* (Göttingen, 1996).

Herodion

Amit, D., "New Data for Dating the High-Level Aqueduct and the Wadi el Biyar Aqueduct, and the Herodion Aqueduct," *Aqueducts of Israel*, op. cit., pp. 253–66.

Corbo, V., "L'Herodion di Jebel Fureidis," *Liber annuus* 13 (1963), pp. 219–77; "L'Herodion di Giabal Fureidis," *Liber annuus* 17 (1967), pp. 65–121; *Herodion. Gli edifici della Reggia Fortezza* (Jerusalem, 1989).

Foerster, G., "Herodion (Notes and News)," *IEJ* 19 (1969), pp. 123–24; "Herodium," *Revue biblique* 77 (1970), pp. 400–401.

Netzer, E., *Greater Herodium* (Jerusalem, 1981).

Netzer, E., Y. Kalman, and R. Laureys, "Lower Herodium's Large Bathhouse," *Judea and Samaria Research Studies* 9 (2000), pp. 113–20 (in Hebrew).

Qumran

The bibliography is immense. For guidance, see: *Encyclopedia of the Dead Sea Scrolls*, L. H. Schiffman and J. C. VanderKam, eds. (New York, 2000).

Broshi, M., and H. Eshel, "Residential Caves at Qumran," *Dead Sea Discoveries* 6 (1999), pp. 328–47.

Davies, P. R., "How Not to Do Archaeology: The Story of Qumran," *Biblical Archaeologist* 51 (1988), pp. 203–7.

De Vaux, R., "La grotte des manuscrits hébreux," *Revue biblique* 56 (1949), pp. 586–609; "Fouille au Khirbet Qumran: Rapport préliminaire," *Revue biblique* 60 (1953), pp. 83–106; "Fouilles de Khirbet Qumrân: Rapport préliminaire sur la deuxième campagne," *Revue biblique* 61 (1954), pp. 206–36; "Fouilles de Khirbet Qumrân: Rapport préliminaire sur les 3e, 4e, et 5e campagnes," *Revue biblique* 63 (1956), pp. 533–77; *Archaeology and the Dead Sea Scrolls*, rev. ed. (Oxford, 1973).

Discoveries in the Judaean Desert: 1. *Qumran Cave 1*, D. Barthélemy and J. T. Milik, eds. (Oxford, 1955); 3. *Les "Petites Grottes" de Qumrân*, M. Baillet, J. T. Milik, and R. de Vaux, eds. (Oxford, 1962); 6. *Qumrân Grotte 4/2*, R. de Vaux and J. T. Milik, eds. (Oxford, 1977).

Donceel-Voûte, P., "Les ruines de Qumran réinterprétées" *Archaeologia* 298 (1994), pp. 24–35.

Donceel-Voûte, R., and P. Donceel-Voûte, "The Archaeology of Qumran," *Methods of Investigation of the Dead Sea Scrolls and the Khirbet Qumran Site*, M. O. Wise et al., eds. (New York, 1994), pp. 1–38.

Golb, N., *Who Wrote the Dead Sea Scrolls? The Search for the Secret of Qumran* (New York, 1994).

Goodman, M., "A Note on the Qumran Sectarians: The Essenes and Josephus," *Journal of Jewish Studies* 46 (1995), pp. 161–66.

Hirschfeld, Y., "Early Roman Manor Houses in Judea and the Site of Khirbet Qumran," *Journal of Near Eastern Studies* 57 (1998), pp. 161–89; "Qumran: Back to the Beginning," *JRA* 16 (2003), pp. 648–52.

Humbert, J.-B., "Qumrân, esséniens et architecture," *Antikes Judentum und fruhes Christentum*, B. Kollman, W. Reinfold, and A. Steudel, eds. (Berlin, 1999), pp. 184–86.

Humbert, J.-B., and A. Chambon, *Fouilles de Khirbet Qumrân et de Aïn Feshkha* (Fribourg, 1994).

Magen, I., and Y. Peleg, "Important New Findings at Qumran (abstr.)," *Qumran: The Site of the Dead Sea Scrolls*, Conference held November 1–19, 2002, Providence, RI.

Magness, J., *The Archaeology of Qumran and the Dead Sea Scrolls* (Grand Rapids, MI, 2002).

Patrich, J., "Khirbet Qumran in Light of New Archaeological Explorations in the Qumran Caves," *Annals of the New York Academy of Sciences* 215 (1995), pp. 72–95.

Regenstorf, K. H., *Hirbet Qumran und die Bibliothek von Toten Meer* (Stuttgart, 1960).

Sussman, A., and R. Peled, *Scrolls from the Dead Sea* (Washington, DC, 1993).

Ullman-Margalit, E., "Writing, Ruins and Their Readings: The Dead Sea Discoveries as a Case Study in Theory Formation and Scientific Interpretation," *Social Research* 65 (1998), pp. 839–70.

Masada

Avi-Yonah, M., N. Avigad, Y. Aharoni, I. Dunayevski, and S. Gutman, eds., *Masada: Survey and Excavation 1955–1956* (Jerusalem, 1957).

Bowersock, G. W., "The Babatha Papyri, Masada and Rome," *JRA* 4 (1991), 344.

Campbell, D., "Dating the Siege of Masada," *ZPE* 73 (1988), pp. 156–58.

Cotton, H. M., "The Date of the Fall of Masada: The Evidence of the Masada Papyri," *ZPE* 78 (1989), pp. 157–62.

Goldfus, H., and B. Arubas, "Excavations at the Roman Siege Complex at Masada—1995," *Limes 18. Proceedings of the 18th International Congress of Roman Frontier Studies*, P. Freeman, J. Bennett, Z. T. Fiema, and B. Hoffmann, eds. (Oxford, 2002), pp. 207–14.

Gutman, S., *With Masada* (Tel Aviv, 1965) (in Hebrew).

Hadas-Lebel, M., *Masada. Histoire et symbole* (Paris, 1995).

Masada Excavation Reports, 6 vols., Y. Yadin, ed. (Jerusalem, 1989–99): 1. Y. Yadin, J. Naveh, and Y. Meshorer, *The Aramaic and Hebrew Ostraca and Jar Inscriptions* (1989); 2. H. Cotton and J. Geiger, *The Latin and Greek Documents* (1989); 3. E. Netzer, *The Buildings: Stratigraphy and Architecture* (1989); 4. G. Foerster, *Art and Architecture* (1995); 5. D. Barag et al., *Lamps, Textiles et alia* (1995); 6. S. Talmon, *Hebrew Fragments from Masada* (1999).

Richmond, I. A., "The Roman Siege-Works of Masada, Israel," *JRS* 52 (1962), pp. 142–55.

Roth, J., "The Length of the Siege of Masada," *SCI* 14 (1995), pp. 87–110.

Schulten, A., "Masada. Die Burg des Herodes und die romischen Lager," *Zeitschrift des Deutschen Palästina Vereins* 56 (1933), pp. 1–179.

The Story of Masada, G. Hurvitz, ed. (Winona Lake, IN, 1997).

Yadin, Y. *Masada. Herod's Fortress and the Zealots' Last Stand* (London, 1966).

Bethlehem

Avi-Yonah, M., and V. Tzaferis, s.v. "Bethlehem," *NEAEHL* 1, pp. 203–10.

Bagatti, B., *Gli antichi edifici sacri di Betlemme*, Studium Biblicum Franciscanum, Collectio Maior 9 (Jerusalem, 1952).

Guérin, V., *Description géographique, historique et archéologique de la Palestine: Judée 1* (Paris, 1868), pp. 120–206.

Hamilton, R. W., *The Church of the Nativity, Bethlehem: A Guide* (Jerusalem, 1947).

Petrozzi, M. T., *Bethlehem* (Jerusalem, 1971).

TIR, p. 83.

Vincent, L. H., and F. M. Abel, *Le sanctuaire de la Nativité* (Paris, 1914).

Hebron

Bagatti, B., *Antichi villaggi cristiani di Giudea e Neghev*, Studium Biblicum Franciscanum, Collectio minor 24 (Jerusalem, 1983), pp. 71–78.

Guérin, V., *Description géographique, historique et archéologique de la Palestine: Judée 1* (Paris, 1868), pp. 214–56.

Mader, A. E., *Altchristliche Basiliken und Localtraditionen in Südjudäa* (Paderborn, 1918), pp. 120–52; *Mambre* (Freiburg im Breisgau, 1957).

Magen, Y., "Mamre. A Cultic Site from the Reign of Herod," *One Land, Many Cultures: Archaeological Studies in Honour of Fr S. Loffreda*, Studium Biblicum Franciscanum, Collectio Maior 42, G. C. Bottini, L. Di Segni, and D. Chrupcala, eds. (Jerusalem, 2003), pp. 245–57; s.v. "Mambre," *NEAEHL* 2, pp. 939–42.

Ofer, A., s.v. "Hebron," *NEAEHL* 2, pp. 606–9.

TIR, p. 141.

Vincent, L. H., E. J. H. Mackay, and F. M. Abel, *Hébron* (Paris, 1923).

Caesarea

Avi-Yonah, M., "The Caesarea Porphyry Statue," *IEJ* 20 (1970), pp. 203–8.

Blakely, J. A., *Caesarea Maritima: The Pottery and Dating of Vault 1: Horreum, Mithraeum, and Later Uses* (Lewiston, 1987).

Bull, R. J., "The Mithraeum of Caesarea Maritima," *Textes et mémoires* 4 (1978), pp. 75–89.

Caesarea Papers: 1. Straton's Tower, Herod's Harbour, and Roman and Byzantine Caesarea, R. L. Vann, ed. (Ann Arbor, 1992); 2. *Herod's Temple, The Provincial Governor's Praetorium and Granaries, the Later Harbor, a Gold Coin Hoard, and Other Studies*, K. G. Holum, A. Raban, and J. Patrich, eds. (Portsmouth, RI, 1999).

Fritsch, C. T., *The Joint Expedition to Caesarea Maritima*, Studies in the History of Cesarea Maritima 1 (Missoula, MT, 1975).

Frova, A., *Cesarea Maritima (Israele). Rapporto preliminare della Ia campagna di scavo della missione archeologica italiana* (Milan, 1959); "L'iscrizione di Ponzio Pilato a Cesarea," *Rendiconti dell'Istituto Lombardo di scienze e lettere* 95 (1961).

Frova, A., et al., *Scavi di Cesarea Maritima* (Rome, 1966).

Holum, K. G., "Inscriptions from the Imperial Revenue Office of Byzantine Caesarea Palaestinae," *The Roman and Byzantine Near East*, J. H. Humphrey, ed. (Ann Arbor, 1995), pp. 333–45.

Humphrey, J. H., "A Summary of the 1974 Excavations in the Caesarea Hippodrome," *BASOR* 218 (1975), pp. 1–24.

King Herod's Dream: Caesarea on the Sea, K. G. Holum, R. L. Hohlfelder, R. J. Bull, and A. Raban, eds. (New York and London, 1988).

Lehmann, C. M., and K. G. Holum, *The Greek and Latin Inscriptions of Caesarea Maritima* (Boston, 2000).

Levine, L. I., *Roman Caesarea: An Archaeological-Topographical Study* (Jerusalem, 1975); *Caesarea under Roman Rule* (Leiden, 1975).

Lifshitz, B., "Césarée de Palestine, son histoire et ses institutions," *ANRW* 1, 8 (Berlin and New York, 1977), pp. 490–518.

Lifshitz, B., and E. Netzer, *Excavations at Caesarea Maritima: 1975, 1976, 1979. Final Report* (Jerusalem, 1986).

Olami, Y., and Y. Peleg, "The Water Supply System of Caesarea Maritima," *IEJ* 27 (1977), pp. 127–37.

Oleson, J., M. Fitzgerald, A. Sherwood, and S. Sidebotham, *The Harbours of Caesarea Maritima: Results of the Caesarea Ancient Harbour Excavations Project 1980–85* (Oxford, 1994).

Patrich, J., "Herod's Hyppodrome-Stadium at Caesarea and the Games Conducted Therein," *What Athens Has to Do with Jerusalem*, L. V. Rutgers, eds. (Leuven, 2002), 29–68; "Urban Space in Caesarea Maritima, Israel," *Urban Centers and Rural Contexts in Late Antiquity*, T. S. Burns and J. W. Eadie, eds. (East Lansing, MI, 2001), pp. 77–110.

Porath, Y., "Herod's 'Amphitheatre' at Caesarea: A Multipurpose Entertainment Building," *The Roman and Byzantine Near East*, op. cit., pp. 15–27; "The Water Supply to Caesarea: A Re-assessment," *Aqueducts of Israel*, op. cit., pp. 105–29.

Raban, A., *The Harbors of Caesarea Maritima. Results of the Caesarea Ancient Harbor Excavation Project, 1980–1985: 1. The Site and the Excavations* (Oxford, 1989).

Raban, A., and K. G. Holum, eds., *Caesarea Maritima: A Retrospective after Two Millennia* (Leiden, 1996).

Ringel, J., *Césarée de Palestine. Étude historique et archéologique* (Paris, 1975).

Vann, R. L., "Early Byzantine Street Construction at Caesarea Maritima," *City, Town and Countryside in the Early Byzantine Era*, R. L. Hohlfelder, ed. (Boulder, 1982).

Wiemken, R. C., and K. G. Holum, "The Joint Expedition to Caesarea Maritima: Eighth Season, 1979," *BASOR* 244 (1981), pp. 27–52.

Ashkelon

Arbel, N., ed., *Ashkelon: 4,000 and Forty More Years* 1 (Ashkelon, 1990), pp. 67–90 (in Hebrew).

Bagatti, B., "Ascalon e Maiuma di Ascalon nel VI secolo," *Studii Biblici Franciscani Liber Annuus* 24 (1974), pp. 227–64.

Guérin, V., *Description géographique, historique et archéologique de la Palestine: Judée* 2 (Paris, 1869), pp. 133–49, 152–71.

Phythian-Adams, W. J., "The History of Askalon," *Palestine Exploration Fund Quarterly Statement* (1921), pp. 76–90.

Sasson, A., Z. Safrai, and N. Sagiv, eds., *Ashkelon, a City on the Seashore* (Tel Aviv, 2001) (in Hebrew); *Ashkelon, Bride of the South: Studies in the History of Ashkelon from the Middle Ages to the Twentieth Century* (Tel Aviv, 2001) (in Hebrew).

Stager, L. E., s.v. "Ashkelon," *NEAEHL* 1, pp. 103–12.

TIR, pp. 68–70.

Gaza

Bagatti, B., *Antichi villaggi cristiani di Giudea e Neghev*, Studium Biblicum Franciscanum, Collectio minor 24 (Jerusalem, 1983), pp. 150–65.

Bitton-Ashkeloni, B., and A. Kofsky, eds., *Christian Gaza in Late Antiquity* (Leiden, New York, and Köln, in press).

Downey, G., *Gaza in the Early Sixth Century* (Norman, OK, 1963).

Glucker, C., *The City of Gaza in the Roman and Byzantine Periods*, BAR International Series 325 (Oxford, 1987).

Guérin, V., *Description géographique, historique et archéologique de la Palestine: Judée* 2 (Paris, 1869), pp. 178–211, 219–21.

Humbert, J.-B., ed., *Gaza méditerranéenne. Histoire et archéologie en Palestine* (Paris, 2000).

Meyer, M. A., *A History of the City of Gaza* (New York, 1907).

Ovadiah, A., s.v. "Gaza," *NEAEHL* 2, pp. 464–67.

Saliou, C., "Gaza dans l'antiquité tardive: Nouveaux documents épigraphiques," *Revue biblique* 107 (2000), pp. 390–411 (a Byzantine church at Jabaliya, 3 km northwest of ancient Gaza).

TIR, pp. 129–31, 175.

Towns of the Negev

Bingen, J., "Sur un dédicace protobyzantine d'Elusa (Negev)," *ZPE* 53 (1983), pp. 123–24.

Bruins, H., *Desert Environment and Agriculture in the Central Negev and Kadesh Barnea during Historical Times* (Nijkerk, 1986).

Colt, H., *Excavations at Nessana* 1 (London, 1962).

Erickson-Gini, T., "Nabataean or Roman? Reconsidering the Date of the Army Camp in Avdat," *Limes 17. Proceedings of the 17th International Congress of Roman Frontier Studies*, P. Freeman, J. Bennett, Z. T. Fiema, and B. Hoffmann, eds. (Oxford, 2002), pp. 113–30.

Evenari, M., L. Shanan, and N. Tadmor, *The Negev: The Challenge of a Desert* (Cambridge, MA, 1982).

Hirschfeld, Y., "Farms and Villages in Byzantine Palestine," *Dumbarton Oaks Papers* 51 (1997), pp. 33–71.

Jaussen, A., R. Savignac, and H. Vincent, "Abdeh," *Revue biblique* 1 (1904), pp. 403–24; 2 (1905), pp. 74–89, 235–44.

———"Sbaita," *Revue biblique* 2 (1905), pp. 256–57.

Kruse, F., et al., eds., *Ulrich Jasper Setzen's Reisen* (Berlin, 1854–59), vol. 3, p. 11.

Lewin, A., "Il Negev dall'età nabatea all'epoca tardoantica," *Mediterraneo antico* 5 (2002), pp. 319–75.

Musil, A., *Arabia Petraea, Edom* (Vienna, 1907).

Negev, A., "The Churches of the Central Negev: An Archaeological Survey," *Revue biblique* 81 (1974), pp. 400–422; *Greek Inscriptions from the Negev* (Jerusalem, 1981); "Survey and Trial Excavations at Haluza (Elusa)," *Israel Exploration Journal* 32 (1982), pp. 134–37; *Nabatean Archaeology Today* (New York, 1986); *The Architecture of Mampsis. Final Report: 1. The Middle and Late Nabataean Period; 2. The Late Roman and Byzantine Periods* (Jerusalem, 1988); "The Temple of Obodas: Excavations at Oboda in July 1989," *IEJ* 41 (1991), pp. 62–80; *The Architecture of Oboda: Final Report* (Jerusalem, 1997).

Palmer, E. H., "The Desert of the Tih and the Country of Moab," *Palestine Exploration Fund Quarterly Statement* (1871), pp.3–80.

Robinson, E., *Biblical Researches in Palestine, Mount Sinai, and Arabia Petraea* (Boston, 1841), vol. 1, pp. 283–98.

Rosenthal-Heginbottom, R., *Die Kirche von Sobota und die Dreiapsidenkirche des Nahens Osten* (Wiesbaden, 1982).

Rubin, R., *The Negev as a Settled Land* (Jerusalem, 1990) (in Hebrew).

Rubin, R., and Y. Shereshevski, "Sa'adon: An Urban Settlement of the Byzantine Period in the Negev," *Qadmoniot* 81–82 (1988), pp. 49–54 (in Hebrew).

Segal, A., *The Byzantine City of Shivta (Esbeita), Negev Desert, Israel* (Oxford, 1983).

Shereshevski, J., *Byzantine Urban Settlements in the Negev Desert* (Beer-Sheva, 1991).

Tsafrir, Y., *Excavations at Rehovot in the Negev: 1. The Northern Church* (Jerusalem, 1988).

Weigand, T., *Sinai* (Berlin, 1920).

Wooley, C.L., and T. E. Lawrence, "The Wilderness of Zin," *Annual of the Palestine Exploration Fund* (1914–15; repr. New York, 1936).

Churches and monasteries

This is only a general bibliography; for individual sites, see the entries in *NEAEHL* and the bibliography in Ovadiah, *Corpus*; for new discoveries, see the two items by Bottini et al.

Avi-Yonah, M., R. Cohen, and A. Ovadiah, s.v. "Churches," *NEAEHL* 1, pp. 305–14.

Bottini, G. C., L. Di Segni, and D. Chrupcala, *One Land, Many Cultures. Archaeological Studies in Honour of Fr S. Loffreda*, Studium Biblicum Franciscanum, Collectio Maior 42 (Jerusalem, 2003).

Bottini, G. C., L. Di Segni, and E. Alliata, *Christian Archaeology in the Holy Land: New Discoveries*, Studium Biblicum Franciscanum, Collectio Maior 36 (Jerusalem, 1990).

Chitty, D. J., *The Desert a City* (Oxford, 1966).

Hirschfeld, Y., *The Judean Desert Monasteries in the Byzantine Period* (New Haven and London, 1992).

Ovadiah, A., *Corpus of the Byzantine Churches in the Holy Land* (Bonn, 1970).

Ovadiah, A., and C. Gomez de Silva, "Supplementum to the Corpus of the Byzantine Churches in the Holy Land (Part I)," *Levant* 13 (1981), pp. 200–261; "Supplementum to id. (Part II)," *Levant* 14 (1982), pp. 122–70; "Supplementum to id. (Part III)," *Levant* 16 (1984), pp. 129–65.

Patrich, J., *Sabas, Leader of Palestinian Monasticism*, Dumbarton Oaks Studies 32 (Washington, DC, 1995).

Patrich, J., and R. Cohen, s.v. "Monasteries," *NEAEHL* 3, pp. 1063–70.

Vailhé, S., "Repertoire alphabetique des monastères de Palestine," *Revue de l'Orient Chrétien* 4 (1899), pp. 512–42; 5 (1900), pp. 12–48, 279–92.

Synagogues

This general bibliography includes the earliest publications of modern research into the synagogues. For individual sites, see the bibliography in Saller and in Hüttenmeister and Reeg, and individual entries in *NEAEHL*.

Gutman, J. ed., *The Synagogue: Studies in Origins, Archaeology and Architecture* (New York, 1975); *Ancient Synagogues: The State of Research* (Chico, CA, 1981).

Hachlili, R., ed., *Ancient Synagogues in Israel, Third–Seventh Century C.E.*, BAR International Series 499 (Oxford, 1989).

Hüttenmeister, F., and G. Reeg, *Die Antike Synagogen in Israel*, 2 vols. (Wiesbaden, 1977).

Ilan, Z., *Synagogues in Galilee and Golan* (Ari'el 52) (Jerusalem, 1987); *Ancient Synagogues in Israel* (Tel Aviv, 1991) (both in Hebrew).

Kohl, H., and C. Watzinger, *Antike Synagogen in Galiläa* (Leipzig, 1916).

Levine, L. I., s.v. "Synagogues," *NEAEHL* 4, pp. 1421–24.

———, ed., *The Synagogue in Late Antiquity*, American Schools of Oriental Research (Philadelphia, 1987); *Ancient Synagogues Revealed* (Jerusalem, 1981).

Magen, Y., s.v. "Samaritan Synagogues," *NEAEHL* 4, pp. 1424–27.

Naveh, J., *On Stone and Mosaic: The Aramaic and Hebrew Inscriptions from Ancient Synagogues* (Tel Aviv, 1978) (in Hebrew).

Roth-Gerson, L., *The Greek Inscriptions from the Synagogues in Eretz Israel* (Jerusalem, 1987) (in Hebrew).

Saller, S., "Ancient Synagogues of the Holy Land," *Studii Biblici Franciscani Liber Annuus* 4 (1953–54), pp. 219–46.

Sukenik, E. L., "The Ancient Synagogue of el-Hamme," *Journal of the Palestine Oriental Society* 15 (1935), pp. 101–80.

Urman, D., and P. V. M. Flesher, eds., *Ancient Synagogues. Historical Analysis and Archaeological Discovery* (Leiden, New York, and Köln, 1994; 2nd ed. 1998).

Index

Italic page references indicate
illustrations.

Abbahu, 151
Absalom, Tomb of, 58, *58*
Aelia Capitolina, 33–34, 47, 58–61
Agrippa I, 21–22, 150–51
Agrippa II, 22–24, *23*, 31, 74
Akiba, 151
Albinus, 24
Alexander (son of Herod), 14–15
Alexander, Tiberius Julius (procura-
    tor of Judea), 22
Alexander III of Macedonia, 11
Alexander Jannaeus (Hasmonean
    ruler), 12, 113, 162
Alexander the Great, 100, 162
Alexandra (Hasmonean ruler), 12,
    113–14
Alföldy, Geza, 30, 154
Ananias, 24
Ananus, 18–19
Ananus the Younger, 23–24, 26
Anastasius, 42, 65, 90, 97
Antigonus, 46
Antiochus III, 11
Antiochus IV, 12, 44
Antipas, 15–17, 21–22, 74, 80
Antipater (governor of Idumea),
    12, 46
Antipater (son of Herod), 15, 115
Antonia Fortress, *13*, 14, 29, *50*, 56
Antoninus Pius, 34, 88, 106, 109
apse, 181, 184, 186
Arabs
    at Gaza, 164, 165
    at Hebron, 146–47
    in Jerusalem, 49
    in Palestine, 42
    at Tiberias, 76
    in towns of Negev, 170
Archelaus, 15, 46, 150
Arch of Titus, 30
Aretas IV, 168, 169
Aristobulus (Hasmonean ruler), 12
Aristobulus (son of Alexandra),
    12–13, 14, 44–46, 113–14
Aristobulus (son of Herod), 15
aron haqodesh, 181, 182
Arsenius, 98
Ascension, Chapel of the, *65*, 186
Ashkelon (Ascalon), 156–61
    archaeological excavations at,
        160–61

basilica of, 160–61
in Byzantine times, 159, 160, 161
Christianity at, 159
exports from, 159–60
in Great Revolt, 158–59
under Hasmonean rule, 156
in Hellenistic times, 156, 159, 161
under Herod, 156–58
Jews at, 158–59, 161
plan of, *156*
in Roman times, 156, *157–60*,
    158–60, 161
synagogue of, 161
Ashkelon Barnea, 161
atrium, 181, 184, 186
Augustus, 15, 150
Augustus, Temple of (Caesarea),
    150, 155
Augustus, Temple of (Samaria-
    Sebaste), 100, 102, *103*
Avdat, 166, *168*, 171–72
    acropolis of, *170*, 171, *171*
    archaeological excavations at,
        171–72
    baths of, 171
    citadel of, *169*, 171
    military fort of, 172
    under Nabataean rule, 168
    role of, 168–69
    on spice road, 168
    vine cultivation of, 171

Babylon, 11
Banyas, *16–17*, 17
Baram synagogue, *179*, 180
Barclay's Gate, 54, 56
Bar Kokhba, Simon. *See* Simon bar
    Kokhba
Bar Yohai, Simeon. *See* Simeon
    bar Yohai
basilican ground plan, 181, 184–86
batei midrash, 82
Beatitudes, Basilica of, 73
Bes, *8*
Beth Alpha synagogue, 182, *183*
Bethesda Pool, 50, 61, 63
Bethlehem, 138–42
    archaeological excavations at,
        141, 142
    Church of the Nativity at, 138–42,
        138–43, 184
    Jews banned from living in, 138
    water supply of, 142
Beth Shean. *See* Scythopolis

Beth Shearim, *7*, 35
Bethther (fortress), 33
Bezetha, 29
Bible
    authors of, 8
    composition of, 8, 11
    on Crucifixion, 20
    Greek translation of, 11
    on Hebron, 144, 147
    on history of Israelites, 8–10
    on Megiddo, 9
    prophecies in, 10
boule, 82
bouleuterion, 94, 97, 160
Broshi, Magen, 124
Buckingham, J. S., 88
Byzantine quarter (Jerusalem), *59*

Caesar, 46
Caesarea, *148*, 148–55, *150*
    amphitheater of, 153–54
    aqueduct of, *152–53*, 154
    archaeological excavations at, 148,
        151, 153, 154, 155
    Christianity at, 151
    earthquake at, 148
    foundation of, 14, 46, 148
    in Great Revolt, 31, 151
    in Hellenistic times, 148
    under Herod, 148–50, 153–54
    Jews at, 151, 155
    population of, 153
    as provincial headquarters, 39
    as Roman city, *149*, 150–53, 154
    Samaritans at, 41, 151
    synagogue of, 155
    theater of, *149*, 154
Caesarea Philippi, *16–17*, 17
Caiaphas, 19
Caligula, 21–22
Capernaum, 66–73
    archaeological excavations in,
        66, 68
    Church of Multiplication of the
        Loaves and Fishes in, 68–73,
        72, 73
    fame of, 66
    House of Saint Peter in, 66,
        68, 183
    synagogue in, 66–68, *69–71*, 180
Caracalla, 108, 109, 169
cardo, 58, 60, *65*, 76, *76*, 81, 84
Cathisma Church, 186
cenoby, 187–88, *189*

Cestius Gallus, 26
Chalcis, 22, 24
Chorazin synagogue, 180, *181*
Choricius of Gaza, 164–65
Christ. *See* Jesus
Christianity
    at Ashkelon, 159
    and Bethlehem, 138
    at Caesarea, 151
    and erosion of rights of Jews, 39
    in Galilee and Golan, 187
    at Gaza, 162–63, 164, 165
    at Hebron, 146, 147
    and Holy Land, 36, 39–40
    in Jerusalem, 36, 39–40, 47–48,
        61–65
    at Neapolis, 108–9
    in Palestine, 40
    at Samaria-Sebaste, 102, 104
    at Scythopolis, 94, 98
    at Tiberias, 76
    in towns of Negev, 170–71
churches, 183–89. *See also specific*
        churches and under specific
        cities
    archaeological exploration
        of, 186
    with basilican ground plan,
        184–86
    Byzantine, 187
    martyrium as, 184, 186
    monumental, 184
    mosaic floors of, 186–87
    with polygonal ground plan, 186
    primitive, 183–84
circumcision, prohibition of, 32, 33
Claudius, 22
client kingdoms, 13–17
Coele-Syria, 11
coins, *18*, 30, 32, 33, 80, 82, 106, *109*
Coliseum, 30
Colt, H. D., 176
Columbarium, *132*
Constantine, 35–36
    Bethlehem under, 138, 141
    and Christianity, 47
    churches built by, 36, 62, 64, 138,
        141, 146, 184
    and Eusebius, 151
    Gaza under, 164
    Hebron under, 146
    Jerusalem under, 61, 62, 64
Constantius II, 36, 39
Coponius, 18

copper scroll, 122
Council of Chalcedon, 40, 48
Council of Nicea, 36
Cumanus, 22–23
Cypros, 13–14, 116
Cyrus the Persian, 11

Damascus Gate, 58, 60, 65
Darius I, 11
David, Tomb of, 58, 63
David's Tower, 50, 51, 63
Dead Sea, 120, 120, 126, 128
Dead Sea Scrolls, 21, 124, 125
decumanus, 58, 60, 84
diadochoi, 44
Diocaesarea, 80
Dio Cassius, 33
Diocletian, 35, 170
Djami el-Kabir, 164
dolia, 151
Domaszewski, Alfred Von, 132
Dome of the Rock, 47
Donceel, Robert, 124
Donceel-Voûte, Pauline, 124
Dormition, Church of the, 64

Ecce Homo arch, 60
Egypt
    Israelites in, 9
    Judea under control of, 11
    synagogues in, 178
Eleazar, 27, 126–131
Elusa. See Haluza
Emmaus, 31
En Gedi synagogue, 182, 182–183
Epiphanius, 184
epitropos, 18
Erickson-Gini, Tali, 172
Eshel, Hanan, 124
Essenes, 21, 31, 120, 122–123
Eudocia, 40, 48, 61, 65, 88, 90
Eudoxiana church (Gaza), 164
Eusebius, 36, 151
Euthymius, 188
Eutropius, 84
Exichius, 39

Felix, 23
First Revolt. See Great Revolt
fiscus iudaicus, 31
Flavia Augusta Caesariensis, 31
Florus, Gessius, 24, 26
Foerster, Gideon, 97, 132, 134

Gabinius, 12, 100, 162
Galilee
    Christianity in, 187
    in Great Revolt, 26
    religious schools in, 34
    synagogues in, 180, 181
Gamaliel VI, 39
Gamla synagogue, 178, 178
Gate of Mercy. See Golden Gate
Gaza, 162–165
    Arabs at, 164, 165
    archaeological excavations at, 165

in Byzantine times, 164, 165
Christianity at, 162–163, 164, 165
destruction of, 162
in Great Revolt, 162
under Hasmonean rule, 162
in Hellenistic times, 162
under Herod, 162
mosaic representation of, 163
plague epidemic at, 164
in Roman times, 162, 164
synagogue of, 165, 165, 181
winter bath complex of, 165
genizah, 137, 180
Gihon, 50
Golan
    Christianity in, 187
    synagogues in, 180, 181
Golb, Norman, 124
Golden Gate, 56, 58
Good Shepherd (statue), 165, 165
Great Revolt (A.D. 66), 24–31
    Ashkelon in, 158–159
    Caesarea in, 31, 151
    death toll of, 30
    events in, 24–30
    Gaza in, 162
    Hebron in, 144–146
    Herodion in, 26, 30
    Jerusalem in, 26–30, 46–47
    Masada in, 24, 26, 30, 126–131
    outcome of, 30–31
    preconditions for, 24
    Scythopolis in, 92
    Sepphoris in, 80
    sicarii in, 24
    Tiberias in, 74, 78
Gutman, Shemaryah, 132

Hadrian
    bronze statue of, 33
    Gaza under, 162
    Jerusalem under, 47
    red porphyry statue of, 155
    and Second Revolt, 32, 33–34, 138
    Sepphoris under, 80
    temple dedicated to, 155
Hadrianeum, 155
Hall of Fountains, 88, 90, 90–91
Hall of Inscriptions, 90
Haluza, 166, 172
    archaeological excavations at, 172
    churches of, 172
    under Nabataean rule, 168
    population of, 172
    on spice road, 168
Hammat Gader, 88–90
    archaeological excavations at, 90
    origin of name of, 88
    pools and baths of, 88–90, 89,
        90–91
    synagogue of, 88, 90
Hammath Tiberias, 76, 78, 78, 79
Haram el-Khalil, 144, 146–147
Hasmonean dynasty, 12–13
    at Ashkelon, 156
    foundation of, 12

at Gaza, 162
at Hebron, 144
Herod ending, 13, 46
at Hyrcanus, 106, 109
at Jericho, 110–113
in Jerusalem, 44–46
at Samaria-Sebaste, 100
at Sepphoris, 80
Hebron, 144–147
    Arabs at, 146–147
    in Bible, 144, 147
    Christianity at, 146, 147
    crusaders at, 146, 147
    in Great Revolt, 144–146
    under Hasmonean rule, 144
    under Herod, 144
    Jews at, 144, 146
    Tomb of Patriarchs at, 144, 144,
        145, 146–147, 147
hekhal, 52
Heptapegon, 68, 73
Heraclius, 42, 49
Herod, 12, 13–15
    Ashkelon under, 156–158
    brutal deeds of, 14–15
    Caesarea under, 148–150, 153–154
    construction under, 14, 48, 49–58
    funeral of, 119
    Gaza under, 162
    Hebron under, 144
    and Herodion, 116–119
    high priest under, 14
    Jericho under, 110, 111, 113,
        114–115
    Jerusalem under, 14, 46, 49–58
    Jewish hostility toward, 13
    Masada under, 128–129, 131–134,
        132–134
    palaces of
        at Caesarea, 153
        at Herodion, 14, 116–119,
            118, 119
        at Jericho, 14, 111, 113, 114–115
        in Jerusalem, 14, 49, 50
        at Masada, 14, 128–129, 131,
            132–134, 133, 134
        Samaria-Sebaste under, 100, 102,
            102, 103
    sons of, 14–17
Herodias, 17
Herodion (city), 116–119
    foundation of, 116
    in Great Revolt, 26, 30
    palace-fortress of, 116–119, 118, 119
    pool complex of, 116, 119
    synagogue of, 178–180
Herodion (hill), 116, 117
Herod of Chalcis, 22, 23
Herodotus, 156
high priest, 11
    and death sentence, 20
    eligibility for, 12–13
    under Herod, 14
    Rome appointing, 18–19
    Seleucid overlords deposing, 12
Hilarion, 39, 170–171

Hippicus Tower, 50, 51
Hirschfeld, Yizhar, 90, 124
Holy Land, 36, 39–40
Holy of Holies, 52
Holy Sepulcher, Church of, 36, 37,
    42, 47, 60, 62, 63, 184
Holy Zion, Church of, 62–63
Honorius, 39
horrea, 151
Huldah Gates, 52, 53, 55
Humbert, J.-B., 124
Hyrcanus I (Hasmonean ruler), 100,
    106, 109, 110–113, 144
Hyrcanus II (son of Alexandra),
    12–13, 14, 44–46, 113–114

Israel, kingdom of, 8–11, 9, 100
Israelites. See also Jews
    archaeologists on history of, 8, 9
    Bible on history of, 8–10
    in Egypt, 9
    in Iron Age Palestine, 8
    and prophets, 10

Jabneh, 31
Jeremiah, 11
Jericho, 110–115
    archaeological excavations at,
        110, 114
    earthquake at, 114
    under Hasmonean rule, 110–113
    under Herod, 110, 111, 113, 114–115
    map of, 110
    mosaic floor at, 115
    palaces at, 110–115, 111, 113
    synagogue of, 178, 181, 182
    water supply of, 113, 114
Jerusalem, 44–65
    as Aelia Capitolina, 33–34, 47,
        58–61
    Arab occupation of, 49
    archaeological excavations in,
        50–52, 54–56, 63–64
    as capital, 9, 12, 44, 46
    cemeteries in, 58
    charitable and building activities
        in, 36, 39–40, 47–48, 61–65
    Christian, 36, 39–40, 47–48, 61–65
    Church of Holy Sepulcher in, 36,
        37, 42, 47, 60, 62, 63, 184
    in Great Revolt, 26–30, 46–47
    hellenization of, 44
    under Herod, 14, 46, 49–58
    Jews banned from living in, 47, 62
    model of, 13, 48, 49, 50
    monasteries in, 187
    Old City, 44, 45, 49, 50
    Persian occupation of, 42, 48
    plan of, 10, 46
    topography of, 49
    Upper City, 49, 50, 54, 60
    water supply of, 50, 61
Jerusalem, Temple of, 11, 12, 48,
    52–58. See also high priest
    under Antipas, 17
    destruction of, 29, 30, 31, 52